AP U.S. HISTORY
ALL ACCESS

D1408127

Gregory Feldmeth, M.A.
Assistant Head of School
Instructor, AP United States History
Polytechnic School
Pasadena, CA

Jerome McDuffie, Ph.D.
Professor of History
University of North Carolina at Pembroke
Pembroke, NC

Gary Piggrem, Ph.D.
Professor of History
DeVry Institute of Technology
Columbus, OH

Steven E. Woodworth, Ph.D.
Assistant Professor of History
Toccoa Falls College
Toccoa, GA

Research & Education Association
Visit our website: www.rea.com/studycenter

Research & Education Association
61 Ethel Road West
Piscataway, New Jersey 08854
E-mail: info@rea.com

AP U.S. HISTORY ALL ACCESS

Library of Congress Control Number 2011941440

ISBN-13: 978-0-7386-1057-3
ISBN-10: 0-7386-1057-7

REA® is a registered trademark of
Research & Education Association, Inc.

Contents

Chapter 8: Jacksonian Democracy and Westward Expansion (1824–1850)   125

Chapter 9: Sectional Conflict and the Causes of the Civil War (1850–1860)   167

Chapter 10: The Civil War and Reconstruction (1860–1877)   187

Chapter 11: Industrialism, War, and the Progressive Era (1877–1912)   215

Chapter 12: Wilson and World War I (1912–1920) 269

Chapter 13: The Roaring Twenties and Economic Collapse (1920–1929) 297

Chapter 14: The Great Depression and the New Deal (1929–1941)　　325

Chapter 17: Watergate, Conservatism's Rise, and Post–Cold War Challenges (1972–2008)   417

Practice Exam (also available online at *www.rea.com/studycenter*)   453

Glossary   505

Index   529

About Research & Education Association

Founded in 1959, Research & Education Association is dedicated to publishing the finest and most effective educational materials—including software, study guides, and test preps—for students in middle school, high school, college, graduate school, and beyond. Today, REA's wide-ranging catalog is a leading resource for teachers, students, and professionals.

Acknowledgments

REA would like to thank Larry B. Kling, Vice President, Editorial, for supervising development; Pam Weston, Publisher, for setting the quality standards for production integrity and managing the publication to completion; John Paul Cording, Vice President, Technology, for coordinating the design and development of the online REA Study Center; Diane Goldschmidt and Michael Reynolds, Managing Editors, for coordinating development of this edition; Claudia Petrilli, Graphic Designer, for interior book design; S4Carlisle Publishing Services for typesetting; and Weymouth Design and Christine Saul for cover design.

Welcome to REA's All Access for AP U.S. History

A new, more effective way to prepare for your AP exam.

There are many different ways to prepare for an AP exam. What's best for you depends on how much time you have to study and how comfortable you are with the subject matter. To score your highest, you need a system that can be customized to fit you: your schedule, your learning style, and your current level of knowledge.

This book, and the free online tools that come with it, will help you personalize your AP prep by testing your understanding, pinpointing your weaknesses, and delivering flashcard study materials unique to you.

Let's get started and see how this system works.

How to Use REA's AP All Access

The REA AP All Access system allows you to create a personalized study plan through three simple steps: targeted review of exam content, assessment of your knowledge, and focused study in the topics where you need the most help.

Here's how it works:

Review the Book	Study the topics tested on the AP exam and learn proven strategies that will help you tackle any question you may see on test day.
Test Yourself & Get Feedback	As you review the book, test yourself. Score reports from your free online tests and quizzes give you a fast way to pinpoint what you really know and what you should spend more time studying.
Improve Your Score	Armed with your score reports, you can personalize your study plan. Review the parts of the book where you are weakest, and use the REA Study Center to create your own unique e-flashcards, adding to the 100 free cards included with this book.

Finding Your Weaknesses: The REA Study Center

The best way to personalize your study plan and truly focus on your weaknesses is to get frequent feedback on what you know and what you don't. At the online REA Study Center, you can access three types of assessment: topic-level quizzes, mini-tests, and a full-length practice test. Each of these tools provides true-to-format questions and delivers a detailed score report that follows the topics set by the College Board.

Topic-Level Quizzes

Short, 15-minute online quizzes are available throughout the review and are designed to test your immediate grasp of the topics just covered.

Mini-Tests

Two online mini-tests cover what you've studied in each half of the book. These tests are like the actual AP exam, only shorter, and will help you evaluate your overall understanding of the subject.

Full-Length Practice Test

After you've finished reviewing the book, take our full-length exam to practice under test-day conditions. Available both in this book and online, this test gives you the most complete picture of your strengths and weaknesses. We strongly recommend that you take the online version of the exam for the added benefits of timed testing, automatic scoring and a detailed score report.

Improving Your Score: e-Flashcards

Once you get your score report, you'll be able to see exactly which topics you need to review. Use this information to create your own flashcards for the areas where you are weak. And, because you will create these flashcards through the REA Study Center, you'll be able to access them from any computer or smartphone.

Not quite sure what to put on your flashcards? Start with the 100 free cards included when you buy this book.

After the Full-Length Practice Test: Crash Course

After finishing this book and taking our full-length practice exam, pick up REA's *Crash Course for AP U.S. History*. Use your most recent score reports to identify any areas where you are still weak, and turn to the *Crash Course* for a rapid review presented in a concise outline style.

REA's Suggested 8-Week AP Study Plan

Depending on how much time you have until test day, you can expand or condense our eight-week study plan as you see fit.

To score your highest, use our suggested study plan and customize it to fit your schedule, targeting the areas where you need the most review.

	Review 1-2 hours	Quiz 15 minutes	e-Flashcards Anytime, anywhere	Mini-Test 30 minutes	Full-Length Practice Test 3 hours, 5 minutes
Week 1	Chapters 1-4	Quiz 1	Access your e-flashcards from your computer or smartphone whenever you have a few extra minutes to study. Start with the 100 free cards included when you buy this book. Personalize your prep by creating your own cards for topics where you need extra study.		
Week 2	Chapters 5-6	Quiz 2			
Week 3	Chapters 7-8	Quiz 3			
Week 4	Chapters 9-10	Quiz 4		Mini-Test 1 (The Mid-Term)	
Week 5	Chapters 11-12	Quiz 5			
Week 6	Chapters 13-14	Quiz 6			
Week 7	Chapters 15-16	Quiz 7			
Week 8	Chapter 17 Review Chapter 2 Strategies	Quiz 8		Mini-Test 2 (The Final)	Full-Length Practice Exam (Just like test day)

Need even more review? Pick up a copy of REA's *Crash Course for AP U.S. History*, a rapid review presented in a concise outline style. Get more information about the *Crash Course* series at the REA Study Center.

Test-Day Checklist

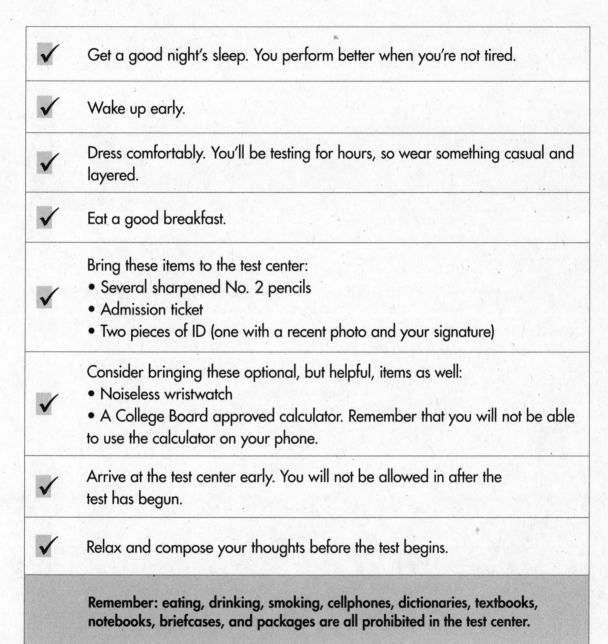

✓	Get a good night's sleep. You perform better when you're not tired.
✓	Wake up early.
✓	Dress comfortably. You'll be testing for hours, so wear something casual and layered.
✓	Eat a good breakfast.
✓	Bring these items to the test center: • Several sharpened No. 2 pencils • Admission ticket • Two pieces of ID (one with a recent photo and your signature)
✓	Consider bringing these optional, but helpful, items as well: • Noiseless wristwatch • A College Board approved calculator. Remember that you will not be able to use the calculator on your phone.
✓	Arrive at the test center early. You will not be allowed in after the test has begun.
✓	Relax and compose your thoughts before the test begins.

Remember: eating, drinking, smoking, cellphones, dictionaries, textbooks, notebooks, briefcases, and packages are all prohibited in the test center.

Strategies for the Exam

What Will I See on the AP U.S. History Exam?

One May morning, you stroll confidently into the school library where you're scheduled to take the AP U.S. History exam. You know your stuff: you paid attention in class, followed your textbook, took plenty of notes, and reviewed your coursework by reading a special test prep guide. You can identify major technological advances, explain the characteristics of different eras of history, and describe the effects of different methods of wars on broad economic and social changes. So, how will you show your knowledge on the test?

The Multiple-Choice Section

First off, you'll complete a lengthy multiple-choice section that tests your ability to not just remember facts about the various eras of U.S. history, but also to apply that knowledge to interpret and analyze historical information. This section will require you to answer 80 multiple-choice questions in just 55 minutes. Here are the major time periods and the approximate percentages of questions found on the AP U.S. History exam relating to each period:

- Pre-Columbian to 1789 (20%)

- 1790 to 1914 (45%)

- 1915 to present (35%)

Topics and their relative percentages on the test include the following:

- Political institutions, behavior, and public policy (35%)

- Social change and cultural history (40%)

- Diplomacy and international relations (15%)

- Economic developments (10%)

So, being able to name which president led the country during the Great Depression (Franklin D. Roosevelt, but you know that, right?) will not do you much good unless you can also explain how Roosevelt's policies shaped the role of U.S. government, the nation's economy, the role of the United States in world affairs, and the day-to-day lives of the nation's people. It sounds like a lot, but by *working quickly and methodically* you'll have plenty of time to address this section effectively. We'll look at this in greater depth later in this chapter.

The Free-Response Section

After time is called on the multiple-choice section, you'll get a short break before diving in the free-response, or essay, section. This section requires you to produce three written responses in 130 minutes. Like the multiple-choice section, the free-response portion of the exam expects you to be able to *apply your own knowledge to analyze historical information,* in addition to being able to provide essential facts and definitions. One of these free-response questions will require you to interpret several primary source documents to create a historical argument. This is known as the document-based question, or DBQ. The other two free-response items will ask you to use your historical knowledge to build a thesis-based essay.

What's the Score?

Although the scoring process for the AP exam may seem quite complex, it boils down to two simple components: your multiple-choice score plus your free-response scores. The multiple-choice section accounts for one-half of your overall score, and is generated by awarding one point toward your "raw score" for each question you've answered correctly. The free-response section also accounts for one-half of your total score. Within the free-response section, the DBQ accounts for 45 percent of your overall score, and the combined total of your two other essay makes up 55 percent of your overall score. Trained graders read students' written responses and assign points according to grading rubrics. The number of points you accrue out of the total possible will form your score on the free-response section.

The College Board scores the AP exam on a scale of 1 to 5. Although individual colleges and universities determine what credit or advanced placement, if any, is awarded to students at each score level, these are the assessments typically associated with each numeric score:

5   Extremely well qualified

4   Well qualified

3   Qualified

2   Possibly qualified

1   No recommendation

Section I: Strategies for the Multiple-Choice Section of the Exam

Because the AP exam is a standardized test, each version of the test from year to year must share many similarities in order to be fair. That means that you can always expect certain things to be true about your AP U.S. History exam.

Which of the following phrases accurately describes a multiple-choice question on the AP U.S. History exam?

(A) always has five choices

(B) may rely on a cartoon, photo, or other visual stimulus

(C) may ask you to find a wrong idea or group related concepts

(D) more likely to test interpretation and application content than names and dates

(E) all of the above*

> Did you pick "all of the above?" Good job!

What does this mean for your study plan? You should focus more on the application and interpretation of various historical events and periods than on nuts and bolts such as names and dates, because the exam will not directly test your ability to memorize these types of details. Keep in mind, too, that many historical concepts overlap. This means that you should consider the connections among ideas and events as you study. This will help you prepare for more difficult interpretation questions and give you a

---

*Of course, on the actual AP exam you won't see any choices featuring "all of the above" or "none of the above." Do, however, watch for "except" questions. We'll cover this kind of item a bit later in this section.

head start on questions that ask you to use Roman numerals to organize ideas into categories. Not sure what this type of question might look like? Let's examine a typical Roman-numeral item:

In the presidential election of 1860,

I. the Democratic Party factionalized and nominated two candidates.

II. the election evolved into a contest between Abraham Lincoln and Stephen A. Douglas in the North and John C. Breckinridge and John Bell in the South.

III. Abraham Lincoln won less than 50 percent of the popular vote.

IV. no candidate received a majority of the popular vote.

(A)   I and II only

(B)   II and III only

(C)   III and IV only

(D)   II, III, and IV only

(E)   I, II, III, and IV

> Take a moment to look over the answer choices before evaluating each Roman numeral statement. You may notice that one numeral appears in more answer choices than do others. In this question, II and III appear in the most choices. Evaluating those first can save you time; if II is false, for example, the only possible correct answer is (C). Remember that the correct answer will include *all* of the applicable Roman numerals.

Types of Questions

You've already seen a list of the general content areas that you'll encounter on the AP U.S. History exam. But how do those different areas translate into questions?

Question Type	Sample Question Stems
Cause and Effect	*Which factor did NOT contribute to Spanish exploration of the Americas?*
Charts, Graphs, and Tables	*Based on the information in the graph, which statement best analyzes population trends during the 1830s?*
Definition	*McCarthyism was primarily an attempt to...*
Diplomatic	*Which of the following was NOT one of the main ideas of Wilson's Fourteen Points?*

Some More Advice

What have you learned about the free-response section? Keep these ideas in mind as you prepare for the AP U.S. History exam. Becoming comfortable with these techniques will make you feel confident and prepared when you sit down to take the exam in May.

- Remember that the DBQ and standard essay questions require different but similar approaches. You should be mentally prepared to address both of these essay types.

- Be sure to thoroughly read and evaluate all of the sources given with the DBQ. Make notes in your test booklet, and think of additional information to further contextualize the provided sources.

- Make a clear and concise outline before you begin writing. This will help you organize your thoughts and speed up the actual writing process.

- Stay on topic and answer the question! Addressing the question fully is the single most important way to earn points on this section.

- Handwriting is important and must be legible! If the AP Reader can't read your writing, you'll get no points, even if your response is correct.

- Leave a few minutes to quickly review and revise your answers. You don't need to check the spelling of every single word, but you do need to make sure that all of your ideas made it onto the page. Skipping lines while you write will leave room for you to add important words and ideas, and make it easier for the scorer to read your handwriting.

Two Final Words: Don't Panic!

The free-response questions can and probably will ask you about specific historical concepts and examples you haven't thought about in much detail before: The effects of the annexation of Texas on sectional disputes before the Civil War? The influence of popular music and television on public perception of the Vietnam War? The possibilities are practically endless. Remember that all free-response questions seek to test your knowledge of big-picture historical themes and concepts and not your ability to write a list of battles or recite the Declaration of Independence. Applying what you know about broad historical causation to these specific scenarios will help you get a great score, even if you're never thought much about the particular event presented in the question.

Pre-Columbian Cultures
(12,000 B.C.E.–1492 C.E.)

While historians disagree as to when the first Americans reached the Western Hemisphere, there is no disagreement as to where: the Bering Strait between Siberia and Alaska. Most scholars place the arrival at between 15,000 and 30,000 years ago; it appears that the receding waters exposed enough of a land bridge over the 56 miles that separate North America and Asia for groups to migrate across on at least two occasions. The Asian immigrants probably followed large game animals, such as mammoths, bison, and giant ground sloths. The small groups gradually spread across North and South America, and there is evidence that some reached the tip of South America by 9000 B.C.E.

DIDYOU**KNOW?**

Although water now covers the area that was once the Bering Land Bridge, the region still connects people on two separate continents. The native peoples of northwestern Alaska and the Russian Far East share a language and other cultural traditions.

2,000 Separate Cultures

The three most advanced civilizations of the more than 2,000 separate cultures that developed in the New World were the Incas, the Mayas, and the Aztecs.

Around 1000 C.E. the Incas successfully conquered neighboring tribes and eventually controlled an area more than 2,500 miles in length. By 1500 the Incas were the largest and richest of the ancient empires of the Americas. The Incas built palaces surrounded by high walls in Peru and connected a series of mountain towns and villages with an elaborate network of roads. They developed a system of terraces to effectively farm on the steep hillsides and used canals and aqueducts to irrigate crops. The potato and the tomato were two of the Incan contributions to world diets. Despite the lack of a written language, the Incan governmental system was well-organized when Spanish conquistador Francisco Pizarro and his brothers Juan, Gonzalo, and Hernando arrived in 1532 with fewer than 200 soldiers. The Pizarros defeated the Incan army and executed their king, Atahualpa, who

had allowed the Spaniards to enter the city because he did not sense a threat from their small force against his 80,000-member army. The Pizarros then captured the capital of Cuzco and looted its wealth of silver and gold.

The Mayas built temples and pyramids surrounding broad plazas in the mountains, deserts, and rain forests of what is now Guatemala, Belize, Honduras, and the Yucatán region of Mexico. The Mayas also constructed observatories, developed accurate calendars, knew of the mathematical concept of zero, and invented their own writing system, which used both syllables and single written characters, known as glyphs. Most of the written record of the Mayas was destroyed by Spanish invaders. The first ceremonial buildings appear to have been constructed about 1000 B.C.E. The Mayas were sophisticated farmers and used raised fields to plant maize, the cereal grain that is the ancestor of modern corn. The Mayas went into a decline in around 800 C.E. and were ruled as smaller city-states when the Spanish conquest began in the 1520s.

Highly Organized Society

The Aztecs were the latest of the three advanced civilizations to develop, having arrived at what is now Mexico City (Tenochtitlán) in the thirteenth century C.E. The city, featuring elaborate temples and canals and boasting a population of over 100,000, was the center of a large empire. The Aztecs developed a highly organized society ruled by a king and included a class of priests and tax collectors, a warrior elite, and an active merchant class. The Aztecs were a warlike people, exacting tribute from other tribes and capturing prisoners for the human sacrifice that was central to their religion. The Aztecs were conquered shortly after the arrival of Spaniard Hernán Cortés in 1519, and their king, Moctezuma, was killed. The Spaniards' accounts say that Moctezuma's attempts to address his subjects, who took a dim view of their leader's submission to Spanish forces, resulted in his being attacked with stones and arrows that inflicted fatal wounds. But the Aztecs' belief that their king had been murdered at the hand of the Spaniards caused the Cortés force heavy loss of life and treasure as it tried to leave the Aztec capital under cover of darkness.

By the time the Aztecs were conquered by the Spanish, the population of Mexico may have numbered 25 million people. Farther north, in what is now the United States and Canada, there were only about 1 million Indians. Most of the inhabitants were nomadic tribes subsisting as hunters or gatherers. Very few, mostly in the American Southwest, settled in one location as farmers.

The Anasazi built five-story pueblos in Chaco Canyon and cliff dwellings in what is now Arizona and New Mexico, and created a system of roads that reached villages 400 miles away. They watered their crops with a system of irrigation canals. But their canals, even combined with other techniques to counter lengthy dry seasons, were not enough to overcome the prolonged drought of the thirteenth century. This drought, the effects of which were compounded by attacks by neighboring tribes, contributed to their decline.

Pueblo peoples also used cliff dwellings (some survive to this day at Mesa Verde, Colorado) that were built during the fourteenth and fifteenth centuries. The Pueblos adopted architectural and religious practices from the Anasazi and, in addition, used plants that were more drought-resistant.

Indian tribes that lived in the Mississippi Valley found conditions that were much less harsh and thus more favorable to continued settlement. The area provided rich soil and a network of rivers that allowed for fishing, hunting, and trade. Beginning about 800 C.E., immigrants to the area, perhaps from the Yucatán Peninsula, planted new strains of maize and beans. The largest settlement, Cahokia, near present-day St. Louis, may have included as many as 40,000 people in the thirteenth century. Even though, as for almost all other New World groups, no written records exist, huge earthen pyramids reveal a sophisticated religious system. Cahokia featured more than 100 of these temple mounds. The main pyramid at Cahokia covers over 15 acres and extended over 35 feet high. Residents traded with groups throughout the eastern half of what is now the United States, including tribes on the Atlantic coastline. As with the Anasazi, the people of Cahokia disappeared for unknown reasons sometime in the fourteenth century, though it is thought that overpopulation, warfare, and urban diseases such as tuberculosis took huge tolls.

One group of Mississippi Valley residents that survived well past the arrival of whites were those known as the Natchez. Their ruler, known as the Great Sun, presided over a class-based society. Advisors to the Great Sun comprised the noble class and served as chiefs of villages. The mass of peasants, called Stinkards, cultivated the land. The Natchez were warlike and practiced torture and human sacrifice. Organized into confederacies of local farming villages, they proved unable to resist the diseases and conquests of the invading Europeans.

The Eastern Woodland Indians of North America occupied the lands east of the Mississippi River. They usually lived in small, self-governing clans of related families and were governed by clan elders. Unlike the Aztec or Mayan rulers, however, these kinship-based systems used consensus, rather than coercion, to govern. The peoples of this region spoke a wide variety of languages belonging to a few language groups. Most of the Indians living between the St. Lawrence River and Chesapeake Bay (Pequots and Delaware, for example) spoke Algonquian languages. The area between the Hudson River and the Great Lakes was home to the Five Nations of the Iroquois (Seneca, Cayuga, Oneida, Onondaga, and Mohawk), who spoke Iroquoian languages. The tribes in the Southeast, such as the Choctaw and Creek, spoke Muskhogean language dialects.

Cahokia Mounds
Cahokia Mounds, the site of the largest pre-Columbian Indian city north of Mexico. This painting, by L. K. Townsend, shows central Cahokia circa 1150 to 1200 B.C.E. Courtesy Cahokia Mounds Historic Site.

Most Eastern Woodland tribes did not live in permanent settlements, though tribes claimed territorial lands as their own. Groups moved about seasonally, gathering berries and seeds, fishing and hunting, and settling in the summer on fertile lands. While men were responsible for hunting and fishing, women controlled agricultural production. In some tribes, such as the Iroquois, the eldest women selected the clan chief, and inheritance of goods was matrilineal, with rights to land and other property passing to daughters from mothers. The economic nature of Eastern Woodland life was primarily one of subsistence agriculture, and these groups never developed large urban centers that the Native Americans of Mexico inhabited.

The arrival of Europeans on the American continent greatly affected Native American cultures. The tribes along the Atlantic Coast were pressured almost immediately to adapt to the white settlers and traders. Some very early contact was peaceful. Trade seemed to be the main interest of many. Whites provided metal tools and weapons in exchange for beaver and other pelts, which were in abundant supply to the Indians.

Often, trading encounters led to efforts of the Europeans to civilize the Indians, attempting to persuade them to live in permanent houses, learn to read and write, and, almost always, to accept Christianity. Jesuits and Franciscan priests and missionaries accompanied Spanish explorers in the American Southwest, and French fur traders in what is now Canada were closely followed by Jesuits who sought to convert the Indians they encountered.

TEST TIP

Beginning in May 2011, the AP U.S. History Exam stopped penalizing test takers for incorrect responses to multiple-choice questions. Entering a response for every question—even a wild guess—may help improve your score.

Some Native Tribes Rendered Nearly Extinct

The interaction between the natives and the new immigrants was largely, but not always, negative. Horses, which had first evolved in the New World, returned with the Spanish in the 1500s and became central to the lives of many peoples, particularly those who lived in the Great Plains. While nomadic before the horse's re-introduction to the continent, they now could range much farther and develop new means of hunting and fighting other tribes. In sum, however, the benefits of the contact with whites were drastically outweighed by the devastation caused by conquest and disease. Superior European weapons resulted in many decisive defeats for Indian groups throughout the Americas. In addition, illnesses such as measles, typhus, and smallpox ravaged Indian groups that had developed no immunities. Within 50 years of Columbus's arrival in the Caribbean, some native tribes on the islands were virtually extinct. On the island of Hispaniola, the population dropped from approximately 1 million to just *500* by

1600. In Peru the population dropped from 9 million in 1530 to 500,000 in 1630. Some historians estimate that in some regions as much as 95 percent of Indian groups died of European diseases in the first century after contact.

In this Columbian exchange, whites fared much better than Indians. While sexually transmitted diseases were carried by sailors returning to Europe, other New World contributions were of great positive value. New agricultural techniques and new crops, such as tomatoes, potatoes, pumpkins, beans, and squash, enriched European diets. Maize (corn), which Columbus brought back to Spain after his first voyage, became an important part of European diets.

In sum, the contact with European civilizations proved disastrous for the Indian residents of the New World. They were devastated by conquering armies and by disease, and made to work as slaves. While vestiges of their cultures have survived to the present day, most of their traditions, cities and villages, and populations have been wiped out.

II chartered the separate royal colony of New Hampshire. It remained economically dependent on Massachusetts.

TEST TIP

Do you get especially nervous when taking tests? Test anxiety is a common concern, particularly for high-stakes exams like the AP exams. If you find yourself getting nervous during the exam, put down your pencil, close your eyes, empty your mind, and take a few deep breaths. A short mental break may help you refocus and save you time in the long run.

Maryland

By the 1630s, the English crown was taking a more direct interest in exercising control over the colonies, and therefore turned away from the practice of granting charters to joint-stock companies, and towards granting such charters to single individuals or groups of individuals known as proprietors. The proprietors would actually own the colony, and would be directly responsible for it to the king, in an arrangement similar to the feudalism of medieval Europe. Though this was seen as providing more opportunity for royal control and less for autonomy on the part of the colonists, in practice proprietary colonies turned out much like the company colonies because settlers insisted on self-government.

The first proprietary colony was Maryland, granted in 1632 to George Calvert, Lord Baltimore. It was to be located just north of the Potomac River and to be at the same time a reward for Calvert's loyal service to the king as well as a refuge for English Catholics, of whom Calvert was one. George Calvert died before the colony could be planted, but the venture was carried forward by his son Cecilius.

From the start, more Protestants than Catholics came. To protect the Catholic minority Calvert approved an Act of Religious Toleration (1649) guaranteeing political rights to Christians of all persuasions. Calvert also allowed a representative assembly. Economically and socially, Maryland developed as a virtual carbon copy of neighboring Virginia.

The Carolinas

In 1663 Charles II, having recently been restored to the throne after a twenty-year Puritan revolution that had seen his father beheaded, moved to reward eight of the noblemen who had helped him regain the crown by granting them a charter for all the lands lying south of Virginia and north of Spanish Florida.

The new colony was called Carolina, after the king. In hopes of attracting settlers, the proprietors came up with an elaborate plan for a hierarchical, almost feudal, society. Not surprisingly this proved unworkable, and despite offers of generous land grants to settlers, the Carolinas grew slowly.

The area of North Carolina developed as an overflow from Virginia with similar economic and cultural features. South Carolina was settled by English planters from the island of Barbados; they founded Charles Town (Charleston) in 1670. These planters brought with them their black slaves; thus, unlike the Chesapeake colonies of Virginia and Maryland, South Carolina had slavery as a fully developed institution from the outset.

New York and New Jersey

Charles II, though immoral and dissolute, was cunning and had an eye for increasing Britain's power. The Dutch colony of New Netherlands, lying between the Chesapeake and the New England colonies, caught his eye as a likely target for British expansion. In 1664 Charles gave his brother, James, Duke of York, title to all the Dutch lands in America, provided James conquered them first. To do this James sent an invasion fleet under the command of Colonel Richard Nicols. New Amsterdam fell almost without a shot and became New York.

James was adamantly opposed to representative assemblies and ordered that there should be none in New York. To avoid unrest Nicols shrewdly granted as many other civil and political rights as possible; but residents, particularly Puritans who had settled on Long Island, continued to agitate for self-government. Finally, in the 1680s, James relented, only to break his promise when he became king in 1685.

To add to the confusion in the newly renamed colony, James granted a part of his newly acquired domain to John Lord Berkeley and Sir George Carteret (two of the Carolina proprietors) who named their new proprietorship New Jersey. James neglected to tell Colonel Nicols of this, with the result that both Nicols, on the one hand, and Carteret and Berkeley, on the other, were granting title to the same land—to different settlers. Conflicting claims of land ownership plagued New Jersey for decades, being used by the crown in 1702 as a pretext to take over New Jersey as a royal colony.

The Colonial World

Life in the Colonies

New England grew not only from immigration but also from natural increase during the 17th century. The typical New England family had more children than the typical English or Chesapeake family, and more of those children survived to have families of their own. A New Englander could expect to live 15 to 20 years longer than his counterpart in the parent country and 25 to 30 years longer than his fellow colonist in the Chesapeake. Because of the continuity provided by these longer lifespans, because the Puritans had migrated as intact family units, and because of the homogeneous nature of the Puritan New England colonies, New England enjoyed a much more stable and well-ordered society than did the Chesapeake colonies.

Puritans placed great importance on the family, which in their society was highly patriarchal. Young people were generally subject to their parents' direction in the matter of when and whom they would marry. Few defied this system, and illegitimate births were rare. Puritans also placed great importance on the ability to read, since they believed everyone should be able to read the Bible, God's word, himself. As a result, New England was ahead of the other colonies educationally and enjoyed extremely widespread literacy.

Since New England's climate and soil were unsuited to large-scale farming, the region developed a prosperous economy based on small farming, home industry, fishing, and especially trade and a large shipbuilding industry. Boston became a major international port.

Life in the Chesapeake colonies was drastically different. The typical Chesapeake colonist lived a shorter, less healthy life than his New England counterpart and was survived by fewer children. As a result the Chesapeake's population steadily declined despite a constant influx of settlers. Nor was Chesapeake society as stable as that of New England. Most Chesapeake settlers came as indentured servants; and since planters desired primarily male servants for work in the tobacco fields, men largely outnumbered women in Virginia and Maryland. This hindered the development of family life. The short lifespans also contributed to the region's unstable family life, as few children reached adulthood without experiencing the death of one or both parents. Remarriage resulted in households that contained children from several different marriages.

The system of indentured servitude was open to serious abuse, with masters sometimes treating their servants brutally or contriving through some technicality to lengthen their terms of indenture. In any case, 40 percent of Chesapeake region indentured servants failed to survive long enough to gain their freedom.

By the late 17th century life in the Chesapeake was beginning to stabilize, with death rates declining and life expectancies rising. As society stabilized, an elite group of wealthy families such as the Byrds, Carters, Fitzhughs, Lees, and Randolphs, among others, began to dominate the social and political life of the region. Aping the lifestyle of the English country gentry, they built lavish manor houses from which to rule their vast plantations. For every one of these, however, there were many small farmers who worked hard for a living, showed deference to the great planters, and hoped someday they, or their children, might reach that level.

On the bottom rung of Southern society were the black slaves. During the first half of the 17th century, blacks in the Chesapeake made up only a small percentage of the population and were treated more or less as indentured servants. In the decades between 1640 and 1670 this gradually changed, and blacks came to be seen and treated as life-long chattel slaves whose status would be inherited by their children. Larger numbers of them began to be imported and with this and rapid natural population growth they came by 1750 to compose 30 to 40 percent of the Chesapeake population.

While North Carolina tended to follow Virginia in its economic and social development (although with fewer great planters and more small farmers), South Carolina developed a society even more dominated by large plantations and chattel slavery. By the early decades of the 18th century, blacks had come to outnumber whites in that colony. South Carolina's economy remained dependent on the cultivation of its two staple crops, rice and, to a lesser extent, indigo.

DIDYOUKNOW?

By 1700, the English colonies had a population of about 275,000. Some 7,000 people lived in Boston, the largest colonial city.

Mercantilism and the Navigation Acts

Beginning around 1650, British authorities began to take more interest in regulating American trade for the benefit of the mother country. A key idea that underlay this policy was the concept of mercantilism. Mercantilists believed the world's wealth was sharply limited, and therefore one nation's gain was automatically another nation's loss. Each nation's goal was to export more than it imported (i.e., to have a "favorable balance of trade"). The difference would be made up in gold and silver, which, so the theory ran, would make the nation strong both economically and militarily. To achieve their goals, mercantilists believed economic activity should be regulated by the government. Colonies could fit into England's mercantilist scheme by providing staple crops, such as rice, tobacco, sugar, and indigo, and raw materials, such as timber, that England would otherwise have been forced to import from other countries.

To make the colonies serve this purpose, Parliament passed a series of Navigation Acts (1651, 1660, 1663, and 1673). These were the foundation of England's worldwide commercial system and some of the most important pieces of imperial legislation during the colonial period. They were also intended as weapons in England's on-going struggle against its chief seventeenth-century maritime rival, Holland. The system created by the Navigation Acts stipulated that trade with the colonies was to be carried on only in ships made in Britain or America and with at least 75 percent British or American crews. Additionally, when certain "enumerated" goods were shipped from an American port, they were to go only to Britain or to another American port. Finally, almost nothing could be imported to the colonies without going through Britain first.

Mercantilism's results were mixed. Though ostensibly for the benefit of all subjects of the British Empire, its provisions benefited some at the expense of others. It boosted the prosperity of New Englanders, who engaged in large-scale shipbuilding (something Britain's mercantilist policy-makers chose to encourage), while it hurt the residents of the Chesapeake by driving down the price of tobacco (an enumerated item). On the whole, the Navigation Acts, as intended, transferred wealth from America to Britain by increasing the prices Americans had to pay for British goods and lowering the prices Americans received for the goods they produced. Mercantilism also helped bring on a series of three wars between England and Holland in the late 1600s.

Charles II and his advisors worked to tighten up the administration of colonies, particularly the enforcement of the Navigation Acts. In Virginia tempers grew short as tobacco prices plunged as a result. Virginians were also angry at Royal Governor Sir William Berkeley, whose high-handed, high-taxing ways they despised and whom they believed was running the colony for the benefit of himself and his circle of cronies.

When, in 1674, an impoverished nobleman of shady past by the name of Nathaniel Bacon came to Virginia and failed to gain admittance to Berkeley's inner circle with its financial advantages, he began to oppose Berkeley at every turn and came to head a faction of like-minded persons. In 1676 disagreement over Indian policy brought the matter to the point of armed conflict. Bacon and his men burned Jamestown, but then the whole matter came to an anticlimactic ending when Bacon died of dysentery.

The British authorities, hearing of the matter, sent ships, troops, and an investigating commission. Berkeley, who had had twenty-three of the rebels hanged in reprisal, was removed. Thenceforth Virginia's royal governors had strict instructions to run the colony for the benefit of the mother country. In response, Virginia's gentry, who had been divided over Bacon's Rebellion, united to face this new threat to their local autonomy. By political means they consistently obstructed the governors' efforts to increase royal control.

The Half-Way Covenant

By the latter half of the seventeenth century many Puritans were coming to fear that New England was drifting away from its religious purpose. The children and grand-children of the first generation were displaying more concern for making money than creating a godly society.

To deal with this, some clergymen in 1662 proposed the "Half-Way Covenant," providing a sort of half-way church membership for the children of members, even though those children, having reached adulthood, did not profess saving grace as was normally required for Puritan church membership. Those who embraced the Half-Way Covenant felt that in an increasingly materialistic society it would at least keep church membership rolls full and might preserve some of the church's influence in society.

Some communities rejected the Half-Way Covenant as an improper compromise, but in general the shift toward secular values continued, though slowly.

TEST TIP

Spelling not your strong point? Don't worry. Spelling errors will not affect your essay score as long as the graders can determine what your intent was.

King Philip's War

As New England's population grew, local Indian tribes felt threatened, and conflict sometimes resulted. Puritans endeavored to convert Indians to Christianity. The Bible was translated into Algonquian; four villages were set up for converted Indians, who by 1650 numbered over a thousand. Still, most Indians remained unconverted.

In 1675 a Wampanoag chief named King Philip (Metacomet) led a war to extermi-nate the whites. Some 2,000 settlers lost their lives before King Philip was killed and his tribe subdued. New England continued to experience Indian troubles from time to time, though not as severe as those suffered by Virginia.

The Dominion of New England

The trend toward increasing imperial control of the colonies continued. In 1684 the Massachusetts charter was revoked in retaliation for that colony's large-scale evasion of the restrictions of the Navigation Acts.

The following year Charles II died and was succeeded by his brother, James II. James was prepared to go even farther in controlling the colonies, favoring the establishment of a unified government for all of New England, New York, and New Jersey. This was to be called the Dominion of New England, and the fact that it would abolish representative assemblies and facilitate the imposition of the Church of England on Congregationalist (Puritan) New England made it still more appealing to James.

To head the Dominion, James sent the obnoxious and dictatorial Sir Edmond Andros. Arriving in Boston in 1686, Andros quickly alienated the New Englanders. When news reached America of England's 1688 Glorious Revolution, replacing the Catholic James with his Protestant daughter Mary and her husband, William of Orange, New Englanders cheerfully shipped Andros back to England.

Similar uprisings occurred in New York and Maryland. William and Mary's new government generally accepted these actions, though Jacob Leisler, leader of Leisler's Rebellion in New York, was executed for hesitating to turn over power to the new royal governor. This unfortunate incident poisoned the political climate of New York for many years.

The charter of Massachusetts, now including Plymouth, was restored in 1691, this time as a royal colony, though not as tightly controlled as others of that type.

The Salem Witch Trials

In 1692 Massachusetts was shaken by an unusual incident in which several young girls in Salem Village (now Danvers) claimed to be tormented by the occult activities of certain of their neighbors. Before the resulting Salem witch trials could be stopped by the intervention of Puritan ministers such as Cotton Mather, some twenty persons had been executed (nineteen by hanging and one crushed under a pile of rocks).

Pennsylvania and Delaware

Pennsylvania was founded as a refuge for Quakers. One of a number of radical religious sects that had sprung up about the time of the English Civil War, the Quakers held many controversial beliefs. They believed all persons had an "inner light" which allowed them to commune directly with God. They believed human institutions were, for the most part, unnecessary and, since they believed they could receive revelation directly from God, placed little importance on the Bible. They were also pacifists and declined to show customary deference to those who were considered to be their social superiors. This and their aggressiveness in denouncing established institutions brought them trouble in both Britain and America.

William Penn, a member of a prominent British family, converted to Quakerism as a young man. Desiring to found a colony as a refuge for Quakers, in 1681 he sought and received from Charles II a grant of land in America as payment of a large debt the king had owed Penn's late father.

Penn advertised his colony widely in Europe, offered generous terms on land, and guaranteed a representative assembly and full religious freedom. He personally went to America to set up his colony, laying out the city of Philadelphia. He succeeded in maintaining peaceful relations with the Indians.

In the years that followed, settlers flocked to Pennsylvania from all over Europe. The colony grew and prospered and its fertile soil made it not only attractive to settlers, but also a large exporter of grain to Europe and the West Indies.

Delaware, though at first part of Pennsylvania, was granted by Penn a separate legislature, but until the American Revolution, Pennsylvania's proprietary governors also functioned as governor of Delaware.

TEST TIP

Remember that the multiple-choice section of the AP U.S. History Exam gives you 55 minutes to answer 80 questions. Plan to spend about 40 seconds on each question. Pacing yourself in this way will help ensure that you have enough time to comfortably respond to every item.

The 18th Century

Economy and Population

British authorities continued to regulate the colonial economy, though usually without going so far as to provoke unrest. An exception was the Molasses Act of 1733, which would have been disastrous for New England merchants. In this case, trouble was averted by the customs agents wisely declining to enforce the act stringently.

The constant drain of wealth from America to Britain, created by the mother country's mercantilistic policies, led to a corresponding drain in hard currency (gold and silver). The artificially low prices that this shortage of money created for American goods was even more advantageous to British buyers. When colonial legislatures responded by endeavoring to create paper money, British authorities blocked such moves. Despite these hindrances, the colonial American economy remained for the most part extremely prosperous.

America's population continued to grow rapidly, both from natural increases due to prosperity and a healthy environment, and from large-scale immigration, not only of English but also of such other groups as Scots-Irish and Germans.

The Germans were prompted to migrate because of wars, poverty, and religious persecution in their homeland. They found Pennsylvania especially attractive and settled there fairly close to the frontier, where land was more readily available. They eventually came to be called the "Pennsylvania Dutch."

The Scots-Irish, Scottish Presbyterians who had been living in northern Ireland for several generations, left their homes because of high rent and economic depression. In America they settled even farther west than the Germans, on or beyond the frontier in the Appalachians.

The Early Wars of the Empire

Between 1689 and 1763 Britain and its American colonies fought a series of four wars with Spain, France, and France's Indian allies, in part to determine who would dominate North America.

Though the first war, known in America as King William's War (1689–1697) but in Europe as the War of the League of Augsburg, was a limited conflict involving no major battles in America, it did bring a number of bloody and terrifying border raids by Indians. It was ended by the Treaty of Ryswick, which made no major territorial changes.

The second war was known in America as Queen Anne's War (1702–1713), but in Europe as the War of the Spanish Succession, and brought America twelve years of sporadic fighting against France and Spain. It was ended by the Treaty of Utrecht, the terms of which gave Britain major territorial gains and trade advantages.

In 1739 war once again broke out with France and Spain. Known in America as King George's war, it was called the War of Jenkins' Ear in Europe (since Captain Robert Jenkins had claimed to have lost an ear to the Spanish coast guards in the Caribbean) and later the War of the Austrian Succession. American troops played an active role, accompanying the British on several important expeditions and suffering thousands of casualties. In 1745 an all-New England army, led by William Pepperrell, captured the powerful French fortress of Louisbourg at the mouth of the St. Lawrence River. To the Americans' disgust, the British in the 1748 Treaty of Aix-la-Chapelle gave Louisbourg back to France in exchange for lands in India.

Georgia

With this almost constant imperial warfare in mind, it was decided to found a colony as a buffer between South Carolina and Spanish-held Florida. A group of British philanthropists, led by General James Oglethorpe, obtained a charter for such a colony in 1732, to be located between the Savannah and Altamaha rivers and to be populated by such poor as could not manage to make a living in Great Britain.

The philanthropist trustees, who were to control the colony for twenty-one years before it reverted to royal authority, made elaborate and detailed rules to mold the new colony's society as they felt best. As a result, relatively few settlers came, and those who did complained endlessly. By 1752 Oglethorpe and his colleagues were ready to acknowledge their efforts a failure.

The Enlightenment

As the eighteenth century progressed, Americans came to be more or less influenced by European ways of thought, culture, and society. Some Americans embraced the European intellectual movement known as the "Enlightenment."

The key concept of the Enlightenment was rationalism—the belief that human reason was adequate to solve all of mankind's problems and, correspondingly, much less faith was needed in the central role of God as an active force in the universe.

A major English political philosopher of the Enlightenment was John Locke. Writing partially to justify England's 1688 Glorious Revolution, he strove to find in the social and political world the sort of natural laws Isaac Newton had recently discovered in the physical realm. He held that such natural laws included the rights of life, liberty, and property; that to secure these rights people submit to governments; and that governments which abuse these rights may justly be overthrown. His writings were enormously influential in America, though usually indirectly, by way of early eighteenth-century English political philosophers. Americans tended to equate Locke's law of nature with the universal law of God.

DIDYOU**KNOW**?

Founded in 1636, Harvard is the nation's oldest college. It takes its name from John Harvard, a Charlestown, Massachusetts, minister who left the institution his library and half of his estate when he died in 1638.

The most notable Enlightenment man in America was Benjamin Franklin. While Franklin never denied the existence of God, he focused his attention on human reason and what it could accomplish.

The Great Awakening

Of much greater impact on the lives of the common people in America was the movement known as the Great Awakening. It consisted of a series of religious revivals occurring throughout the colonies from the 1720s to the 1740s. Preachers such as the Dutch Reformed Theodore Frelinghuysen, the Presbyterians William and Gilbert Tennent, and the Congregationalist Jonathan Edwards—best known for his sermon "Sinners in the Hands of an Angry God"—proclaimed a message of personal repentance and faith in Jesus Christ for salvation from an otherwise certain eternity in hell. The most dynamic preacher of the Great Awakening was the Englishman George Whitefield, who traveled through the colonies several times, speaking to crowds of up to 30,000.

The Great Awakening had several important results. America's religious community came to be divided between the "Old Lights," who rejected the great Awakening, and the "New Lights," who accepted it—and sometimes suffered persecution because of their fervor. A number of colleges were founded (many of them today's "Ivy League" schools), primarily for the purpose of training New-Light ministers. The Great Awakening also fostered a greater readiness to lay the claims of established authority (in this case religious) alongside a fixed standard (in this case the Bible) and to reject any claims it found wanting.

The French and Indian War

The Treaty of Aix-la-Chapelle (1748), ending King George's War, provided little more than a breathing space before the next European and imperial war. England and France continued on a collision course as France determined to take complete control of the Ohio Valley and western Pennsylvania.

British authorities ordered colonial governors to resist this, and Virginia's Robert Dinwiddie, already involved in speculation on the Ohio Valley lands, was eager to comply. George Washington, a young major of the Virginia militia, was sent to western Pennsylvania to request the French to leave. When the French declined, Washington was sent in 1754 with 200 Virginia militiamen to expel them. After success in a small skirmish, Washington was forced by superior numbers to fall back on his hastily built Fort Necessity and then to surrender.

The war these operations initiated spread to Europe two years later, where it was known as the Seven Years' War. In America it later came to be known as the French and Indian War.

While Washington skirmished with the French in western Pennsylvania, delegates of seven colonies met in Albany, New York, to discuss common plans for defense. Delegate

Benjamin Franklin proposed a plan for an intercolonial government. While the other colonies showed no support for the idea, it was an important precedent for the concept of uniting in the face of a common enemy.

To deal with the French threat, the British dispatched Major General Edward Braddock with several regiments of British regular troops. Braddock marched overland toward the French outpost of Fort Duquesne, at the place where the Monongahela and Allegheny rivers join to form the Ohio. About eight miles short of his goal he was ambushed by a small force of French and Indians. Two-thirds of the British regulars, including Braddock himself, were killed. However, Britain bounced back from this humiliating defeat and several others that followed, and under the leadership of its capable and energetic prime minister, William Pitt, had by 1760 taken Quebec and Montreal and virtually liquidated the French empire in North America.

By the Treaty of Paris of 1763, which officially ended hostilities, Britain gained all of Canada and all of what is now the United States east of the Mississippi River. France lost all of its North American holdings.

Americans at the end of the French and Indian War were proud to be part of the victorious British Empire and proud of the important role they had played in making it so. They felt affection for Great Britain, and thoughts of independence would not have crossed their minds.

(Before taking the quiz noted below, please review the summary timeline for this chapter on the following pages.)

Time for a quiz
- Review strategies in Chapter 2
- Take Quiz 1 at the REA Study Center
  (www.rea.com/studycenter)

The Colonial Period (1500–1763)

Historical Timeline (1500–1763)

Year	Event
1517	Martin Luther challenges Roman Catholic authority, beginning Protestant Reformation in Europe
1521	Cortés conquers Aztecs in Mexico Magellan circumnavigates the globe
1533	Pizarro captures Inca capital in Peru
1539	De Soto explores southeastern U.S.
1540	Coronado explores southwestern U.S.
1555	Elizabeth I takes throne in England
1585	Roanoke Island colony established off Virginia coast, then disappears
1607	Jamestown colony founded
1608	Champlain founds Quebec
1611	First Virginia tobacco crop harvested
1619	First Africans arrive in Virginia
1620	Plymouth Colony founded House of Burgesses established in Virginia
1622	Powhatan Confederacy attacks Virginia settlers
1630	Massachusetts Bay Colony founded
1635	Roger Williams establishes Rhode Island colony
1636	Harvard College founded
1660	Anne Hutchinson expelled from Massachusetts Bay Colony

In March 1776, Washington placed on Dorchester Heights, overlooking Boston, some of the large cannon that had been captured at Ticonderoga, forcing the British to evacuate the city.

The British shipped their troops to Nova Scotia and then, together with large reinforcements from Britain, landed that summer at New York City. They hoped to find many loyalists there and make that city the key to their campaign to subdue America.

Washington anticipated the move and was waiting at New York, which Congress had ordered should be defended. However, the under-trained, under-equipped, and badly outnumbered American army was no match for the powerful forces under the Howes. Defeated at the Battle of Long Island (August 27, 1776), Washington narrowly avoided being trapped there (an escape partially due to the Howes' slowness). Defeated again at the Battle of Washington Heights (August 29–30, 1776) on Manhattan, Washington was forced to retreat across New Jersey with the aggressive British General Lord Cornwallis, a subordinate of Howe, in pursuit. By December, what was left of Washington's army had made it into Pennsylvania.

WASHINGTON, CROSSING THE DELAWARE.

Washington preparing to cross the Delaware. Currier and Ives print.

With his victory almost complete, Howe decided to wait till spring to finish annihilating Washington's army. Scattering his troops in small detachments so as to hold all of New Jersey, he went into winter quarters.

Washington, with his small army melting away as demoralized soldiers deserted, decided on a bold stroke. On Christmas night 1776, his army crossed the Delaware River and struck the Hessians at Trenton. The Hessians, still groggy from their hard-drinking Christmas party, were easily defeated. A few days later Washington defeated a British force at Princeton (January 3, 1777).

Howe was so shocked by these two unexpected defeats that he pulled his outposts back close to New York. Much of New Jersey was regained. Those who had signed British loyalty oaths in the presence of Howe's army were now at the mercy of their patriot neighbors. And Washington's army was saved from disintegration.

DIDYOUKNOW?

During the American Revolution, about one-third of American colonists were loyalists who supported Great Britain. Perhaps the most famous loyalist was William Franklin, the illegitimate son of Benjamin Franklin. The famed statesman never forgave his son for his loyalist beliefs, essentially writing him out of his will with the comment, "The part he acted against me in the late war, which is of public notoriety, will account for my leaving him no more of an estate he endeavoured to deprive me of."

Early in the war France began making covert shipments of arms to the Americans. This it did, not because the French government loved freedom (it did not), but because it hated Britain and saw the war as a way to weaken Britain by depriving it of its colonies. Arms shipments from France were vital for the Americans.

Saratoga and Valley Forge

For the summer of 1777 the British home authorities adopted an elaborate plan of campaign urged on them by General Burgoyne. According to the plan, Burgoyne himself would lead an army southward from Canada along the Lake Champlain corridor while another army under Howe moved up the Hudson River to join hands with Burgoyne at Albany. This, it was hoped, would cut off New England and allow the British to subdue that region, which they considered the hotbed of the "rebellion."

Howe had other ideas and shipped his army by sea to Chesapeake Bay, hoping to capture the American capital, Philadelphia, and destroy Washington's army at the same time. At Brandywine Creek (September 1, 1777) Washington tried but failed to stop Howe's advance. Yet the American army, though badly beaten, remained intact. Howe occupied Philadelphia as the Congress fled westward to York, Pennsylvania.

In early October, Washington attempted to drive Howe out of Philadelphia; but his attack at Germantown, though at first successful, failed at least partially due to thick fog and the still imperfect level of training in the American army, both of which contributed to confusion among the troops. Thereafter Howe settled down to comfortable winter quarters in Philadelphia, and Washington and his army to very uncomfortable ones at nearby Valley Forge, while far to the north, the British strategy that Howe had ignored was going badly awry.

Burgoyne's advance began well but slowed as the Americans placed obstructions on the rough wilderness trails by which his army, including numerous cannon and much bulky baggage, had to advance. A diversionary force of British troops and Iroquois Indians under the command of Colonel Barry St. Leger swung east of Burgoyne's column, but although it defeated and killed American General Nicholas Herkimer at the Battle of Oriskany (August 6, 1777), it was finally forced to withdraw to Canada.

In mid-August, a detachment of Burgoyne's force was defeated by New England militia under General John Stark near Bennington in what is now Vermont. By autumn Burgoyne found his way blocked by an American army: continentals (American regular troops such as those that made up most of Washington's army, paid, in theory at least, by Congress); and New England militia, under General Horatio Gates, at Saratoga, about thirty miles north of Albany. Burgoyne's two attempts to break through (September 19 and October 7, 1777) were turned back by the Americans under the brilliant battlefield leadership of Benedict Arnold. On October 17, 1777, Burgoyne surrendered to Gates.

The American victory at Saratoga convinced the French to join openly in the war against England. Eventually the Spanish (1779) and the Dutch (1780) joined as well, and England was faced with a world war.

The British Move South

The new circumstances brought a change in British strategy. With fewer troops available for service in America, the British would have to depend more on loyalists, and since they imagined that larger numbers of these existed in the South than elsewhere, it was there they turned their attention.

Howe was relieved and replaced by General Henry Clinton, who was ordered to abandon Philadelphia and march to New York. In doing so, he narrowly avoided defeat at the hands of Washington's army—much improved after a winter's drilling at Valley Forge under the direction of Prussian nobleman Baron von Steuben—at the Battle of Monmouth, New Jersey (June 28, 1778).

Clinton was thenceforth to maintain New York as Britain's main base in America while detaching troops to carry out the new Southern strategy. In November 1778 the British easily conquered Georgia. Late the following year Clinton moved on South Carolina with a land and naval force, and in May 1780, U.S. General Benjamin Lincoln surrendered Charleston. Clinton then returned to New York, leaving Cornwallis to continue the Southern campaign.

Congress, alarmed at the British successes, sent General Horatio Gates to lead the forces opposing Cornwallis. Gates blundered to a resounding defeat at the Battle of Camden, in South Carolina (August 16, 1780).

The general outlook seemed bad for America at that point in the war. Washington's officers grumbled about their pay in arrears. The army was understrength and then suffered successive mutinies among the Pennsylvania and New Jersey troops. Benedict Arnold went over to the British. In short, the British seemed to be winning the contest of endurance. This outlook was soon to change.

In the West, George Rogers Clark, acting under the auspices of the state of Virginia, led an expedition down the Ohio River and into the area of present-day Illinois and Indiana, defeating a British force at Vincennes, Indiana, and securing the area north of the Ohio River for the United States.

TEST TIP

You don't have to answer every multiple-choice question correctly in order to get a great score on the AP Exam. However, you'll need to choose the right answers for at least 50 multiple-choice items to get a score of 3 or above (Source: College Board).

In the South, Cornwallis began to move northward toward North Carolina, but on October 7, 1780, a detachment of his force under Major Patrick Ferguson was defeated by American frontiersmen at the Battle of Kings Mountain in northern South Carolina. To further increase the problems facing the British, Cornwallis had unwisely moved north without bothering to secure South Carolina first. The result was that the British would no sooner leave an area than American militia or guerilla bands, such as that under Francis Marion ("the Swamp Fox"), were once again in control and able to deal with those who had expressed loyalty to Britain in the presence of Cornwallis's army.

To command the continental forces in the South, Washington sent his most able subordinate, military genius Nathaniel Greene. Greene's brilliant strategy led to a crushing victory at Cowpens, South Carolina (January 17, 1781), by troops under Greene's subordinate, General Daniel Morgan of Virginia. It also led to a near victory by Greene's own force at Guilford Court House, North Carolina (March 15, 1781).

Yorktown

The frustrated and impetuous Cornwallis now abandoned the Southern strategy and moved north into Virginia. Clinton, disgusted at this departure from plan, sent instructions for Cornwallis to take up a defensive position and await further orders. Against his better judgment Cornwallis did so, selecting Yorktown, Virginia, on a peninsula that reaches into Chesapeake Bay between the York and James rivers.

Washington now saw and seized the opportunity this presented. With the aid of a French fleet which took control of Chesapeake Bay and a French army that joined him in sealing off the land approaches to Yorktown, Washington succeeded in trapping Cornwallis. After three weeks of siege, Cornwallis surrendered on October 17, 1781.

The War at Sea

Britain had other problems as well. Ships of the small but daring U.S. Navy as well as privateers (privately owned vessels outfitted with guns and authorized by a warring government to capture enemy merchant ships for profit) preyed on the British merchant marine. John Paul Jones, the most famous of American naval leaders, captured ships and carried out audacious raids along the coast of Britain itself. French and Spanish naval forces also struck against various outposts of the British Empire.

The Treaty of Paris of 1783

News of the debacle at Yorktown brought the collapse of Lord North's ministry, and the new Cabinet opened peace negotiations. The extremely able American negotiating team was composed of Benjamin Franklin, John Adams, and John Jay. The negotiations continued for some time, delayed by French and Spanish maneuvering. When it became apparent that France and Spain were planning to achieve an agreement unfavorable to the United States, the American envoys negotiated a separate treaty with Britain.

The final agreement became known as the Treaty of Paris of 1783. Its terms stipulated the following: 1) The United States was recognized as an independent nation by the major European powers, including Britain; 2) Its western boundary was set at the

Mississippi River; 3) Its southern boundary was set at 31° north latitude (the northern boundary of Florida); 4) Britain retained Canada but had to surrender Florida to Spain; 5) Private British creditors would be free to collect any debts owed by U.S. citizens; and 6) Congress was to recommend that the states restore confiscated loyalist property.

The Creation of New Governments

The State Constitutions

After the collapse of British authority in 1775, it became necessary to form new state governments. By the end of 1777 ten new state constitutions had been formed.

Connecticut and Rhode Island kept their colonial charters, which were republican in nature, simply deleting references to British sovereignty. Massa-chusetts waited until 1780 to complete the adoption of its new constitution. The constitutions ranged from such extremely democratic models as the virtually unworkable Pennsylvania constitution (soon abandoned), in which a unicameral legislature ruled with little check or balance, to more reasonable frameworks such as those of Maryland and Virginia, which included more safeguards against popular excesses.

Massachusetts voters set an important example by insisting that a constitution should be made by a special convention rather than the legislature. This would make the constitution superior to the legislature and, it was hoped, assure that the legislature would be subject to the constitution.

Most state constitutions included bills of rights—lists of things the government was not supposed to do to the people.

The Articles of Confederation

In the summer of 1776, Congress appointed a committee to begin devising a framework for national government. When completed, this document was known as the Articles of Confederation. John Dickinson, who had played a leading role in writing the Articles, felt a strong national government was needed; but by the time Congress finished revising them, the Articles went to the opposite extreme of preserving the sovereignty of the states and creating a very weak national government.

The Articles of Confederation provided for a unicameral Congress in which each state would have one vote, as had been the case in the Continental Congress. Executive authority under the Articles would be vested in a committee of thirteen, one member from each state. In order to amend the Articles, the unanimous consent of all the states was required.

The Articles of Confederation government was empowered to make war, make treaties, determine the amount of troops and money each state should contribute to the war effort, settle disputes between states, admit new states to the Union, and borrow money. More importantly, however, was that it was not empowered to levy taxes, raise troops, or regulate commerce.

Ratification of the Articles of Confederation was delayed by a disagreement over the future status of the lands that lay to the west of the original thirteen states. Some states, notably Virginia, held extensive claims to these lands based on their original colonial charters. Maryland, which had no such claim, withheld ratification until in 1781 Virginia agreed to surrender its western claims to the new national government.

DIDYOUKNOW?

Although George Washington is commonly identified as the first president of the United States, seven presidents actually served before him—under the Articles of Confederation. The first of these largely forgotten presidents was John Hanson, who governed from November 1781 to November 1782.

Declaration of Independence

Meanwhile, the country was on its way to deep financial trouble. Unable to tax, Congress resorted to printing large amounts of paper money to finance the war; but these inflated "Continentals" were soon worthless. Other financial schemes fell through, and only grants and loans from France and the Netherlands staved off complete financial collapse. A plan to amend the Articles to give Congress power to tax was stopped by the lone opposition of Rhode Island. The army, whose pay was far in arrears, threatened mutiny. Some of those who favored a stronger national government welcomed this development and in what became known as the Newburgh Conspiracy (1783) consulted with army second-in-command Horatio Gates as to the possibility of using the army to force the states to surrender more power to the national government. This movement was stopped by a moving appeal to the officers by Washington himself.

TEST TIP

Essay questions ask you to respond to a direct question using historical facts and interpretation. Because the most important thing that you must do to score well on these questions is fully answer the question, you should begin by asking yourself what, exactly, the question wishes you to do. Try to rephrase the question in your own words.

The Trans-Appalachian West and the Northwest Ordinance

For many Americans the enormous trans-Appalachian frontier represented an opportunity to escape the economic hard times that followed the end of the war.

In 1775, Daniel Boone opened the "Wilderness Road" through the Cumberland Gap and on to the "Bluegrass" region of Kentucky. Others scouted down the Ohio River from Pittsburgh. By 1790, over 100,000 had settled in Kentucky and Tennessee, despite the risk of violent death at the hands of Indians. This risk was made worse by the presence of the British in northwestern military posts that should have been evacuated at the end of the war. From these posts they supplied the Indians with guns and encouraged them to use them on Americans. The Spaniards on the Florida frontier behaved in much the same way.

The settlement of Kentucky and Tennessee increased the pressure for the opening of the lands north of the Ohio River. To facilitate this, Congress passed three land ordinances in the years from 1784 to 1787.

The Land Ordinance of 1784 provided for territorial government and an orderly system by which each territory could progress to full statehood (this ordinance is sometimes considered part of the Land Ordinance of 1785).

The Land Ordinance of 1785 provided for the orderly surveying and distribution of land in townships six miles square, each composed of thirty-six one-square-mile (640 acre) sections, of which one should be set aside for the support of education. (This ordinance is sometimes referred to as the "Northwest Ordinance of 1785").

The Northwest Ordinance of 1787 provided a bill of rights for settlers and forbade slavery north of the Ohio River.

These ordinances were probably the most important legislation of the Articles of Confederation government.

DIDYOU**KNOW?**

Along with the designation of one section for the use of public schools in each township, the federal government reserved four sectors of each township for land bounties to veterans of the American Revolution under the Northwest Ordinance.

The Jay-Gardoqui Negotiations

Economic depression followed the end of the war as the United States remained locked into the disadvantageous commercial system of the British Empire but without the trade advantages that this system had provided.

One man who thought he saw a way out of the economic quagmire was Congress's secretary of foreign affairs, John Jay. In 1784, Jay began negotiating with Spanish minister Gardoqui a treaty that would have granted lucrative commercial privileges—benefiting large east-coast merchants such as Jay—in exchange for U.S. acceptance of Spain's closure of the Mississippi River as an outlet for the agricultural goods of the rapidly growing settlements in Kentucky and Tennessee. This the Spanish desired because they feared that extensive settlement in what was then the western part of the United States might lead to American hunger for Spanish-held lands.

When Jay reported this to Congress in the summer of 1786, the West and South were outraged. Negotiations were broken off. Some, angered that Jay could show so little concern for the other sections of the country, talked of dissolving the Union; this helped spur to action those who desired not the dissolution but the strengthening of the Union.

Shays' Rebellion

Nationalists were further stimulated to action by Shays' Rebellion (1786). Economic hard times coupled with high taxes intended to pay off the state's war debt drove western Massachusetts farmers to desperation. Led by war veteran Daniel Shays, they shut down courts to prevent judges from seizing property or condemning people to debtors' prison for failing to pay their taxes.

The unrest created a disproportionate amount of panic in the rest of the state and the nation. The citizens of Boston subscribed money to raise an army to suppress the rebels. The success of this army together with timely tax relief caused the "rebellion" to fizzle out fairly quickly.

Amid the panic caused by the news of the uprising, many came to feel that a stronger government was needed to control such violent public outbursts as those of the western Massachusetts farmers.

TEST TIP

Before you begin writing your response to an essay question on the AP Exam, create an outline of your thoughts. Your outline should include a thesis statement and the main points you wish to include in your essay. To help organize your essay, you may wish to divide up your ideas paragraph by paragraph or list them in the order in which you plan to discuss them.

The American Revolution (1763–1783)

Historical Timeline (1763–1783)

1763	Proclamation Line of 1763
1764	Stamp Act Currency Act
1765	Stamp Act Sons of Liberty formed
1767	Townshend Duties Dickinson's "Letters of a Pennsylvania Farmer"
1770	Boston Massacre Lord North becomes British prime minister
1772	H.M.S. *Gaspee* burned off coast of Rhode Island
1773	Tea Act Boston Tea Party
1774	Intolerable Acts First Continental Congress
1775	Lexington and Concord Battle of Bunker Hill
1776	*Common Sense* published by Thomas Paine Declaration of Independence Battle of New York City Battle of Trenton
1777	British surrender 5,800 men at Saratoga American army at Valley Forge
1778	French-American alliance established British begin Southern strategy and capture Savannah
1780	British capture Charleston French army lands in Connecticut
1781	Articles of Confederation approved Gen. Cornwallis surrenders at Yorktown
1783	Treaty of Paris ends war, grants American independence Newburgh Conspiracy of American army officers

The United States Constitution (1785–1789)

Development and Ratification

Toward a New Constitution

As time went on, the inadequacy of the Articles of Confederation became increasingly apparent. Congress could not compel the states to comply with the terms of the Treaty of Paris of 1783 regarding debts and loyalists' property. The British used this as an excuse for not evacuating their Northwestern posts, hoping to be on hand to make the most of the situation when, as they not unreasonably expected, the new government fell to pieces. In any case, Congress could do nothing to force them out of the posts, nor to solve any of the nation's other increasingly pressing problems.

In these dismal straits, some called for disunion, others for monarchy. Others felt that republican government could still work if given a better constitution, and they made it their goal to achieve this.

In 1785 a meeting of representatives of Virginia, Maryland, Pennsylvania, and Delaware was held at George Washington's residence, Mt. Vernon, for the purpose of discussing current problems of interstate commerce. At their suggestion the Virginia legislature issued a call for a convention of all the states on the same subject, to meet the following summer in Annapolis, Maryland.

The Annapolis Convention met in September of 1786, but only five states were represented. Among those present, however, were such nationalists as Alexander Hamilton, John Dickinson, and James Madison. With so few states represented it was decided instead to call for a convention of all the states to meet the following summer in Philadelphia for the purpose of revising the Articles of Confederation.

The Constitutional Convention

The men who met in Philadelphia in 1787 were remarkably able, highly educated, and exceptionally accomplished. For the most part they were lawyers, merchants and planters. Though representing individual states, most thought in national terms. Prominent among them were James Madison, Alexander Hamilton, Gouverneur Morris, Robert Morris, John Dickinson, and Benjamin Franklin.

George Washington was unanimously elected to preside, and the enormous respect that he commanded helped hold the convention together through difficult times (as it had the Continental Army) and make the product of the convention's work more attractive to the rest of the nation. The delegates then voted that the convention's discussions should be secret, to avoid the distorting and confusing influence of the press and publicity.

The delegates shared a basic belief in the innate selfishness of man, which must somehow be kept from abusing the power of government. For this purpose the document that they finally produced contained many checks and balances, designed to prevent the government, or any one branch of the government, from gaining too much power.

Madison, who has been called the "father of the Constitution," devised a plan of national government and persuaded fellow Virginian Edmund Randolph, who was more skilled at public speaking, to introduce it. Known as the "Virginia Plan," it called for an executive branch and two houses of Congress, each based on population.

Smaller states, who would thus have seen their influence decreased, objected and countered with William Paterson's "New Jersey Plan," calling for the continuation of a unicameral legislature with equal representation for the states as well as sharply increased powers for the national government.

A temporary impasse developed that threatened to break up the convention. At this point Benjamin Franklin played an important role in reconciling the often wrangling delegates, suggesting that the sessions of the convention henceforth begin with prayer (they did) and making various other suggestions that eventually helped the convention arrive at the "Great Compromise." The Great Compromise provided for a Presidency, a Senate with all states represented equally (by two Senators each), and a House of Representatives with representation according to population.

Another crisis involved North-South disagreement over the issue of slavery. Here also a compromise was reached. Slavery was neither endorsed nor condemned by the Constitution. Each slave was to count as three-fifths of a person for purposes of apportioning representation and direct taxation on the states (the Three-Fifths Compromise). The federal government was prohibited from stopping the importation of slaves prior to 1808.

The third major area of compromise was the nature of the Presidency. This was made easier by the virtual certainty that George Washington would be the first president and the universal trust that he would not abuse the powers of the office or set a bad example for his successors. The result was a strong Presidency with control of foreign policy and the power to veto Congress's legislation. Should the president commit an actual crime, Congress would have the power to impeach him. Otherwise the president would serve for a term of four years and be re-electable without limit. As a check to the possible excesses of democracy, the president was to be elected by an Electoral College, in which each state would have the same number of electors as it did Senators and Representatives combined. The person with the second highest total in the Electoral College would be Vice-President. If no one gained a majority in the Electoral College, the President would be chosen by the House of Representatives.

> ## DID YOU KNOW?
>
> As president of the Constitutional Convention, George Washington regularly sat in a chair that had been decorated with a painting of the sun. After the group finally agreed on the text of the Constitution, a pleased Benjamin Franklin famously remarked, "I have . . . often . . . looked at that [sun] behind the president without being able to tell whether it was rising or setting; but now at length I have the happiness to know that it is a rising and not a setting Sun." (John R. Vile, The Constitutional Convention of 1787, Volume 2.)

The new Constitution was to take effect when nine states, through special state conventions, had ratified it.

The Struggle for Ratification

As the struggle over ratification got under way, those favoring the Constitution astutely took for themselves the name Federalists (i.e., advocates of centralized power) and labeled their opponents Antifederalists. The Federalists were effective in explaining the convention and the document it had produced. *The Federalist Papers*, written as a series of eighty-five newspaper articles by Alexander Hamilton, James Madison, and John Jay, brilliantly expounded the Constitution and demonstrated how it was designed to prevent the abuse of power from any direction. These essays are considered to be the best commentary on the Constitution by those who helped write it.

At first, ratification progressed smoothly, with five states approving in quick succession. In Massachusetts, however, a tough fight developed. By skillful maneuvering, Federalists were able to win over to their side such popular opponents of the Constitution as Samuel Adams and John Hancock. Others were won over by the promise that a bill of rights would be added to the Constitution, limiting the federal government just as the state governments were limited by their bills of rights. With such promises, Massachusetts ratified by a narrow margin.

By June 21, 1788, the required nine states had ratified, but the crucial states of New York and Virginia still held out. In Virginia, where George Mason and Patrick Henry opposed the Constitution, the influence of George Washington and the promise of a bill of rights finally prevailed and ratification was achieved there as well. In New York, where Alexander Hamilton led the fight for ratification, *The Federalist Papers*, the promise of a bill of rights, and the news of Virginia's ratification were enough to carry the day.

Only North Carolina and Rhode Island still held out, but they both ratified within the next fifteen months.

In March 1789, George Washington was inaugurated as the nation's first president.

Outline of The United States Constitution

Articles of the Constitution

Preamble

"We the People of the United States, in order to form a more perfect Union, establish justice, insure domestic tranquility, provide for the common defense, promote the general welfare, and secure the blessings of liberty to ourselves and our posterity, do ordain and establish this Constitution for the United States of America."

Article I – Legislature

The legislature is divided into two parts—the House of Representatives (435 members currently; determined by proportional representation of the population) and the Senate (100 members currently; two from each state).

The House of Representatives may bring impeachment charges. All bills which concern money must originate in the House. Because of the size of the body, debate is limited except in special cases, where all representatives may meet as the Committee of the Whole. The Speaker of the House presides over the proceedings. Terms of representatives are two years, re-electable without limit, to persons who are at least 25 years of age.

The Senate, originally elected by state legislatures but now by direct election (17th Amendment), approves or rejects presidential nominations and treaties, and serves as the court and jury in impeachment proceedings. Debate within the Senate is unlimited. The President pro tempore usually presides, but the Vice-President of the United States is the presiding officer, and may vote to break a tie. Senate elected terms are for six years, re-electable without limit, to persons who are at least 30 years of age.

Article II – Executive

The President of the United States is elected for a four-year term, originally electable without limit (the 22nd Amendment limits election to two terms), and must be at least 35 years old.

Responsibilities for the President as outlined in the Constitution include acting as the Chief of State, the Chief Executive, Commander-in-Chief of the Armed Forces, the Chief Diplomat, and Chief Legislature.

Article III – Judiciary

While the Constitution describes the Supreme Court in Article 111, the actual construction of the court system was accomplished by the Judiciary Act of 1789. The Supreme Court has jurisdiction for federal courts and appellate cases on appeal from lower courts.

Article IV – Interstate Relations

This article guarantees that court decisions and other legal actions (marriage, incorporation, etc.) valid in one state are valid in another. Extradition of criminals (and, originally, runaway slaves) and the exchange of citizenship benefits are likewise guaranteed. Article IV also provides for the admission of new states and guarantees federal protection against invasion and violence for each state. States admitted maintain the same status as the original states. All states are guaranteed a republican form of government.

Article V – Amendment Process

Amendments are proposed by a two-thirds vote of each house of Congress or by a special convention called by Congress upon the request of two-thirds of the state legislatures. Amendments are ratified by three-fourths of the state legislatures or state conventions.

Article VI – Supremacy Clause

Article VI sets up the hierarchy of laws in the United States. The Constitution is the "supreme law of the land," and supersedes treaties. Treaties supercede federal laws, federal laws (later to include federal regulatory agency directives) supercede state constitutions, state laws and local laws, respectively. All federal and state officials, including judges, must take an oath to support and defend the Constitution.

Article VII – Ratification

This article specified the ratification process necessary for the Constitution to take effect. Nine of the original thirteen states had to ratify the Constitution before it became operative.

Amendments to the Constitution

The Amendments to the Constitution guarantee certain individual rights and amend original dictates of the Constitution. The first ten amendments are known as the Bill of Rights, for which Thomas Jefferson provided the impetus.

1 – protects the freedom of religion, speech, press, assembly, as well as the right to petition the government for the redress of grievances (1791)

2 – protects the right to bear arms* (1791)

3 – ensures that troops will not be housed in private citizens' homes (1791)

4 – protects against unreasonable search and seizure (need for search warrant) (1791)

5 – protects the rights for the accused, including required indictments, double jeopardy, self-incrimination, due process, and just compensation (1791)

6 – guarantees a speedy and public trial, the confrontation by witnesses, and the right to call witnesses on one's own behalf (1791)

7 – guarantees a jury trial (1791)

8 – protects against excessive bail and cruel and unusual punishment (1791)

9 – says that all rights not enumerated are nonetheless retained by the people (1791)

10 – says that all powers not specifically delegated to the federal government are retained by the states (1791)

---

*In the 2008 decision, *District of Columbia v. Heller,* the Supreme Court struck down the sweeping ban on handguns in Washington, D.C., thus breathing new life into the Second Amendment. The high court had only examined the Second Amendment once before, in 1939, since the Constitution was ratified in 1791.

provincial town, with muddy streets and muggy summers. Most of its inhabitants moved out when Congress was not in session.

Jefferson the President

The new president tried to project an image of democratic simplicity, sometimes appearing so casually dressed as to appear slovenly. But he was a brilliant thinker and a shrewd politician. He appointed men to his Cabinet who agreed with his political philosophy: James Madison as Secretary of State and Albert Gallatin to the Treasury.

specimens, Jefferson was most interested in the possibility of a Northwest Passage by water to the Pacific. The expedition was also an attempt to gain information about the activities of British and French fur-trappers, who had been in the area for years.

Jefferson chose Captain Meriwether Lewis as the leader of this Corps of Discovery and Lewis immediately asked an old friend, William Clark, to be his co-commander. While officially still a second lieutenant, Lewis from the start treated Clark as an equal and referred to him as "Captain" with the men of the Corps, which consisted of 33 members. The Corps left from Camp River Dubois, near present-day Hartford, Illinois, on May 14, 1804. They traveled up the Missouri and passed the last white settlement at La Charrette. On August 20, 1804, the Corps of Discovery lost one member, Sergeant Charles Floyd, who apparently died from acute appendicitis. That was their only fatality of the nearly three-year journey. They spent the winter of 1804–1805 at Fort Mandan, in present-day North Dakota. They hired a French Canadian, Toussaint Charbonneau, as a guide. Charbonneau's Shoshone wife, Sacagawea, also accompanied the Corps and proved to be an invaluable guide and source of information. She had a son, Jean Baptiste (or Pomp, as he was called by Clark), who was born just before the expedition left the Mandans. Because the Corps traveled with a woman and a child, the Indian tribes they encountered recognized that this strange group of whites (and one African-American, York, Clark's slave) was not a war party and mostly aided the voyage.

The journey up the Missouri River was difficult because of heat, injuries, mosquitoes, and the river itself, which was difficult to navigate. The Corps employed a keelboat and two smaller boats, called pirogues, on the voyage and averaged 15 miles per day. The expedition followed the Missouri through what are now the states of Missouri, Nebraska, North Dakota, and Montana, where they discovered the Missouri's headwaters. They then crossed the Rocky Mountains and reached the West Coast of North America by paddling down the Clearwater River, the Snake River, and the Columbia River through what is now Oregon until they reached the Pacific Ocean in December 1805. The trip ran into several huge obstacles, such as the need for horses to cross the Rockies, but the expedition was aided in that quest by the chance encounter of Sacagawea with her brother, Kamahweit, and his tribe of Shoshones, from whom she had been kidnapped as a girl years earlier. It was from the Shoshones that the expedition was able to purchase the horses it needed. When the Corps reached the Pacific, they camped on the south side of the Columbia River and built Fort Clatsop near the modern town of Astoria, Oregon. When a hoped-for European ship never showed up during their rain-soaked wait, they started a return trip across the continent on March 23, 1806, and arrived back in St. Louis on September 23.

The Corps of Discovery traveled over 8,000 miles, lost only one member of their party, and cost the government the small sum of $40,000. The Lewis and Clark expedition made a major contribution in mapping a vastly unexplored segment of the North American continent. The journals of Lewis and Clark documented valuable information about the natural history of the area and the Native Americans living there. Hundreds of new plant and animal species were identified. Perhaps most importantly, they focused the attention of the nation on the West and paved the way for the many emigrants who would follow on the Oregon Trail to the Pacific Northwest.

Conflict with the Judges

Marbury vs. Madison

William Marbury, one of Adams' "midnight appointments," sued Secretary of State Madison to force delivery of his commission as a justice of the peace in the federal district. John Marshall, as Supreme Court justice, refused to rule on the request, claiming that the law which gave the Supreme Court jurisdiction over such matters had exceeded the Constitutional grant of powers and thus was unconstitutional. Marshall thus asserted the power of judicial review over federal legislation, a power which has become the foundation of the Supreme Court's check on the other two branches of government.

The Impeachment Episodes

Jefferson began a campaign to remove Federalist judges by impeachment. One district judge was removed, and proceedings were begun to impeach Supreme Court Justice Samuel Chase. That effort failed, but the threat had encouraged the judiciary to be less blatantly political.

Domestic Affairs

Enforcement of the Alien and Sedition Acts was immediately suspended, and the men convicted under those laws were released.

The federal bureaucracy was reduced and expenses were drastically cut. The size of the army was reduced and the expansion program of the Navy was cancelled.

The excise taxes were repealed and federal income was limited to land sale proceeds and customs duties. Federal land sale policy was liberalized, smaller parcels were authorized, and less cash was required—policies which benefitted small farmers.

The 12th Amendment was adopted and ratified in 1804, ensuring that a tie vote between candidates of the same party could not again cause the confusion of the Jefferson-Burr affair.

Following the Constitutional mandate, the importation of slaves was stopped by law in 1808.

The Louisiana Purchase

Napoleon, in an effort to regain some of France's New World empire, had obtained the old French trans-Mississippi territory from Spain by political pressure. Jefferson sent a delegation to Paris to try to buy New Orleans, lest the new French officials close it to American traffic. Napoleon's defeat in Santo Domingo persuaded him that Louisiana could not be exploited, and indeed was now subject to potential American incursions. So he offered to sell the entire territory to the United States for $15 million. The American delegation accepted the offer in April 1803, even though they had no authority to buy more than the city of New Orleans.

> **DID YOU KNOW?**
>
> The territory included in the Louisiana Purchase was so vast that it included all of the land that is now the states of Louisiana, Missouri, Arkansas, Iowa, North Dakota, South Dakota, Nebraska, and Oklahoma, along with much of the land that is now Kansas, Colorado, Wyoming, Montana, and Minnesota.

The Constitutional Dilemma

Jefferson's stand on the strict interpretation of the Constitution would not permit him to purchase land without Congressional approval. But he accepted his advisors' counsel that his treaty-making powers included the authority to buy the land. Congress concurred, after the fact, and the purchase price was appropriated, thus doubling the territory of the nation overnight.

Exploring the West

Even before Napoleon's offer, Jefferson had authorized an expedition to explore the Western territory to the Pacific. The Lewis and Clark group, with 48 men, left St. Louis in 1804, and returned two years later with a wealth of scientific and anthropological information, and having strengthened the United States' claim to the Oregon territory. At the same time, Zebulon Pike and others had been traversing the middle parts of Louisiana and mapping the land.

The Essex Junto (1804)

Some New England Federalists saw the Western expansion as a threat to their position in the Union, and they tried to organize a secessionist movement. They courted Aaron Burr's support by offering to back him in a bid for the governorship of New

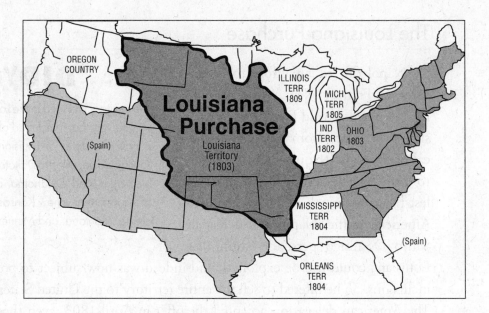

The Louisiana Purchase, in 1803, doubled the size of the U.S.

York. Hamilton led the opposition to that campaign and when Burr lost the election, he challenged Hamilton to a duel, which resulted in Hamilton's death.

The Burr Conspiracy

Aaron Burr was now a fugitive, without a political future. He became involved in a scheme to take Mexico from Spain and establish a new nation in the West.

In the fall of 1806, he led a group of armed men down the Mississippi River system toward New Orleans. He was arrested in Natchez and tried for treason in Richmond, Virginia. Judge John Marshall's decision for acquittal helped to narrow the legal definition of treason. Jefferson's attempts to influence and prejudice the trial were justified by his claims of "executive privilege," but they were fruitless.

John Randolph and the Yazoo Claims

Jefferson's Republican opponents, under the leadership of his cousin John Randolph of Roanoke, called themselves the "Quids." They accused the president of complicity in the Yazoo Land controversy which had followed Georgia's cession of her western lands to the federal government. This created serious strife within the Republican party and weakened Jefferson's effectiveness in his second term.

TEST TIP

On the AP Exam, a question using a painting or photograph will never ask you to simply identify what person, place, or event the image shows. Instead, you will be asked to apply your knowledge about the contents of the painting or photograph to a broader historical situation or theme.

International Involvement

The Barbary War

In 1801 Jefferson sent a naval force to the Mediterranean to break the practice of the North African Muslim rulers of exacting tribute from Western merchant ships. Intermittent undeclared war dragged on until 1805, with no decisive settlement.

The Napoleonic Wars

War continued in Europe between France under Napoleon and the European powers led by Britain. Both sides tried to prevent trade with their enemies by neutral powers, especially the United States. Napoleon's "Continental System" was answered by Britain's "Orders in Council." American ships were seized by both sides and American sailors were "impressed" into the British navy.

The Chesapeake-Leopard Affair (1807)

The British ship *H.M.S. Leopard* stopped the *U.S.S. Chesapeake* off the Chesapeake Bay, and four alleged British deserters were taken off. Public outcry for war followed, and Jefferson was hard pressed to remain neutral.

The Embargo of 1807

Jefferson's response to the cry for war was to draft a law prohibiting American ships from leaving port for any foreign destination, thus avoiding contact with vessels of either belligerent. The result was economic depression, particularly in the heavily commercial Northeast. This proved to be his most unpopular policy of both terms in office.

Madison's Administration, 1809–1817

The Election of 1808

Republican James Madison won the election over Federalist Charles Pinckney, but the Federalists gained seats in both houses of the Congress. The embargo-induced depression was obviously a heavy political liability, and Madison was to face growing pressures to deal with the international crisis. He was a brilliant man but with few social or political skills. His greatest asset was probably his wife, the vivacious and energetic Dolley.

The War of 1812

Congress had passed a modified embargo just before Madison's inauguration, known as the Non-Intercourse Act, which opened trade to all nations except France and Britain. When it expired in 1810, it was replaced by Macon's Bill No. 2, which gave the president power to prohibit trade with any nation that violated our neutrality.

The Indian tribes of the Northwest and the Mississippi Valley were resentful of the government's policy of pressured removal to the West, and the British authorities in Canada were exploiting their discontent by encouraging border raids against the American settlements.

The Shawnee chief Tecumseh set out to unite the Mississippi Valley tribes and reestablish Indian dominance in the Old Northwest. With the help of his brother, the Prophet, and the timely New Madrid earthquake, he persuaded a sizeable force of warriors to join him. On November 11, 1811, General William Henry Harrison destroyed Tecumseh's village on Tippecanoe Creek and dashed his hopes for an Indian confederacy.

Southern frontiersmen coveted Spanish Florida, which included the southern ranges of Alabama, Mississippi and Louisiana. They resented Spanish support of Indian depredations against the borderlands, and since Spain was Britain's ally, they saw Britain as the background cause of their problems.

The Congress in 1811 contained a strong pro-war group called the War Hawks, led by Henry Clay and John C. Calhoun. They gained control of both houses and began agitating for war with the British. On June 1, 1812, President Madison asked for a declaration of war, and Congress complied.

A three-pronged invasion of Canada met with disaster on all three fronts, and the Americans fell back to their own borders. At sea, American privateers and frigates, including "Old Ironsides," scored early victories over British warships, but were soon driven back into their home ports and blockaded by the powerful British ships-of-the-line.

Admiral Oliver Hazard Perry constructed a fleet of ships on Lake Erie and on September 10, 1813, defeated a British force at Put-In Bay and established control of the lake. His flagship flew the banner, "Don't Give Up the Ship." This victory opened the way for William Henry Harrison to invade Canada in October and defeat a combination British and Indian force at the Battle of the Thames.

The War in the Southwest

Andrew Jackson led a force of frontier militia into Alabama in pursuit of Creek Indians who had massacred the white inhabitants of Fort Mims. On March 27, 1814, he crushed the Indians at Horseshoe Bend, and then seized the Spanish garrison at Pensacola.

British Strategy Changes, 1814

A British force came down Lake Champlain and met defeat at Plattsburgh, New York, in September. A British armada sailed up the Chesapeake Bay and sacked and burned Washington, D.C. It then proceeded toward Baltimore, which was guarded by Fort McHenry. That fort held firm through the British bombardment, inspiring Key's "Star Spangled Banner."

DIDYOUKNOW?

Francis Scott Key set "The Star-Spangled Banner" to the tune of a popular English song of the time called "To Anacreon in Heaven." The original song was the theme of a London music club known as the Anacreontic Society, named for the ancient Greek poet Anacreon.

The Battle of New Orleans

The most serious British threat came at the port of New Orleans. A powerful invasion force was sent there to close the mouth of the Mississippi River, but Andrew Jackson decisively defeated it with a polyglot army of frontiersmen, blacks, creoles and pirates. The battle was fought on January 8, 1815, two weeks after a peace treaty had been signed at the city of Ghent, in Belgium.

THE TAKING of the CITY of WASHINGTON in AMERICA

The War of 1812 forced the President and the Congress to flee from Washington as the British set public buildings ablaze. From Reginald Horsman, *The War of 1812*, 1969, London, Eyre & Spottiswoode Ltd.

The Treaty of Ghent, Christmas Eve, 1814

With the European wars ended, the major causes for the dispute with Britain had ceased to be important, so both sides were eager for peace. The treaty provided for the acceptance of the status quo at the beginning of hostilities and so both sides restored their wartime conquests to the other.

The Hartford Convention, December 1814

The Federalists had become increasingly a minority party. They vehemently opposed the war and Daniel Webster and other New England congressmen consistently blocked the Administration's efforts to prosecute the war effort. On December 15, 1814, delegates from the New England states met in Hartford, Connecticut, and drafted a set of resolutions suggesting nullification—and even secession—if their interests were not protected against the growing influence of the South and the West.

Soon after the convention adjourned the news of the victory at New Orleans was announced and their actions were discredited. The Federalist party ceased to be a political force from this point on.

Postwar Developments

Protective Tariff (1816)

The first protective tariff in the nation's history was passed in 1816 to slow the flood of cheap British manufactures into the country.

Rush-Bagot Treaty (1817)

An agreement was reached in 1817 between Britain and the United States to stop maintaining armed fleets on the Great Lakes. This first "disarmament" agreement is still in effect.

Jackson's Florida Invasion (1817)

Indian troubles in the newly acquired areas of western Florida prompted General Andrew Jackson, acting under dubious authority, to invade Spanish East Florida and to hang two British subjects whom he suspected of selling guns and supplies to the Indians. Then he reoccupied Pensacola and raised the American flag, a clear violation of international law. Only wide public support prevented his arrest and prosecution by the government.

Indian Policy

The government began to systematically pressure all the Indian tribes remaining in the East to cede their lands and accept new homes west of the Mississippi, a policy which met with disappointing results. Most declined the offer.

The Barbary Wars (1815)

In response to continued piracy and extortion in the Mediterranean, Congress declared war on the Muslim state of Algiers in 1815, and dispatched a naval force to the area under Stephen Decatur. He quickly defeated the North African pirates and forced them to pay indemnities for past tribute they had exacted from American ship captains. This action finally gained the United States free access to the Mediterranean basin.

The Adams-Onis Treaty (1819)

Spain had decided to sell the remainder of the Florida territory to the Americans before they took it anyway. Under this agreement, the Spanish surrendered all their claims to the territory and drew the boundary of Mexico all the way to the Pacific. The United States in exchange agreed to assume $5 million in debts owed to American merchants.

The Monroe Doctrine

Around 1810, national revolutions had begun in Latin America, so the colonial populations refused to accept the rule of the new Napoleonic governments in Europe. Leaders like San Martin and Bolivar had declared independence for their countries and, after Napoleon's fall in 1814, were defying the restored Hapsburg and Bourbon rulers of Europe.

British and American leaders feared that the new European governments would try to restore the former New World colonies to their erstwhile royal owners.

In December 1823, President Monroe included in his annual message to Congress a statement that the American hemisphere was "henceforth not to be considered as subjects for future colonization by any European powers." Thus began a thirty-year period of freedom from serious foreign involvement for the United States.

TEST TIP

It's okay to skip an item that you're unsure about or that you would like to come back to later. Be careful to also skip that line on your answer sheet, however, so that you continue to bubble in your answers on the correct line.

Internal Development, 1820–1830

The years following the War of 1812 were years of rapid economic and social development. Too rapid, in fact, and they were followed by a severe depression in 1819. But this slump was temporary, and it became obvious that the country was moving rapidly from its agrarian origins toward an industrial, urban future. Westward expansion accelerated, and the mood of the people became very positive. In fact, these years were referred to as the "Era of Good Feelings."

The Monroe Presidency, 1817–1825

James Monroe, the last of the "Virginia Dynasty," had been hand-picked by the retiring Madison and he was elected with only one electoral vote opposed: a symbol of national unity.

Postwar Boom

The years following the war were characterized by a high foreign demand for American cotton, grain and tobacco; commerce flourished. The Second National Bank, through its overly liberal credit policies, proved to be an inflationary influence, and the price level rose rapidly.

The Depression of 1819

Inventories of British manufactured goods had built up during the war, and English merchants began to dump their products on the American market at cut-rate prices. American manufacturers suffered from this influx of imports. The U.S. Bank tried to slow the inflationary spiral by tightening credit, and a sharp business slump resulted.

This depression was most severe in the newly expanding West, partly because of its economic dependency, partly because of heavy speculation in Western lands.

The Marshall Court

John Marshall delivered the majority opinions in a number of critical decisions in these formative years, all of which served to strengthen the power of the federal government and restrict the powers of state governments.

Marbury v. Madison (1803)

This case established the Supreme Court's power of judicial review over federal legislation.

Fletcher v. Peck (1810)

The Georgia legislature had issued extensive land grants in a shady deal with the Yazoo Land Company. A subsequent legislative session repealed that action because of the corruption that had attended the original grant. The Court decided that the original action by the Georgia Assembly had constituted a valid contract which could not be broken regardless of the corruption which had followed. This was the first time a state law was voided on the grounds that it violated a principle of the U.S. Constitution.

Dartmouth College v. Woodward (1819)

The quarrel between the president and the trustees of the New Hampshire college became a political issue when the Republicans backed the president and the Federalists supported the trustees. The president tried to change Dartmouth from a private to a public institution by having its charter revoked. The Court ruled that the charter, though issued by the king during colonial days, still constituted a contract, and thus could not be arbitrarily changed or revoked without the consent of both parties. The result of this decision was to severely limit the power of state governments to control the corporation, which was the emerging form of business organization.

McCulloch v. Maryland (1819)

The state of Maryland had tried to levy a tax on the Baltimore branch of the Bank of the United States, and so protect the competitive position of its own state banks. Marshall's ruling declared that no state has the right to control an agency of the federal government. Since "the power to tax is the power to destroy," such state action violated Congress' "implied powers" to establish and operate a national bank.

Gibbons v. Ogden (1824)

The State of New York had granted a monopoly to Ogden to operate a steamboat between New York and New Jersey. Gibbons obtained a Congressional permit to operate a steamboat line in the same waters. When Ogden sued to maintain his monopoly, the New York courts ruled in his favor. Gibbons' appeal went to the Supreme Court. John Marshall ruled that commerce included navigation, and that only Congress has the right to regulate commerce among states. Thus the state-granted monopoly was void.

TEST TIP

On the AP Exam, you'll never be asked to recall specific dates. However, you'll need to understand sequence and cause-and-effect relationships among events in order to answer questions effectively.

Statehood: A Balancing Act

The Missouri Compromise (1820)

The Missouri Territory, the first to be organized from the Louisiana Purchase, applied for statehood in 1819. Since the Senate membership was evenly divided between slave-holding and free states at that time, the admission of a new state was obviously going to give the voting advantage either to the North or to the South. Slavery was already well-established in the new territory, so the Southern states were confident in their advantage, until Representative Tallmadge of New York proposed an amendment to the bill which would prohibit slavery in Missouri.

The Southern outcry was immediate, and the ensuing debate grew hot. The Senate was dead-locked.

Henry Clay's Compromise Solution

As the debate dragged on, the northern territory of Massachusetts applied for admission as the state of Maine. This offered a way out of the dilemma, and House Speaker Clay formulated a package that both sides could accept. The two admission bills were combined, with Maine coming in free and Missouri as a slave state. To make the package palatable for the House, a provision was added to prohibit slavery in the remainder of the Louisiana Territory, north of the southern boundary of Missouri (latitude 36° 30′). Clay guided this bill through the House and it became law, thus maintaining the balance of power.

The debates in Congress had reminded everyone of the deep division between the sections, and some saw it as evidence of trouble to come. Thomas Jefferson, in retirement at Monticello, remarked that the news from Washington was like a "fire-ball in the night."

The Expanding Economy

The Growing Population

The population continued to double every 25 years. The migration of people to the West increased in volume and by 1840 over one-third of all Americans lived west of the Alleghenies. Immigration from abroad was not significant until 1820; then it began to increase rapidly, mostly from the British Isles.

The Farming Sector

The growth of markets for farm products in the expanding cities, coupled with liberal land sale policies by the federal government, made the growing of staple agricultural crops more profitable. More and more land was put into cultivation, and the prevailing system of clearing and planting became more wasteful of timber as well as of the fertility of the land.

The Cotton Kingdom

The new lands in the Southwest, then constituting Alabama, Mississippi, Louisiana and Texas, proved ideal for the production of short-staple cotton. Eli Whitney's invention of the cotton gin solved the problem of separating the seeds from the fibers, and the cotton boom was under way.

The growing market for food and work animals in the cotton South provided the opportunity for the new Western farmers to specialize in those items and further stimulated the westward movement.

TEST TIP

Some questions on the AP Exam ask you to evaluate items identified with Roman numerals. Roman-numeral questions may ask you to group events or concepts into categories, or to identify one or more true statements out of several statements. When addressing Roman-numeral items, it's important to carefully consider each option listed next to a numeral. You may notice that one numeral appears in more answer choices than do others. Evaluate those statements first to help save time by either eliminating the statements immediately or identifying them as a possible answer.

Fishing

New England and Chesapeake fishing proved very profitable. Deep-sea whaling became a significant enterprise, particularly from the Massachusetts/Rhode Island ports.

Lumbering

The expanding population created a need for building materials, and timber remained a profitable export item. Shipbuilding thrived in a number of Eastern Seaboard and Gulf Coast ports.

Fur Trade

John Jacob Astor and others opened up business all the way to the Northwest coast. "Mountain men" probed deeper and deeper into the Rocky Mountain ranges in search of the beaver.

Trade with the Spanish

The Santa Fe Trail, which ran from New Mexico northeast to Independence, Missouri, became an active trading corridor, opening up the Spanish territories to American migration and influence, and also providing the basis for future territorial claims.

The Transportation Revolution

The first half of the 19th century witnessed an extraordinary sequence of inventions and innovations which produced a true revolution in transport and communications.

River Traffic

The steamboats built by Robert Fulton, the *Clermont* in 1807 and the *New Orleans* in 1811, transformed river transport. As shipment times and freight rates both plummeted, regular steam service was established on all the major river systems.

Road Building

By 1818, the National Road, which was built with federal funds, had been completed from Cumberland, Maryland, to Wheeling, Virginia, linking the Potomac with the Ohio River. A network of privately owned toll roads (turnpikes) began to reach out from every sizeable city. They were usually built for only a few miles out, and they never accounted for a significant share of the total freight tonnage moved, but they formed the nucleus of a growing road system in the new nation.

The Canal Era

The Erie Canal, linking the Hudson River at Albany, New York, with Lake Erie, was completed in 1825 and became the first and most successful example of an artificial waterway. It was followed by a rash of construction until canals linked every major waterway system east of the Mississippi River.

Canals were the first development projects to receive large amounts of public funding. They ran east-west and so tied the new West to the old East, with later implications for sectional divisions.

The Rise of New York City

Its location as a transport hub, coupled with innovations in business practices, boosted New York City into a primary trade center, and made it America's largest city by 1830. One such innovation was the packet boats, which operated on a guaranteed schedule and helped to rationalize commerce, both internal and international.

New York soon dominated the domestic market for cotton, a situation which progressively reduced the South to the status of an economic colony.

TEST TIP

When writing your essays, be sure to use neat, legible handwriting. Printing may be a better choice than writing in cursive if your handwriting tends to be messy. The essay graders cannot grade what they cannot read!

Industrialization

The Rise of the Factory System

Samuel Slater had migrated from Britain in 1789, having served as an apprentice under inventor Richard Arkwright and then as a mill manager. He used his knowledge to build the first successful cotton-spinning mill in this country. The first cotton manufacturing plant in the world to include all the elements of manufacturing under one roof was built in Boston in 1813.

Eli Whitney's development and application of the principle of interchangeable parts, first used in his firearms factories, helped to speed the growth of mass-production operations.

The expansion of markets in Latin America and the Far East, as well as domestic markets, both resulted from and helped to develop the factory system.

Manufacturers and industrialists found it necessary to organize banks, insurance companies, and real estate firms to meet the needs of their growing business organizations.

The Corporation

The corporate form, with its limited liability and its potential for raising and utilizing large amounts of capital, became the typical type of business organization. By the 1830s, most states had enacted general laws for incorporating.

The Labor Supply

In the early days, the "Lowell System" became a popular way to staff the New England factories. Young women were hired from the surrounding countryside, brought to town and housed in dormitories in the mill towns. They were paid low wages for hard work under poor conditions, but they were only working for a short time, to earn a dowry or help out with the family income, so they soon went back home. This "rotating labor supply" was ideal for the owners, since the girls were not motivated to agitate for better wages and conditions.

Labor was always in short supply in this country, so the system depended on technology to increase production. This situation always placed a premium on innovation in machinery and technique.

The Growth of Unions

The factory system separated the owners from the workers and thus depersonalized the workplace. It also made the skilled artisan less important, since the repetitive processes of the mill could be performed by relatively unskilled laborers.

Although the first organized strike took place in 1828, in Paterson, New Jersey, by child workers, periodic economic downturns helped keep workers relatively dependent and passive until the 1850s.

A major goal of early unions was the 10-hour day, and this effort sparked a period of growth in organized labor which was later effectively quenched by the depression of 1837.

Educational Development

The Growth of Public Schools

Before 1815, there were no public schools to speak of in this country. Some states had endorsed the idea of free schools for the people, but they shrank from the task of financing such a system. Jefferson had outlined such a plan for Virginia, but it came to nothing.

Schools were primarily sponsored by private institutions—corporate academies in the Northeast and religious institutions in the South and mid-Atlantic states. Most were aristocratic in orientation, training the nation's leaders, and few had any interest in schooling the children of the poor.

Women were likewise considered unfit for academic training, and those female schools which existed concentrated on homemaking skills and the fine arts which would make "ornaments" of the young ladies enrolled.

The New York Free School, one of those rare examples of a school for the poor, experimented for a time with the Lancastrian system, in which older students tutored the younger ones, thus stretching scarce budget dollars.

Higher Education

Although the numbers of institutions of higher learning increased sharply in the early years of the nineteenth century, none was truly public. All relied upon high tuition rates for survival, so less than one in ten young men, and no women, ever attended a college or university.

The training these schools provided was very limited as well. The only professional training was in theology, and only a scattering of colleges offered brief courses of study in law or medicine. The University of Pennsylvania, for example, offered one year of medical schooling, after which a person could obtain a license to practice the healing arts. Needless to say, medical practice was quite primitive.

The Growth of Cultural Nationalism

Jeffersonian Americans tried to demonstrate their newly-won independence by championing a strong sense of cultural nationalism, a feeling that their young republic represented the "final stage" of civilization, the "last great hope of mankind."

Literary Nationalism

Although most Americans had access to one or more newspapers, the market for native authors was quite limited. Publishers preferred to print works from British authors or to import books from Europe. A few Americans who were willing to pay the costs of publishing their own works found a growing number of readers.

Significant American Authors

Washington Irving was by far the best-known native writer in America. He excelled in the telling of folk tales and local color stories, and is best remembered for his portraits of Hudson River characters.

Mercy Otis Warren, the revolutionary pamphleteer, published a multi-volume *History of the Revolution* in 1805.

"Parson" Mason Weems wrote the best-seller *Life of Washington* in 1806, which was short on historical accuracy but long on nationalistic hero-worship.

Educational Literature

Early schoolbooks, like Noah Webster's *Blue Backed Speller*, as well as his dictionary of the "American" language, reflected the intense desire to promote patriotism and a feeling of national identity.

DIDYOU**KNOW?**

Noah Webster introduced many Americanized spellings of words that are widely used today, including the dropped "u" from words such as "color" and "humor" and respellings of words like "jail" and "draft." However, not all of his new spellings caught on, including "wimmen" (women), "tung" (tongue), and "sley" (sleigh).

Developments in Religious Life

The Post-Revolution Years

The Revolutionary War weakened the position of the traditional, established churches. The doctrines of the Enlightenment became very popular, and its religious expression, deism, gained a considerable following among the educated classes. Rationalism, Unitarianism, and Universalism all saw a period of popularity. Thomas Paine's

Lithograph of a religious revival meeting in a western forest. Lippincott, Grambo & Co., 1854.
U.S. Library of Congress

exposition of the rationalist posture, *The Age of Reason*, attacked the traditional Christian values and was read widely.

The Second Great Awakening

The reaction to the trend toward rationalism, the decline in church membership, and the lack of piety, was a renewal of personal, heart-felt evangelicalism. A second Great Awakening began in 1801 at Cane Ridge, Kentucky, in the first "camp meeting."

As the revival spread, its characteristics became more uniform—an emphasis on personal salvation, an emotional response to God's grace, an individualistic faith. Women took a major part in the movement. Blacks were also heavily involved, and the individualistic emphasis created unrest among their ranks, particularly in the slave-holding South.

The revival produced strong nationalistic overtones, and the Protestant ideas of a "called nation" were to flourish later in some of the Manifest Destiny doctrines of expansionism. The social overtones of this religious renewal were to spark the great reform movements of the 1830s and 1840s.

The New Nation (1789–1824)

Historical Timeline (1789–1824)

Year	Event
1789	Judiciary Act sets up federal court system
1791	Bill of Rights approved First Bank of United States chartered
1793	Washington issues Proclamation of Neutrality Louis XVI executed in France Cotton gin patented by Eli Whitney
1794	Whiskey Rebellion
1795	Jay Treaty Pinckney Treaty Treaty of Greenville
1796	Adams defeats Jefferson for presidency
1798	XYZ Affair Alien and Sedition Acts Virginia and Kentucky Resolutions
1800	Jefferson defeats Adams for presidency Prosser's Rebellion
1801	John Marshall becomes Chief Justice Midnight judges appointed by Adams
1803	*Marbury v. Madison* decision Louisiana Purchase
1804	Lewis and Clark Expedition
1807	Chesapeake-Leopard incident Embargo Act Robert Fulton builds *Clermont*, first steamboat
1811	Battle of Tippecanoe

(continued)

The New Nation (1789–1824)

(continued)

Historical Timeline (1789–1824)

Year	Event
1812	Congress declares war on Britain
1814	British burn Washington, D.C. Treaty of Ghent ends War of 1812 Hartford Convention
1815	Jackson defeats British at New Orleans
1819	First section of Erie Canal is opened Panic of 1819 *McCullough v. Maryland* decision
1820	Missouri Compromise
1823	Monroe Doctrine
1824	Congress sets protective tariffs *Gibbons v. Ogden* decision promotes interstate trade

Jacksonian Democracy and Westward Expansion (1824–1850)

The Jacksonian Democracy, 1829–1841

While the "Age of Jackson" did not bring perfect political, social or economic equality to all Americans, it did mark a transformation in the political life of the nation that attracted the notice of European travelers and observers. Alexis de Tocqueville observed an "equality of condition" here that existed nowhere else in the world, and an egalitarian spirit among the people that was unique. Certainly the electorate had become broadened so that all white males had access to the polls, even if blacks and women were still outside the system. It was, in that sense, the "age of the common man." As to whether Andrew Jackson and his party were actually working for the good of those common men is another matter.

The Election of 1824

The Expansion of the Electorate

Most states had already eliminated the property qualifications for voting before the campaigns for this election began. The new Massachusetts state constitution of 1820 had led the way in this liberalization of the franchise, and most Northern states followed soon after, usually with some conservative opposition, but not violent reactions. In Rhode Island, Thomas Dorr led a bloodless "rebellion" in an effort to expand the franchise in that state, and though he was briefly imprisoned for his efforts, the incident led the conservative legislature to relent and grant the vote to non-property owners. The movement for reform was much slower in the Southern states.

Free blacks were excluded from the polls across the South, and in most of the Northern states. In those areas where they had held the franchise, they were gradually excluded from the social and economic mainstream—as well as from the political arena—in the early years of this period.

National elections had never attracted much enthusiasm until 1824. Legislative caucuses had made the presidential nominations and kept the ruling cliques in power by excluding the voters from the process. But this year the system failed, and the caucuses were bypassed.

The members of the electoral college were now being almost universally elected by the people, rather than by the state legislatures, as in the early days.

The Candidates

Secretary of the Treasury William H. Crawford of Georgia was the pick of the Congressional caucus. Secretary of State John Quincy Adams held the job which traditionally had been the stepping-stone to the executive office. Speaker of the House Henry Clay presented the only coherent program to the voters, the "American System," which provided a high tariff on imports to finance an extensive internal improvement package. Andrew Jackson of Tennessee presented himself as a war hero from the 1812 conflict. All four candidates claimed to be Republicans.

The Election

Jackson won 43 percent of the popular vote, but the four-way split meant that he only received 38 percent of the electoral votes. Under the provisions of the 12th Amendment, the top three candidates were voted on by the House of Representatives. This left Henry Clay out of the running, and he threw his support to Adams. The votes had no sooner been counted when the new president, Adams, appointed Henry Clay his Secretary of State.

Andrew Jackson and his supporters immediately cried "foul!" and accused Clay of making a deal for his vote. The rallying cry of "corrupt bargain" became the impetus for their immediate initiation of the campaign for the 1828 election.

The Adams Administration

The new president pushed for an active federal government in areas like internal improvements and Native American affairs. These policies proved unpopular in an age of increasing sectional jealousies and conflicts over states' rights.

Adams was frustrated at every turn by his Jacksonian opposition, and his unwillingness, or inability, to compromise further antagonized his political enemies. For example, his refusal to endorse and enforce the Creek Native Americans' land cession to the state of Georgia was negated by their recession of their lands under pressure from Georgia's Jacksonian government.

John C. Calhoun and Nullification

In 1828, Congress passed a new tariff bill which was originally supported by Southern congressmen in order to embarrass the administration. The finished bill, however, included higher import duties for many goods which were bought by Southern planters, so they bitterly denounced the law as the "Tariff of Abominations."

John C. Calhoun was serving as Adams' vice president, so to protest the tariff and still protect his position, he anonymously published the "South Carolina Exposition and Protest," which outlined his theory of the "concurrent majority": that a federal law which was deemed harmful to the interests of an individual state could be declared null and void within that state by a convention of the people. Thus, a state holding a minority position could ignore a law enacted by the majority which they considered unconstitutional (shades of Thomas Jefferson).

The Election of 1828

Adams' supporters now called themselves the National Republicans, and Jackson's party ran as the Democratic Republicans. Andrew Jackson had aggressively campaigned since his defeat in the House in 1825.

It was a dirty campaign. Adams' people accused Jackson of adultery and of the murder of several militiamen who had been executed for desertion during the War of 1812. Jackson's followers in turn defamed Adams and his programs and accused him of extravagance with public funds.

When the votes were counted, Jackson had won 56 percent of the popular vote and swept 178 of the 261 electoral votes. John C. Calhoun was elected vice president.

Andrew Jackson as President

Jackson was popular with the common man. He seemed to be the prototype of the self-made Westerner: rough-hewn, violent, vindictive, with few ideas but strong convictions. He ignored his appointed Cabinet officers and relied instead on the counsel of his "Kitchen Cabinet," a group of partisan supporters who had the ear and the confidence of the president.

Andrew Jackson's Inauguration, March 4, 1829. U.S. Library of Congress.

Jackson expressed the conviction that government operations could be performed by untrained, common folk, and he threatened the dismissal of large numbers of government employees, to replace them with his supporters. Actually, he talked more about this "spoils system" than he acted on it.

He exercised his veto power more than any other president before him. A famous example was the Maysville Road, a project in Kentucky which would require a federal subsidy. Jackson opposed it because it would exist only within the boundaries of a single state.

DIDYOUKNOW?

Andrew Jackson lived during a time of great industrial advances. As such, he was the first president to enjoy a system of running water in the White House.

Jacksonian Indian Policy

Jackson supported the removal of all Indian tribes to west of the Mississippi River. The Indian Removal Act in 1830 provided for federal enforcement of that process.

The portion of the Cherokee Nation which occupied northern Georgia claimed to be a sovereign political entity within the boundaries of that state. The Supreme Court supported that claim in its decision in *Worcester v. Georgia* (1832), but President Jackson refused to enforce the court's decision.

The result of this policy was the Trail of Tears, the forced march, under U.S. Army escort, of thousands of Cherokees to the West. A quarter or more of the Indians, mostly women and children, perished on the journey.

The Webster-Hayne Debate (1830)

Federal Land Policy

The method of disposing of government land raised sectional differences. Westerners wanted cheap lands available to the masses. Northeasterners opposed this policy because it would lure away their labor supply and drive up wages. Southerners supported the West, hoping to weaken the ties between East and West.

The Senate Confrontation

Senator Robert Hayne of South Carolina made a speech in support of cheap land and he used Calhoun's anti-tariff arguments to support his position. In his remarks, he referred to the possibility of nullification.

Daniel Webster's famous replies to this argument moved the debate from the issue of land policy to the nature of the Union and states' rights within it. Webster argued for the Union as indissoluble and sovereign over the individual states. His concluding statements have become a part of our rhetorical heritage: "It is, Sir, the people's Constitution, the people's government, made for the people, made by the people, and answerable to the people. . . . Liberty and Union, now and for ever, one and inseparable!"

The Second Nullification Crisis

The final split between Andrew Jackson and his vice president, John C. Calhoun, came over the new Tariff of 1832, and over Mrs. Calhoun's snub of Peggy Eaton, the wife of Secretary of War John Eaton.

Mrs. Eaton was a commoner, and the aristocratic Mrs. Calhoun refused to include her on the guest lists for the Washington parties. Jackson, no doubt remembering the slights to his own dear Rachel, defended his friends Peggy and John, and demanded that they be included in the social life of the capital.

Jackson was a defender of states' rights, but within the context of a dominant Union. When he supported the higher rates of the new tariff, Calhoun resigned his office in a huff and went home to South Carolina. There he composed an Ordinance of Nullification, which was duly approved by a special convention, and the customs officials were ordered to stop collecting the duties at the port of Charleston.

Jackson's response was immediate and decisive. He obtained a Force Bill from Congress (1833), which empowered him to use federal troops to enforce the collection of the taxes. And he suggested the possibility of hanging Calhoun. At the same time, he offered a gradual reduction in the levels of the duties. Calhoun backed down, both sides claimed victory, and the crisis was averted.

The War on the Bank

The Controversy

The Bank of the United States had operated under the direction of Nicholas Biddle since 1823. He was a cautious man, and his conservative economic policy enforced conservatism among the state and private banks—which many bankers resented. Many of the Bank's enemies opposed it simply because it was big and powerful. Many still disputed its constitutionality.

The Election of 1832

Andrew Jackson freely voiced his antagonism toward the Bank and his intention to destroy it. During the campaign for the presidency in 1832, Henry Clay and Daniel Webster promoted a bill to recharter the Bank, even though its charter did not expire until 1836. They feared that Jackson would gain support over time and could kill the Bank as a parting shot as he retired. The Congress passed the recharter bill, but Jackson vetoed it. This left that institution a lame duck agency.

Jackson soundly defeated Henry Clay in the presidential race and he considered his victory a mandate from the people to destroy the Bank. His first move was to remove the federal government's deposits from Biddle's vaults and distribute the funds to various state and local banks, called by his critics the "pet banks." Biddle responded by tightening up on credit and calling in loans, hoping to embarrass the government and force a withdrawal by Jackson. Jackson stood firm and the result was a financial recession.

The Panic of 1837

When Biddle was forced to relent through pressure from business interests, the economy immediately rebounded. With credit policies relaxed, inflation began to pick up. The government contributed to this expansion by offering millions of acres of western land for sale to settlers at low prices.

In 1836, Jackson ordered a distribution of surplus funds and thus helped to further fuel the inflationary rise in prices. Finally, even Jackson recognized the danger, and tried to slow the spiral by issuing the Specie Circular, which required payment for public land in hard money; no more paper or credit. Depression quickly followed this move.

The business recession lasted well into the 1840s. Our national economy was by this time so tied in with international business and finance that the downturn affected the entire Atlantic community, and was in turn worsened by the global impact. But most Americans blamed everyone in power, including Jackson, and our institutions and business practices. This disillusionment helped to initiate and intensify the reform movement which so occupied this nation in the 19th century's second quarter.

The Election of 1836

Jackson had handpicked his Democratic successor, Martin Van Buren of New York. The Whigs ran three regional candidates in hopes of upsetting the Jacksonians. The Whig Party had emerged from the ruins of the National Republicans and other groups who opposed Jackson's policies. The name was taken from the British Whig tradition, which simply refers to the "opposition."

Van Buren's Presidency

Van Buren, known as Old Kinderhook (O.K.), inherited all the problems and resentments generated by his mentor. He spent most of his term in office dealing with the financial chaos left by the death of the Second Bank. The best he could do was to eventually persuade Congress to establish an Independent Treasury to handle government funds. It began functioning in 1840.

TEST TIP

Let's face it: cramming doesn't work. A 2008 study by University of California-San Diego psychologists found that if you review material relatively close to when you first learned it, you will remember it better (*www.popsci.com*). According to the study, the best time is after a wait of 10 percent of the time between when you first learned the material and when you'll need to know it for the test. So if you have a history lesson on Monday and a quiz on the following Monday, the best time to study for the quiz would be Wednesday.

The Election of 1840

The Candidates

The Whigs nominated William Henry Harrison, "Old Tippecanoe," Western Indian fighter. Their choice for vice president was John Tyler, a former Democrat from Virginia. The Democrats put up Van Buren again, but they could not agree on a vice presidential candidate, so they ran no one.

The Campaign

This election saw the largest voter turnout to date. The campaign was a dramatic one. The Whigs stressed the depression and the opulent lifestyle of the incumbent in contrast to the simple "log cabin" origins of their candidate.

Harrison won a narrow popular victory, but swept 80 percent of the electoral vote. Unfortunately for the Whigs, President Harrison died only a month after the inauguration, having served the shortest term in presidential history.

The Meaning of Jacksonian Politics

The Party System

The Age of Jackson was the beginning of the modern party system. Popular politics, based on emotional appeal, became the accepted style. The practice of meeting in mass conventions to nominate national candidates for office was established during these Jackson years.

The Strong Executive

Jackson, more than any president before him, used his office to dominate his party and the government to such an extent that he was called "King Andrew" by his critics.

The Changing Emphasis Towards States' Rights

Andrew Jackson supported the authority of the states against the national government, but he drew the line at the concept of nullification. He advocated a strong union made up of sovereign states, and this created some dissonance in his political thinking.

owned 20 or more. But this minority of large slave owners exercised political and economic power far beyond what their numbers would indicate. They became a class to which all others paid deference, and they dominated the political and social life of their region.

The Yeoman Farmers

The largest group of Southern whites was the independent small farmers who worked their land with their family, sometimes side-by-side with one or two slaves, to produce their own food, with sometimes enough surplus to sell for a little extra cash. These simple folk predominated in the upland South and constituted a sizeable element even in the lower cotton-producing states. Their major crop was corn, and indeed the South's corn crop was more valuable than its cotton. The corn was used at home for dinner tables and for animal feed, however, and so ranked behind cotton as an item of export. These people were generally poorer than their Northern counterparts.

The Poor Whites

Perhaps a half-million white Southerners lived on the edge of the agrarian economy, in varying degrees of poverty. These "crackers," or "sandhillers," occupied the barren soils of the red hills or sandy bottoms, and they lived in squalor worse than the slaves. They formed a true underclass.

The Institution of Slavery

As the necessary concomitant of this expanding plantation system, the "Peculiar Institution" of black slavery fastened itself upon the Southern people, even as it isolated them from the rest of the world.

Slavery as a Labor System

The utilization of slave labor varied according to the region and the size of the growing unit. The large plantations growing cotton, sugar or tobacco used the gang system, in which white overseers directed black drivers, who supervised large groups of workers in the fields, all performing the same operation. In the culture of rice, and on the smaller farms, slaves were assigned specific tasks, and when those tasks were finished, the worker had the remainder of the day to himself.

House servants usually were considered the most favored since they were spared the hardest physical labor and enjoyed the most intimate relationship with the owner's family. This could be considered a drawback, since they were frequently deprived of the social communion of the other slaves, enjoyed less privacy, and were more likely to suffer the direct wrath of a dissatisfied master or mistress.

It is still debated as to whether the living conditions of the Southern plantation slaves were better or worse than the Northern wage laborers. Certainly their lot was better than their counterparts in South America and the Carribean.

Urban Slavery in the Southern City

A sizeable number of black slaves worked in the towns, serving as factory hands, domestics, artisans, and construction workers. They lived fairly independent lives and indeed a good number purchased their freedom with their savings, or quietly crossed the color line and disappeared into the general population. As the 19th century progressed, these people were increasingly seen as a bad model and a threat to the institution, and so urban slavery practically disappeared.

The Slave Trade

The most significant demographic shift in these decades was the movement of blacks from the Old South to the new Southwest. Traders shipped servants by the thousands to the newly opened cotton lands of the gulf states. A prime field hand fetched an average price of $800, as high as $1,500 in peak years. Families were frequently split apart by this miserable traffic. Planters freely engaged in this trade, but assigned very low status to the traders who carried it out.

Although the importation of slaves from abroad had been outlawed by Congress since 1808, they continued to be smuggled in until the 1850s. The import ban kept the price up and encouraged the continuation of the internal trade.

Slaves' Reaction to Slavery

Blacks in bondage suffered varying degrees of repression and deprivation. The harsh slave codes were comprehensive in their restrictions on individual freedom, but they were unevenly applied, and so there was considerable variety in the severity of life. The typical slave probably received a rough but adequate diet and enjoyed crude but sufficient housing and clothing.

But the loss of freedom and the injustice of the system produced a variety of responses. Many "soldiered" on the job, and refused to work hard, or they found ways to sabotage the machinery or the crops. There was an underground system of ridicule toward the masters which was nurtured, as reflected in such oral literature as the "Br'er Rabbit" tales.

Violent reaction to repression was not uncommon. Gabriel Prosser in Richmond (1800), Denmark Vesey in Charleston (1822), and Nat Turner in coastal Virginia (1831) all plotted or led uprisings of blacks against their white masters. Rumors of such uprisings kept whites in a state of constant apprehension.

The ultimate rebellion was to simply leave, and many tried to run away, some successfully. Especially from the states bordering the North, an ever increasing number of slaves fled to freedom, many with the aid of the "underground railroad" and smugglers such as Harriet Tubman, who led over 300 of her family and friends to freedom after she herself had escaped.

Most of those in bondage, however, were forced simply to adapt, and they did. A rich culture was developed within the confines of the system, and included distinctive patterns of language, music and religion.

INSPECTION AND SALE OF A NEGRO.

"Inspection and Sale of a Negro," an 1854 engraving by Whitney, Jocelyn & Annin, depicts an African man being inspected for sale into slavery. U.S. Library of Congress.

Commerce and Industry

The lack of manufacturing and business development has frequently been blamed for the South's losing its bid for independence in 1861–1865. Actually the South was highly industrialized for its day, and compared favorably with most European nations in the development of manufacturing capacity. Obviously, it trailed far behind the North, so much so that when war erupted in 1861, the Northern states owned 81 percent of the factory capacity in the United States.

Manufacturing

The Southern states saw considerable development in the 1820s and 1830s in textiles and iron production and in flour milling. Richmond's Tredegar Iron Works compared favorably with the best in the North. Montgomery Bell's forges in Tennessee produced a good proportion of the ironware used in the upper South. Even so, most of the goods manufactured in these plants were for plantation consumption rather than for export, and they never exceeded two percent of the value of the cotton crop.

Commercial Activity

The businessmen of the South worked primarily with the needs and products of the plantation and the factors of New Orleans and Charleston had to serve as bankers and insurance brokers as well as the agents for the planters. An organized network of commerce never developed in the South, even though the planters themselves must be recognized as businessmen, since they operated large, complex staple-producing units.

Voices for Change

There were those who saw their native South sinking ever more into the position of dependency upon Northern bankers and businessmen, and they cried out for reform. James B.D. DeBow's *Review* advocated commercial development and agricultural diversification, but his cries fell largely on deaf ears.

Why were Southerners so wedded to the plantation system, in the face of much evidence that it was retarding development? Certainly one reason is that cotton was profitable. Over the long run, capital return on plantation agriculture was at least as good as on Northern industrial capital. Even though skilled slaves abounded and could have manned factories, they were more profitable in the field.

Since most of the planter's capital was tied up in land and slaves, there was little left to invest in commerce or manufacturing. Most important, perhaps, was the value system of the Southern people, who put great store in traditional rural ideals: chivalry, leisure, genteel elegance. Even the yeoman farmer held these values, and hoped someday to attain to the position the planters held.

TEST TIP

The AP U.S. History Exam will always contain one question that asks you to interpret and apply historical documents. The document-based question (DBQ) will present you with an essay prompt along with several written or visual primary source documents. Before you can begin writing, you must spend 15 minutes reviewing the documents. You may take notes on the documents in your DBQ booklet. DBQs rarely present you with documents that you're likely to be familiar with, so you will need to use what you know about the topic in order to interpret the documents. Your score will not depend on which position you choose to argue; DBQs usually support multiple viewpoints. Rather, your score depends on how well you state a thesis and support it with both your own historical knowledge and the evidence provided.

Life in the Southern States
The Role of Women

The position of the Southern woman was similar in many ways to her Northern counterpart, but also very different. She had fewer opportunities for anything but home life. The middle-class wife was heavily involved in the operation of the farm, and served as supervisor and nurse for the servants, as well as manager of the household, while the upper class women served merely as ornaments. Education was rare, and centered on the "domestic arts." High birth and death rates took their toll on childbearing women, and many men outlived several wives. The half-breed slave children were constant reminders of the planters' dalliances and produced constant tension and frustration among plantation wives.

Education

Schooling beyond literacy training was available only to the sons of the well-to-do. Academics and colleges abounded, but not for the working classes, and what public schools there were were usually inferior and ill-supported. By 1860, one-half of all the illiterates in the United States lived in the South.

Daily Life in the South

The accounts of travelers in the Southern states provide us with vivid pictures of living conditions on the average homestead. Housing was primitive, one- or two-room cabins being the rule. Corn, sweet potatoes, and pork formed the staples of the Southern diet and health problems reflected the resulting vitamin deficiencies. Rickets and pellagra were common ailments.

Although the prevalence of violence has probably been overstated, it certainly existed and the duel remained an accepted avenue for settling differences well into the nineteenth century.

Southern Response to the Anti-Slavery Movement

As the crusade for abolition intensified in the North, the South assumed an ever more defensive position. Biblical texts were used to justify the enslavement of an "inferior race." Scientific arguments were advanced to prove the inherent inferiority of the black African. Southern postal authorities refused to deliver any mail that contained information antagonistic to the slave system. Any kind of dissent was brutally suppressed, and the South became more and more a closed society. Literature and scholarship shriveled, and creative writers like Edgar Allan Poe and William Gilmore Simms became the rare exception.

The last serious Southern debate over the institution of slavery took place in the Virginia legislature in 1832, in the aftermath of Nat Turner's revolt. That discussion squelched any move toward emancipation. In 1836 Southern members of the U.S. House of Representatives pushed through the infamous "gag rule," which forbade any discussion on the question of slavery on the floor of the House. That rule remained in effect until 1844.

The most elaborate product of this ferment was John C. Calhoun's theory of the "concurrent majority," in which a dual presidency would insure a South independent of Northern dominance, and would forever keep majority rule at bay.

Beginning in 1837, regular conventions were held across the South to discuss ways to escape Northern economic and political hegemony.

As the decade of the 1840s opened, the two sections were becoming more and more estranged, and the channels of compromise were becoming more and more poisoned by the emotional responses to black slavery. The development which contributed most to keeping the sore festering was westward expansion.

Manifest Destiny and Westward Expansion

Although the term "Manifest Destiny" was not actually coined until 1844, the belief that the American nation was destined to eventually expand all the way to the Pacific Ocean, and to possibly embrace Canada to the North, and Mexico to the South, had been voiced for years by many who believed that American liberty and ideals should be shared with everyone possible, by force if necessary. The rising sense of nationalism which followed the War of 1812 was fed by the rapidly expanding population, the reform impulse of the 1830s, and the desire to acquire new markets and resources for the burgeoning economy of "Young America."

Louisiana and the Far West Fur Trade

The Lewis and Clark expedition had scarcely filed its reports before a variety of adventurous entrepreneurs began to penetrate the newly acquired territory and the lands beyond. "Mountain men" like Jim Bridges trapped the Rocky Mountain streams and the headwaters of the Missouri River system for the greatly prized beaver pelts, while explorers like Jedediah Smith mapped the vast territory which stretched from the Rockies to the Sierra Nevada range and on into California. John Jacob Astor established a fur post at the mouth of the Columbia River which he named Astoria, and challenged the British claim to the northwest. Though he was forced to sell out his establishment to the British, he lobbied Congress to pass trade restrictions against British furs, and eventually became the first American millionaire from the profits of the American Fur Company. The growing trade with the Orient in furs and other specialty goods was sharpening the desire of many businessmen for American ports on the Pacific coast.

"Fur Traders Descending the Missouri," 1845, a painting by George Caleb Bingham. This image characterized the impact of the opening of new territory following the Lewis and Clark expedition. Metropolitan Museum of Art.

The Oregon Country

The Adams-Onis Treaty of 1819 had set the northern boundary of Spanish possessions near the present northern border of California. The territory north of that line and west of the vague boundaries of the Louisiana Territory had been claimed over the years by Spain, England, Russia, France, and the United States. By the 1820s, all these claims had been yielded to Britain and the United States. The Hudson's Bay Company had established a fur trading station at Fort Vancouver, and claimed control south to the Columbia. The United States claimed all the way north to the 54° 40′ parallel. Unable to settle the dispute, they had agreed on a joint occupation of the disputed land.

In the 1830s American missionaries followed the traders and trappers to the Oregon country, and began to publicize the richness and beauty of the land, sending back official reports on their work which were published in the new, inexpensive "penny press" papers. Everyone read these reports, and the result was the "Oregon Fever" of the 1840s, as thousands of settlers trekked across the Great Plains and the Rocky Mountains to settle the new Shangri-La.

The Texas Question: 1836–1845

Texas had been a state in the Republic of Mexico since 1822, following the Mexican revolution against Spanish control. The United States had offered to buy the territory at the time, since it had renounced its claim to the area in the Adams-Onis agreement of 1819. The new Mexican government indignantly refused to sell, but immediately began to invite immigration from the north by offering land grants to Stephen Austin and other Americans. They needed to increase the population of the area and to produce revenue for the infant government. The Americans responded in great numbers, and by 1835 approximately 35,000 "gringos" were homesteading on Texas land.

The Mexican officials saw their power base eroding as the foreigners flooded in, and so they moved to tighten control, through restrictions on new immigration, and through tax increases. The Texans responded in 1836 by proclaiming independence and establishing a new republic. The ensuing war was short-lived. The Mexican dictator Antonio López de Santa Anna advanced north and annihilated the Texan garrisons at the Alamo and at Goliad. On April 23, 1836, Sam Houston defeated him at San Jacinto, and the Mexicans were forced to let Texas go its way.

Houston immediately asked the American government for recognition and annexation, but President Andrew Jackson feared the revival of the slavery issue since the new state would come in on the slave-holding side of the political balance, and he also feared war with Mexico, so he did nothing. When Van Buren followed suit, the new republic sought foreign recognition and support, which the European nations eagerly provided, hoping thereby to create a counterbalance to rising American power and influence in the Southwest. France and England both quickly concluded trade agreements with the Texans.

> **DID**YOU**KNOW?**
>
> When the United States annexed Texas in 1845, it agreed to allow up to four additional states be formed from the territory contained in the Republic of Texas.

New Mexico and California

The district of New Mexico had, like Texas, encouraged American immigration, and for the same reasons. Soon that state was more American than Mexican. The Santa Fe Trail—from Independence, Missouri, to the town of Santa Fe—created a prosperous trade in mules, gold and silver, and furs which moved north in exchange for manufactured goods which went south. American settlements sprung up all along the route.

Though the Mexican officials in California had not encouraged it, American immigration nevertheless had been substantial. First traders and whaling crews, then merchants, arrived to set up stores and developed a brisk trade. As the decade of the 1830s passed, the number of newcomers increased. Since the Missouri Compromise had established the northern limits for slavery at the 36° 30′ parallel, most of this Mexican territory lay in the potential slave-holding domain, and many of the settlers had carried their bondsmen with them.

Manifest Destiny and Sectional Stress

The question of expansion was universally discussed. Although the strongest sentiment was found in the North and West, the South had its own ambitions, and they usually involved the extension of their "peculiar institution."

The Democrats generally favored the use of force, if necessary, to extend American borders. The Whigs favored more peaceful means, through diplomacy. Some Whigs, like Henry Clay, feared expansion under any circumstances, because of its potential for aggravating the slavery issue.

Clay was closest to the truth. As the decade of the 1840s opened, the questions of Texas, California and the New Mexican territory were increasingly prominent, and the sectional tension which they produced was destined to light the fires of civil war.

Tyler, Polk, and Continued Westward Expansion

Tyler and the Whigs

When William Henry Harrison became president, he immediately began to rely on Whig leader Henry Clay for advice and direction, just as Clay had planned and expected he would. He appointed to his Cabinet those whom Clay suggested, and at Clay's behest he called a special session of Congress to vote the Whig legislative program into action. To the Whigs' dismay, Harrison died of pneumonia just one month into his term, to be replaced by Vice President John Tyler.

A states' rights Southerner and a strict constitutionalist who had been placed on the Whig ticket to draw Southern votes, Tyler rejected the entire Whig program of a national bank, high protective tariffs, and federally funded internal improvements (roads, canals, etc.). Clay stubbornly determined to push the program through anyway. In the resulting legislative confrontations, Tyler vetoed a number of Whig-sponsored bills.

The Whigs were furious. Every Cabinet member but one resigned in protest. Tyler was officially expelled from the party and made the target of the first serious impeachment attempt. (It failed.) In opposition to Tyler over the next few years the Whigs, under the leadership of Clay, transformed themselves from a loose grouping of diverse factions to a coherent political party with an elaborate organization.

One piece of important legislation that did get passed during Tyler's administration was the Preemption Act (1841), allowing settlers who had squatted on unsurveyed federal lands first chance to buy the land (up to 160 acres at low prices) once it was put on the market.

The Webster-Ashburton Treaty

The member of Tyler's Cabinet who did not immediately resign in protest was Secretary of State Daniel Webster. He stayed on to negotiate the Webster-Ashburton Treaty with Great Britain.

There were at this time several causes of tension between the U.S. and Great Britain:

1) The Canada-Maine boundary in the area of the Aroostook Valley was disputed. British efforts to build a military road through the disputed area led to reaction by Maine militia in a bloodless confrontation known as the "Aroostook War" (1838).

2) The Caroline Affair (1837) involved an American ship, the *Caroline*, that had been carrying supplies to Canadian rebels. It was burned by Canadian loyalists who crossed the U.S. border in order to do so.

3) In the Creole Incident, Britain declined to return escaped slaves who had taken over a U.S. merchant ship, the *Creole*, and sailed to the British-owned Bahamas.

4) British naval vessels, patrolling the African coast to suppress slave-smuggling, sometimes stopped and searched American ships.

The Webster-Ashburton Treaty (1842) dealt with these problems in a spirit of mutual concession and forbearance:

1) Conflicting claims along the Canada-Maine boundary were compromised.

2) The British expressed regret for the destruction of the *Caroline*.

3) The British promised to avoid "officious interference" in freeing slaves in cases such as that of the *Creole*.

4) Both countries agreed to cooperate in patrolling the African coast to prevent slave-smuggling.

The Webster-Ashburton Treaty was also important in that it helped create an atmosphere of compromise and forebearance in U.S.-British relations.

After negotiating the treaty, Webster too resigned from Tyler's Cabinet.

TEST TIP

During the AP Exam, you will have a break of just five minutes between the multiple-choice and free-response sections. Although you cannot eat or drink anything during the test, you may bring along a snack or a bottle of water for your break time.

The Texas Issue

Rejected by the Whigs and without ties to the Democrats, Tyler was a politician without a party but not without ambitions. Hoping to gather a political following of his own, he sought an issue with powerful appeal and believed he had found it in the question of Texas annexation.

The Republic of Texas had gained its independence from Mexico in 1836 and, since most of its settlers had come from the U.S., immediately sought admission as a state. It was rejected because anti-slavery forces in Congress resented the presence of slavery in Texas and because Mexico threatened war should the U.S. annex Texas.

To excite American jealousy and thus hasten annexation, Texas President Sam Houston made much show of negotiating for closer relations with Great Britain. Southerners feared that Britain, which opposed slavery, might bring about its abolition in Texas and then use Texas as a base from which to undermine slavery in the American South. Other Americans were disturbed at the possibility of a British presence in Texas because of the obstacle it would present to what many Americans were coming to believe—and what New York journalist John L. O'Sullivan would soon express—as America's "manifest destiny to overspread the continent."

Tyler's new secretary of state, John C. Calhoun, negotiated an annexation treaty with Texas. Calhoun's identification with extreme pro-slavery forces and his insertion in the treaty of pro-slavery statements brought the treaty's rejection by the Senate (1844). Nevertheless, the Texas issue had been injected into national politics and could not be made to go away.

The Election of 1844

Democratic front-runner Martin Van Buren and Whig front-runner Henry Clay agreed privately that neither would endorse Texas annexation and that it would not become a campaign issue, but expansionists at the Democratic convention succeeded in dumping Van Buren in favor of James K. Polk. Polk, called "Young Hickory" by his supporters, was a staunch Jacksonian who opposed protective tariffs and a national bank but, most important, favored territorial expansion, including not only annexation of Texas but also occupation of all the Oregon country (up to latitude 54° 40′) hitherto jointly occupied by the U.S. and Britain. The latter claim was expressed in his campaign slogan, "Fifty-four forty or fight."

Tyler, despite his introduction of the issue that was to decide that year's presidential campaign, was unable to build a party of his own and withdrew from the race.

The Whigs nominated Clay, who continued to oppose Texas annexation but, sensing the mood of the country was against him, began to equivocate. His wavering cost him votes among those Northerners who were extremely sensitive to the issue of slavery and believed that the settlement, independence, and proposed annexation of Texas was a gigantic plot to add slave states to the Union. Some of these voters shifted to the Liberty party.

The anti-slavery Liberty party nominated James G. Birney. Apparently because of Clay's wavering on the Texas issue, Birney was able to take enough votes away from Clay in New York to give that state, and thus the election, to Polk.

Tyler, as a lame-duck president, made one more attempt to achieve Texas annexation before leaving office. By means of a joint resolution, which unlike a treaty required only a simple majority rather than a two-thirds vote, he was successful in getting the measure through Congress. Texas was finally admitted to the Union (1845).

Polk as President

Though a relatively unknown "dark horse" at the time of his nomination for the Presidency, Polk had considerable political experience within his home state of Tennessee and was an adept politician. He turned out to be a skillful and effective president.

As a good Jacksonian, Polk favored a low, revenue-only tariff rather than a high, protective tariff. This he obtained in the Walker Tariff (1846). He also opposed a national debt and a national bank and re-established Van Buren's Independent Sub-Treasury system, which then remained in effect until 1920.

The Settlement of Oregon

A major issue in the election campaign of 1844, Oregon at this time comprised all the land bounded on the east by the Rockies, the west by the Pacific, the south by latitude 42°, and the north by the boundary of Russian-held Alaska at 54° 40′. Oregon had been visited by Lewis and Clark and in later years by American fur traders and especially missionaries such as Jason Lee and Marcus Whitman. Their reports sparked interest in Oregon's favorable soil and climate. During the first half of the 1840s, some 6,000 Americans had taken the 2,000-mile, six-month journey on the Oregon Trail, from Independence, Missouri, across the plains along the Platte River, through the Rockies at South Pass, and down the Snake River to their new homesteads. Most of them settled in the Willamette Valley, south of the Columbia River.

The area had been under the joint occupation of the U.S. and Great Britain since 1818, but Democrats in the election of 1844 had called for U.S. ownership of all of Oregon. Though this stand had helped him win the election, Polk had little desire to fight the British for land he considered unsuitable for agriculture and unavailable for slavery, which he favored. This was all the more so since trouble seemed to be brewing with Mexico over territory Polk considered far more desirable.

The British, for their part, hoped to obtain the area north of the Columbia River, including the natural harbor of Puget Sound (one of only three on the Pacific coast), with its adjoining Strait of Juan de Fuca.

By the terms of the Oregon Treaty (1846), a compromise solution was reached. The existing U.S.-Canada boundary east of the Rockies (49°) was extended westward to the Pacific, thus securing Puget Sound and shared use of the Strait of Juan de Fuca for the U.S. Some northern Democrats were angered and felt betrayed by Polk's failure to insist on all of Oregon, but the Senate readily accepted the treaty.

The Mormon Migration

Aside from the thousands of Americans who streamed west on the Oregon Trail during the early 1840s, and the smaller number who migrated to what was then Mexican-held California, another large group of Americans moved west but to a different destination and for different reasons. These were the Mormons.

Mormonism is a unique religion founded in 1832 by Joseph Smith at Palmyra, New York. Mormons were often in trouble with their neighbors, and had been forced to migrate to Kirtland, Ohio; then Clay County, Missouri; and finally, Nauvoo, Illinois.

There, on the banks of the Mississippi River, they built the largest city in the state, had their own militia, and were a political force to be reckoned with.

In 1844 Mormon dissidents published a newspaper critical of church leader Smith and his newly announced doctrine of polygamy. Smith had their printing press destroyed. Arrested by Illinois authorities, Smith and his brother were confined to a jail in Carthage, Illinois, but later killed by a crowd of hostile non-Mormons who forced their way into the jail.

The Mormons then decided to migrate to the Far West, preferably someplace outside U.S. jurisdiction. Their decision to leave was hastened by pressure from their non-Mormon neighbors, among whom anti-Mormon feeling ran high as a response to polygamy and the Mormons' monolithic social and political structure.

Under the leadership of new church leader Brigham Young, some 85,000 Mormons trekked overland in 1846 to settle in the valley of the Great Salt Lake in what is now Utah (but was then owned by Mexico). Young founded the Mormon republic of Deseret and openly preached (and practiced) polygamy.

After Deseret's annexation by the U.S. as part of the Mexican Cession, Young was made territorial governor of Utah. Nevertheless, friction developed with the federal government. By 1857 public outrage over polygamy prompted then-President James Buchanan to replace Young with a non-Mormon governor. Threats of Mormon defiance led Buchanan to send 2500 army troops to compel Mormon obedience to federal law. Young responded by calling out the Mormon militia and blocking the passes through which the army would have to advance. This standoff, known as the "Mormon War," was resolved in 1858, with the Mormons accepting the new governor and Buchanan issuing a general pardon.

DIDYOU**KNOW?**

As of 2005, Mormons made up an estimated 60 percent of Utah's population. Some analysts believe that the proportion of Mormons in the state will drop below 50 percent by 2030 as people move to Utah from other parts of the country and the non-Mormon population grows (www.sltrib.com).

The Coming of War with Mexico

For some time American interest had been growing in the far western lands then held by Mexico:

1) Since the 1820s Americans had been trading with Santa Fe and other Mexican settlements along the Rio Grande by means of the Santa Fe Trail. Though not extensive enough to be of economic importance the trade aroused further American interest in the area.

2) Also, since the 1820s, American "mountain men," trappers who sought beaver pelts in the streams of the Rockies, had explored the mountains of the Far West, opening new trails and discovering fertile lands. They later served as guides for settlers moving west.

3) At the same time whaling ships and other American vessels had carried on a thriving trade with the Mexican settlements on the coast of California.

4) Beginning in 1841, American settlers came overland to California by means of the California Trail, a branch from the Oregon Trail that turned southwest in the Rockies and crossed Nevada along the Humboldt River. By 1846 several hundred Americans lived in California.

The steady flow of American pioneers into Mexican-held areas of the Far West led to conflicting territorial desires and was thus an underlying cause of the Mexican War. Several more immediate causes existed:

1) Mexico's ineffective government was unable to protect the lives and property of American citizens in Mexico during the country's frequent and recurring revolutions and repeatedly declined to pay American claims for damages even when such claims were supported by the findings of mutually agreed upon arbitration.

2) Mexico had not reconciled itself to the loss of Texas and considered its annexation by the U.S. a hostile act.

3) The southern boundary of Texas was disputed. Whereas first the independent Republic of Texas and now the U.S. claimed the Rio Grande as the boundary, Mexico claimed the Nueces River, 130 miles farther north, because it had been the boundary of the province of Texas when it had been part of Mexico.

4) Mexican suspicions had been aroused regarding U.S. designs on California when, in 1842, a U.S. naval force under Commodore Thomas Catsby Jones had seized the province in the mistaken belief that war had broken out between the U.S. and Mexico. When the mistake was discovered, the province was returned and apologies made.

5) Mexican politicians had so inflamed the Mexican people against the U.S. that no Mexican leader could afford to take the risk of appearing to make concessions to the U.S. for fear of being overthrown.

Though Mexico broke diplomatic relations with the U.S. immediately upon Texas' admission to the Union, there still seemed to be some hope of a peaceful settlement.

In the fall of 1845 Polk sent John Slidell to Mexico City with a proposal for a peaceful settlement of the differences between the two countries. Slidell was empowered to cancel the damage claims and pay $5 million for the disputed land in southern Texas. He was also authorized to offer $25 million for California and $5 million for other Mexican territory in the Far West. Polk was especially eager to obtain California because he feared the British would snatch it from Mexico's extremely weak grasp.

Nothing came of these attempts at negotiation. Racked by coup and countercoup, the Mexican government refused even to receive Slidell.

Polk thereupon sent U.S. troops into the disputed territory in southern Texas. A force under General Zachary Taylor (who was nicknamed "Old Rough and Ready") took up a position just north of the Rio Grande. Eight days later, on April 5, 1846, Mexican troops attacked an American patrol. When news of the clash reached Washington, Polk sought and received from Congress a declaration of war against Mexico, on May 13, 1846.

The Mexican War

Americans were sharply divided about the war. Some favored it because they felt Mexico had provoked the war or because they felt it was the destiny of America to spread the blessings of freedom to oppressed peoples. Others opposed the war. Some, primarily Polk's political enemies the Whigs, accused the president of having provoked it. Others, generally Northern abolitionists, saw in the war the work of a vast conspiracy of Southern slaveholders greedy for more slave territory.

In planning military strategy, Polk showed genuine skill. American strategy consisted originally of a three-pronged attack, consisting of a land movement westward through New Mexico into California, a sea movement against California, and a land movement southward into Mexico.

The first prong of this three-pronged strategy, the advance through New Mexico and into California, was led by Colonel Stephen W. Kearny. Kearny's force easily secured New Mexico, entering Santa Fe on August 16, 1846, before continuing west to California. There American settlers, aided by an Army exploring party under John C. Fremont, had already revolted against Mexico's weak rule in what was called the Bear Flag Revolt.

As part of the second prong of U.S. strategy, naval forces under Commodore John D. Sloat had seized Monterey and declared California to be part of the United States. Forces put ashore by Commodore Robert Stockton joined with Kearny's troops to defeat the Mexicans at the Battle of San Gabriel in January 1847, and complete the conquest of California.

The third prong of the American strategy, an advance southward into Mexico, was itself divided into two parties:

1) Troops under Colonel Alexander W. Doniphan defeated Mexicans at El Brazito (December 25–28, 1846) to take El Paso, and then proceeded southward, winning the Battle of Sacramento (February 28, 1847) to take the city of Chihuahua, capital of the Mexican province of that name.

2) The main southward thrust, however, was made by a much larger American army under General Zachary Taylor. After badly defeating larger Mexican forces at the battles of Palo Alto (May 7, 1846) and Resaca de la Palma (May 8, 1846), Taylor advanced into Mexico and defeated an even larger Mexican force at the Battle of Monterey (September 20–24, 1846). Then, after substantial numbers of his troops had been transferred to other sectors of the war, he successfully withstood, though badly outnumbered, an attack by a Mexican force under Antonia Lopez de Santa Anna at the Battle of Buena Vista, February 22–23, 1847.

Despite the success of all three parts of the American strategy, the Mexicans refused to negotiate. Polk therefore ordered U.S. forces under General Winfield Scott to land on the east coast of Mexico, march inland, and take Mexico City.

> **DID**YOU**KNOW?**
>
> Like the Louisiana Purchase, the Mexican Cession added a vast amount of territory to the United States. The Mexican Cession included all of what is now the states of California, Nevada, and Utah, along with parts of what is now Arizona, Colorado, New Mexico, Utah, and Wyoming.

Scott landed at Veracruz March 9, 1847, and by March 27 had captured the city with the loss of only twenty American lives. He advanced from there, being careful to maintain good discipline and avoid atrocities in the countryside. At Cerro Cord (April 18, 1847), in what has been called "the most important single battle of the war," Scott outflanked and soundly defeated a superior enemy force in a seemingly impregnable position. After beating another Mexican army at Churubusco (August 19–20, 1847), Scott paused outside Mexico City to offer the Mexicans another chance to negotiate. When they declined, U.S. forces stormed the fortress of Chapultepec (September 13, 1847) and the next day entered Mexico City. Still Mexico refused to negotiate a peace and instead carried on guerilla warfare.

Negotiated peace finally came about when the State Department clerk Nicholas Trist, though his authority had been revoked and he had been ordered back to Washington two months earlier, negotiated and signed the Treaty of Guadalupe-Hidalgo

(February 2, 1848), ending the Mexican War. Under the terms of the treaty Mexico ceded to the U.S. the territory Polk had originally sought to buy, this time in exchange for a payment of $15 million and the assumption of $3.25 million in American citizens' claims against the Mexican government. This territory, the Mexican Cession, included the natural harbors at San Francisco and San Diego, thus giving the U.S. all three of the major west-coast natural harbors.

Despite the appropriation of vast territories, many, including Polk, felt the treaty was far too generous. There had been talk of annexing all of Mexico or of forcing Mexico to pay an indemnity for the cost of the war. Still, Polk felt compelled to accept the treaty as it was, and the Senate subsequently ratified it.

On the home front many Americans supported the war enthusiastically and flocked to volunteer. Some criticized the war, among them Henry David Thoreau, who, to display his protest, went to live at Walden Pond and refused to pay his taxes. Jailed for this, he wrote "Civil Disobedience."

Although the Mexican War increased the nation's territory by one-third, it also brought to the surface serious political issues that threatened to divide the country, particularly the question of slavery in the new territories.

(Before taking the quiz noted below, please review the summary timeline for this chapter on the following pages.)

Time for a quiz
- Review strategies in Chapter 2
- Take Quiz 3 at the REA Study Center
  (www.rea.com/studycenter)

Jacksonian Democracy and Westward Expansion (1824–1850)

Historical Timeline (1824–1850)

Year	Event
1825	John Quincy Adams wins Corrupt Bargain presidential election
1828	Tariff of Abominations Jackson wins presidency
1830	Jackson vetoes Maysville Road extension Baltimore & Ohio becomes first railroad company Joseph Smith publishes *Book of Mormon*
1831	*Cherokee Nation v. Georgia* denies Indian claim of nationhood Nat Turner's Rebellion
1832	Jackson vetoes U.S. Bank re-charter Nullification crisis in South Carolina
1834	Women workers at Lowell, Massachusetts, stage first strike
1836	Texas independence fight Gag rule prevents discussion of slavery in Congress
1837	Panic of 1837
1838	Trail of Tears
1842	*Commonwealth v. Hunt* legalizes unions
1845	Annexation of Texas
1846	U.S. declares war on Mexico Oregon Treaty
1847	Winfield Scott captures Mexico City
1848	Gold discovered in northern California Treaty of Guadalupe Hidalgo Seneca Falls statement of women's rights
1849	California gold rush

Chapter 9

Sectional Conflict and the Causes of the Civil War (1850–1860)

The Crisis of 1850 and America at Mid-Century

The Wilmot Proviso

The Mexican War had no sooner started when, on August 8, 1846, freshman Democratic Congressman David Wilmot of Pennsylvania introduced his Wilmot Proviso as a proposed amendment to a war appropriations bill. It stipulated that "neither slavery nor involuntary servitude shall ever exist" in any territory to be acquired from Mexico. It was passed by the House, and though rejected by the Senate it was reintroduced again and again amid increasingly acrimonious debate.

The Wilmot Proviso aroused intense sectional feelings. Southerners, who had supported the war enthusiastically, felt they were being treated unfairly. Northerners, some of whom had been inclined to see the war as a slaveholders' plot to extend slavery, felt they saw their worst suspicions confirmed by the Southerners' furious opposition to the Wilmot Proviso. There came to be four views regarding the status of slavery in the newly acquired territories.

The Southern position was expressed by John C. Calhoun, now serving as senator from South Carolina. He argued that the territories were the property not of the U.S. federal government, but of all the states together, and therefore Congress had no right to prohibit in any territory any type of "property" (by which he meant slaves) that was legal in any of the states.

Anti-slavery Northerners, pointing to the Northwest Ordinance of 1787 and the Missouri Compromise of 1820 as precedents, argued that Congress had the right to make what laws it saw fit for the territories, including, if it so chose, laws prohibiting slavery.

A compromise proposal favored by President Polk and many moderate Southerners called for the extension of the 36° 30′ line of the Missouri Compromise westward through the Mexican Cession to the Pacific, with territory north of the line to be closed to slavery and territory south of it open to slavery.

Another compromise solution, favored by Northern Democrats such as Lewis Case of Michigan and Stephen A. Douglas of Illinois, was known as "squatter sovereignty" and later as "popular sovereignty." It held that the residents of each territory should be permitted to decide for themselves whether or not to allow slavery, but it was vague as to when they might exercise that right.

The Election of 1848

Both parties sought to avoid as much as possible the hot issue of slavery in the territories as they prepared for the 1848 election campaign.

The Democrats nominated Lewis Cass, and their platform endorsed his middle-of-the-road popular sovereignty position with regard to slavery in the territories.

The Whigs dodged the issue even more effectively by nominating General Zachary Taylor, whose fame in the Mexican War made him a strong candidate. Taylor knew nothing of the current political issues, had never voted, and liked to think of himself as above politics. He took no position at all with respect to slavery in the territories.

Some anti-slavery Northern Whigs and Democrats, disgusted with their parties' failure to take a clear stand against the spread of slavery, deserted the party ranks to form another antislavery third party. They were known as "Conscience" Whigs (because they voted their conscience) and "Barnburner" Democrats (because they were willing to burn down the whole Democratic "barn" to get rid of the pro-slavery "rats"). Their party was called the Free Soil Party, since it stood for keeping the soil of new western territories free of slavery. Its candidate was Martin Van Buren.

The election excited relatively little public interest. Taylor won a narrow victory, apparently because Van Buren took enough votes from Cass in New York and Pennsylvania to throw those states into Taylor's column.

Gold in California

The question of slavery's status in the Western territories was made more immediate when, on January 24, 1848, gold was discovered at Sutter's Mill, not far from Sacramento, California. The next year gold-seekers from the eastern U.S. and from many foreign countries swelled California's population from 14,000 to 100,000.

Once in the gold fields these "forty-niners" proved to contain some rough characters, and that fact, along with the presence, or at least the expectation, of quick and easy riches, made California a wild and lawless place. No territorial government had been organized since the U.S. had received the land as part of the Mexican Cession, and all that existed was an inadequate military government. In September 1849, having more than the requisite population and being much in need of better government, California petitioned for admission to the Union as a state.

Since few slaveholders had chosen to risk their valuable investments in human property in the turbulent atmosphere of California, the people of the area not surprisingly sought admission as a free state, touching off a serious sectional crisis back east.

DIDYOU**KNOW?**

Gold and other mineral discoveries drew thousands of people to places, creating boomtowns across the West. The town of Bodie, California, grew to include some 8,500 residents and 2,000 buildings within two decades of the discovery of gold there in 1859. As resources were exhausted, however, populations of these boomtowns plummeted. By 1886, Bodie's population dropped to just 1,500, and it eventually became a ghost town (www.parks.ca.gov).

The Compromise of 1850

President Zachary Taylor, though himself a Louisiana slaveholder, opposed the further spread of slavery. Hoping to sidestep the dangerously divisive issue of slavery in the territories, he encouraged California as well as the rest of the Mexican Cession to organize and seek admission directly as states, thus completely bypassing the territorial stage.

Southerners were furious. They saw admission of a free-state California as a backdoor implementation of the hated Wilmot Proviso they had fought so hard to turn back in Congress. They were also growing increasingly alarmed at what was becoming the minority status of their section within the country. Long outnumbered in the House of Representatives, the South would now find itself, should California be admitted as a free state, also outvoted in the Senate.

Other matters created friction between North and South. A large tract of land was disputed between Texas, a slave state, and the as-yet-unorganized New Mexico Territory, where slavery's future was at best uncertain. Southerners were angered by the small-scale but much-talked-of efforts of Northern abolitionists' "underground railroad" to aid escaped slaves in reaching permanent freedom in Canada. Northerners were disgusted by the presence of slave pens and slave markets in the nation's capital. Radical southerners talked of secession and scheduled an all-Southern convention to meet in Nashville in June 1850 to propose ways of protecting Southern interests, inside or outside the Union.

At this point the aged Henry Clay attempted to compromise the various matters of contention between North and South. He proposed an eight-part package deal that he hoped would appeal to both sides.

For the North, the package contained these aspects: California would be admitted as a free state; the land in dispute between Texas and New Mexico would go to New Mexico; New Mexico and Utah Territories (all of the Mexican Cession outside of California) would not be specifically reserved for slavery, but its status there would be decided by popular sovereignty; and, the slave trade would be abolished in the District of Columbia.

For the South, the package offered the following: A tougher Fugitive Slave Law would be enacted; the federal government would pay Texas' $10,000,000 pre-annexation debt; Congress would declare that it did not have jurisdiction over the interstate slave trade; and, Congress would promise not to abolish slavery itself in the District of Columbia.

What followed the introduction of Clay's compromise proposal was eight months of heated debate, during which Clay, Calhoun, and Daniel Webster, the three great figures of Congress during the first half of the 19th century— all three aged and none of them with more than two years to live—made some of their greatest speeches. Clay called for compromise and "mutual forbearance." Calhoun gravely warned that the only way to save the Union was for the North to grant all the South's demands and keep quiet on the issue of slavery. Webster abandoned his previous opposition to the spread of slavery (as well as most of his popularity back in his home state of Massachusetts) to support the Compromise in an eloquent speech.

The opponents of the Compromise were many and powerful and ranged from President Taylor, who demanded admission of California without reference to slavery, to Northern extremists such as Senator William Seward of New York, who spoke of a "higher law" than the Constitution, forbidding the spread of slavery, to Southern extremists such as Calhoun or Senator Jefferson Davis of Mississippi. By mid-summer all seemed lost for the Compromise, and Clay left Washington exhausted and discouraged.

Then the situation changed dramatically. President Taylor died (apparently of gastroenteritis) July 9, 1850, and was succeeded by Vice President Millard Fillmore, a quiet but efficient politician and a strong supporter of compromise. In Congress the fight for the Compromise was taken up by Senator Stephen A. Douglas of Illinois. Called the "Little Giant" for his small stature and large political skills, Douglas broke Clay's proposal into its component parts so that he could use varying coalitions to push each part through Congress. This method proved successful, and the Compromise was adopted.

The Compromise of 1850 was received with joy by most of the nation. Sectional harmony returned, for the most part, and the issue of slavery in the territories seemed to have been permanently settled. That this was an illusion became apparent within a few years.

The Election of 1852

The 1852 Democratic convention deadlocked between Cass and Douglas and so instead settled on dark horse Franklin Pierce of New Hampshire. The Whigs, true to form, chose General Winfield Scott, a war hero of no political background.

The result was an easy victory for Pierce, largely because the Whig Party, badly divided along North-South lines as a result of the battle over the Compromise of 1850, was beginning to come apart. The Free Soil Party's candidate, John P. Hale of New Hampshire, fared poorly, demonstrating the electorate's weariness with the slavery issue.

Pierce and "Young America"

Americans eagerly turned their attention to railroads, cotton, clipper ships, and commerce. The world seemed to be opening up to American trade and influence.

President Pierce expressed the nation's hope that a new era of sectional peace was beginning. To assure this he sought to distract the nation's attention from the slavery issue to an aggressive program of foreign economic and territorial expansion known as "Young America."

In 1853 Commodore Matthew Perry led a U.S. naval force into Tokyo Bay on a mission to open Japan—previously closed to the outside world—to American diplomacy and commerce.

By means of the Reciprocity Treaty (1854) Pierce succeeded in opening Canada to greater U.S. trade. He also sought to annex Hawaii, increase U.S. interest in Central America, and acquire territories from Mexico and Spain.

From Mexico he acquired in 1853 the Gadsden Purchase, a strip of land in what is now southern New Mexico and

Arizona along the Gila River. The purpose of this purchase was to provide a good route for a trans-continental railroad across the southern part of the country.

Pierce sought to buy Cuba from Spain. When Spain declined, three of Pierce's diplomats, meeting in Ostend, Belgium, sent him the Ostend Manifesto urging military seizure of Cuba should Spain remain intransigent.

Pierce was the first "doughface" president—"a northern man with southern principles"—and his expansionist goals, situated as they were in the South, aroused suspicion and hostility in anti-slavery northerners. Pierce's administration appeared to be dominated by southerners, such as Secretary of War Jefferson Davis, and whether in seeking a southern route for a trans-continental railroad or seeking to annex potential slave territory such as Cuba, it seemed to be working for the good of the South.

Economic Growth

The chief factor in the economic transformation of America during the 1840s and 1850s was the dynamic rise of the railroads. In 1840 America had less than 3000 miles of railroad track. By 1860 that number had risen to over 30,000 miles. Railroads pioneered big-business techniques, and by improving transportation helped create a nationwide market. They also helped link the Midwest to the Northeast rather than the South, as would have been the case had only water transportation been available.

Water transportation during the 1850s saw the heyday of the steamboat on inland rivers and the clipper ship on the high seas. The period also saw rapid and sustained industrial growth. The factory system began in the textile industry, where Elias Howe's invention of the sewing machine (1846) and Isaac Singer's improved model (1851) aided the process of mechanization, and spread to other industries.

Agriculture varied according to region. In the South, large plantations and small farms existed side by side for the most part, and both prospered enormously during the 1850s from the production of cotton. Southern leaders referred to the fiber as "King Cotton," an economic power that no one would dare fight against.

In the North the main centers of agricultural production shifted from the Middle Atlantic states to the more fertile lands of the Midwest. The main unit of agriculture was the family farm, and the main products were grain and livestock. Unlike the South, where 3.5 million slaves provided abundant labor, the North faced incentives to introduce labor-saving machines. Cyrus McCormick's mechanical reaper came into wide use, and by 1860 over 100,000 were in operation on Midwestern farms. Mechanical threshers also came into increasing use.

> # DIDYOUKNOW?
>
> Steam power fueled the expansion of the railroad system during the mid-nineteenth century. The first steam-powered locomotive in the United States was the Tom Thumb, which reached an unheard-of speed of 30 miles per hour during an early journey in 1830.

Decline of the Two-Party System

Meanwhile, ominous developments were taking place in politics. America's second two-party system, which had developed during the 1830s, was in the process of breaking down. The Whig Party, whose dismal performance in the election of 1852 had signaled its weakness, was now in the process of complete disintegration. Partially this was the result of the issue of slavery, which tended to divide the party along North-South lines. Partially, though, it may have been the result of the nativist movement.

The nativist movement and its political party, the American, or, as it was called, the Know-Nothing Party, grew out of alarm on the part of native-born Americans at the rising tide of German and Irish immigration during the late 1840s and early 1850s. The Know-Nothing Party, so called because its members were told to answer "I know nothing" when asked about its secret proceedings, was anti-foreign and, since many of the foreigners were Catholic, also anti-Catholic. It surged briefly to become the country's second-largest party by 1855 but faded even more quickly due to the ineptness of its leaders and the growing urgency of the slavery question, which, though ignored by the Know-Nothing Party, was rapidly coming to overshadow all other issues. To some extent the Know-Nothing movement may simply have benefitted from the already progressing disintegration of the Whig Party, but it may also have helped to complete that disintegration.

All of this was ominous because the collapse of a viable nationwide two-party system made it much more difficult for the nation's political process to contain the explosive issue of slavery.

The Return of Sectional Conflict

Continuing Sources of Tension

While Americans hailed the apparent sectional harmony created by the Compromise of 1850 and enjoyed the rapid economic growth of the decade that followed, two items which continued to create tension centered on the issue of slavery.

The Strengthened Fugitive Slave Law

The more important of these was a part of the Compromise itself, the strengthened federal Fugitive Slave Law. The law enraged Northerners, many of whom believed it little better than a legalization of kidnapping. Under its provisions blacks living in the North and claimed by slave catchers were denied trial by jury and many of the other protections of due process. Even more distasteful to anti-slavery Northerners was the provision that required all U.S. citizens to aid, when called upon, in the capture and return of alleged fugitives. So violent was Northern feeling against the law that several riots erupted as a result of attempts to enforce it. Some Northern states passed personal liberty laws in an attempt to prevent the working of the Fugitive Slave Law.

The effect of all this was to polarize the country even further. Many Northerners who had not previously taken an interest in the slavery issue now became opponents of slavery as a result of having its injustices forcibly brought home to them by the Fugitive Slave Law. Southerners saw in Northern resistance to the law further proof that the North was determined to tamper with the institution of slavery.

Uncle Tom's Cabin

One Northerner who was outraged by the Fugitive Slave Act was Harriet Beecher Stowe. In response, she wrote *Uncle Tom's Cabin*, a fictional book depicting what she perceived as the evils of slavery. Furiously denounced in the South, the book became an overnight best-seller in the North, where it turned many toward active opposition to slavery. This, too, was a note of harsh discord among the seemingly harmonious sectional relations of the early 1850s.

Chapter 1

The Civil War and Reconstruction (1860–1877)

Hostilities Begin

Fort Sumter

Lincoln did his best to avoid angering the slave states that had not yet seceded. In his inaugural address he urged Southerners to reconsider their actions but warned that the Union was perpetual, that states could not secede, and that he would therefore hold the federal forts and installations in the South.

Of these only two remained in federal hands: Fort Pickens, off Pensacola, Florida; and Fort Sumter, in the harbor of Charleston, South Carolina. Lincoln soon received word from Major Robert Anderson, commanding the small garrison at Sumter, that supplies were running low. Desiring to send in the needed supplies, Lincoln informed the governor of South Carolina of his intention but promised that no attempt would be made to send arms, ammunition, or reinforcements unless Southerners initiated hostilities.

Not satisfied, Southerners determined to take the fort. Confederate General P. G. T. Beauregard, acting on orders from President Davis, demanded Anderson's surrender. Anderson said he would if not resupplied. Knowing supplies were on the way, the Confederates opened fire at 4:30 a.m. on April 12, 1861. The next day the fort surrendered.

The day following Sumter's surrender Lincoln declared the existence of an insurrection and called for the states to provide 75,000 volunteers to put it down. In response to this, Virginia, Tennessee, North Carolina, and Arkansas declared their secession.

The remaining slave states, Delaware, Kentucky, Maryland, and Missouri, wavered to varying degrees but stayed with the Union. Delaware, which had few slaves, gave little serious consideration to the idea of secession. Kentucky declared itself neutral and then sided with the North when the South failed to respect this neutrality. Maryland's incipient secession movement was crushed by Lincoln's timely imposition of martial law. Missouri was saved for the Union by the quick and decisive use of federal troops as well as the sizeable population of pro-Union, anti-slavery German immigrants living in St. Louis.

Relative Strengths at the Outset

An assessment of available assets at the beginning of the war would not have looked favorable for the South.

The North enjoyed at least five major advantages over the South. It had overwhelming preponderance in wealth and thus was better able to finance the enormous expense of the war. The North was also vastly superior in industry and thus capable of producing the needed war materials; the South, as a primarily agricultural society, often had to improvise or do without.

The North furthermore had an advantage of almost three-to-one in manpower, and over one-third of the South's population was composed of slaves, whom Southerners would not use as soldiers. Unlike the South, the North received large numbers of immigrants during the war. The North retained control of the U.S. Navy, and thus would command the sea and be able, by blockading, to cut the South off from outside sources of supply.

Finally, the North enjoyed a far superior system of railroads, while the South's relatively sparse railroad net was composed of a number of smaller railroads, often not interconnected and with varying gauges of track. They were more useful for carrying cotton from the interior to port cities than for moving large amounts of war supplies or troops around the country.

The South did, however, have several advantages of its own. It was vast in size, and this would make it difficult to conquer; it did not need to conquer the North, but only resist being conquered itself. Its troops would also be fighting on their own ground, a fact that would give them the advantage of familiarity with the terrain, as well as the added motivation of defending their homes and families. Its armies would often have the opportunity of fighting on the defensive, a major advantage in the warfare of that day.

At the outset of the war the South drew a number of highly qualified senior officers, such as Robert E. Lee, Joseph E. Johnston, and Albert Sidney Johnston, from the U.S. Army. By contrast, the Union command structure was already set when the war began, with the aged Winfield Scott, of Mexican War fame, at the top. It took young and talented officers, such as Ulysses S. Grant and William T. Sherman, time to work up to high rank. Meanwhile, Union armies were often led by inferior commanders as Lincoln experimented while in search of good generals.

At first glance, the South might also have seemed to have an advantage in its president. Jefferson Davis had extensive military and political experience and was acquainted with the nation's top military men and, presumably, with their relative abilities. On the other hand, Lincoln had been, up until his election to the presidency, less successful politically and had virtually no military experience. In fact, Lincoln was much superior to Davis as a war leader, showing firmness, flexibility, mental toughness, great political skill, and, eventually, an excellent grasp of strategy.

Opposing Strategies

Both sides were full of enthusiasm for the war. In the North the battle cry was "On to Richmond," the new Confederate capital established after the secession of Virginia. In the South it was "On to Washington." Yielding to popular demand, Lincoln ordered General Irvin McDowell to advance on Richmond with his army. At a creek called Bull Run near the town of Manassas Junction, Virginia, just southwest of Washington, D.C., they met a Confederate force under generals P. G. T. Beauregard and Joseph E. Johnston, July 21, 1861. In the First Battle of Bull Run (called First Battle of Manassas in the South) the Union army was forced to retreat in confusion back to Washington.

Bull Run demonstrated the unpreparedness and inexperience of both sides. It also demonstrated that the war would be long and hard, and, particularly in the North, that greater efforts would be required. Lincoln would need an overall strategy. To supply this, Winfield Scott suggested his Anaconda Plan to squeeze the life out of the Confederacy. This plan included a naval blockade to shut out supplies from Europe, a campaign to take the Mississippi River, thereby splitting the South in two, and the taking of several strategic points, then waiting for pro-Union sentiment in the South to overthrow the secessionists. Lincoln liked the first two points of Scott's strategy but considered the third point unrealistic.

He ordered a naval blockade, an overwhelming task considering the South's long coastline. Yet under Secretary of the Navy Gideon Welles the Navy was expanded enormously and the blockade, derided in the early days as a "paper blockade," became increasingly effective.

Lincoln also ordered a campaign to take the Mississippi River. A major step in this direction was taken when naval forces under Captain David G. Farragut took New Orleans in April 1862.

Rather than waiting for pro-Unionists in the South to gain control, Lincoln hoped to raise huge armies and apply overwhelming pressure from all sides at once until the Confederacy collapsed. The strategy was good; the problem was finding good generals to carry it out.

The Union Preserved

Lincoln Tries McClellan

To replace the discredited McDowell, Lincoln chose General George B. McClellan. McClellan was a good trainer and organizer and was loved by the troops, but was unable to effectively use the powerful army (now called the Army of the Potomac) he had built up. Despite much prodding from Lincoln, McClellan hesitated to advance, badly overestimating his enemy's numbers.

Finally, in the spring of 1862, he took the Army of the Potomac by water down Chesapeake Bay to land between the York and James rivers in Virginia. His plan was to advance up the peninsula formed by these rivers directly to Richmond.

The operations that followed were known as the Peninsula Campaign. McClellan advanced slowly and cautiously toward Richmond, while his equally cautious Confederate opponent, General Joseph E. Johnston, drew back to the outskirts of the city before turning to fight at the Battle of Seven Pines. May 31–June 1, 1862. In this inconclusive battle Johnston was wounded. To replace him Jefferson Davis appointed his military advisor, General Robert E. Lee.

Lee summoned General Thomas J. "Stonewall" Jackson and his army from the Shenandoah Valley (where Jackson had just finished defeating several superior federal forces, causing consternation in Washington) and with the combined forces attacked McClellan.

After two days of bloody but inconclusive fighting, McClellan lost his nerve and began to retreat. In the remainder of what came to be called the Battle of the Seven Days, Lee continued to attack McClellan, forcing him back to his base, though at great cost in lives. McClellan's army was loaded back onto its ships and taken back to Washington.

Before McClellan's army could reach Washington and be completely deployed in northern Virginia, Lee saw and took an opportunity to thrash Union General John Pope, who was operating in northern Virginia with another Northern army, at the Second Battle of Bull Run.

Union Victories in the West

In the western area of the war's operations, (essentially everything west of the Appalachian Mountains,) matters were proceeding in a much different fashion. The Northern commanders there, Henry W. Halleck and Don Carlos Buell, were no more enterprising than McClellan, but Halleck's subordinate, Ulysses S. Grant, definitely was.

Seeking and obtaining permission from Halleck, Grant mounted a combined operation—army troops and navy gunboats—against two vital Confederate strongholds, Forts Henry and Donelson, which guarded the Tennessee and Cumberland rivers in northern Tennessee, and which were the weak point of the thin-stretched Confederate line under General Albert Sidney Johnston. When Grant captured the forts in February 1862, Johnston was forced to retreat to Corinth in northern Mississippi.

TEST TIP

Some questions on the AP U.S. History Exam ask you to interpret a political cartoon. Political cartoons give opinions about events taking place at the time of their creation. Because of this, the cartoons may reference specific people or events with which you are unfamiliar. However, you don't need to focus on identifying the individuals in the cartoon. Focus instead on the broad historical themes and symbolism behind the cartoon, which will give you all the information you need to answer the question.

Grant pursued but, ordered by Halleck to wait until all was in readiness before proceeding, Grant halted his troops at Pittsburg Landing on the Tennessee River, twenty-five miles north of Corinth. On April 6, 1862, Johnston, who had received reinforcements and been joined by General P. G. T. Beauregard, surprised Grant there, but in the two-day battle that followed (Shiloh) failed to defeat him. Johnston himself was among the many killed in what was, up to this point, the bloodiest battle in American history.

Grant was severely criticized in the North for having been taken by surprise. Yet with other Union victories and Farragut's capture of New Orleans, the North had taken all of the Mississippi River except for a 110-mile stretch between the Confederate fortresses of Vicksburg, Mississippi, and Port Hudson, Louisiana.

The Success of Northern Diplomacy

Many Southerners believed Britain and France would rejoice in seeing a divided and weakened America. The two countries would likewise be driven by the need of their factories for cotton and thus intervene on the Confederacy's behalf. So strongly was this view held that during the early days of the war, when the Union blockade was still too weak to be very effective, the Confederate government itself prohibited the export of cotton in order to hasten British and French intervention.

This view proved mistaken for several reasons. Britain already had on hand large stocks of cotton from the bumper crops of the years immediately prior to the war. During the war the British were successful in finding alternative sources of cotton, importing the fiber from India and Egypt. British leaders may also have weighed their country's need to import wheat from the northern United States against its desire for cotton from the Southern states. Finally, British public opinion opposed slavery.

Skillful Northern diplomacy had a great impact. In this, Lincoln had the extremely able assistance of Secretary of State William Seward, who took a hard line in warning Europeans not to interfere, and of Ambassador to Great Britain Charles Francis Adams. Britain therefore remained neutral and other European countries, France in particular, followed its lead.

One incident nevertheless came close to fulfilling Southern hopes for British intervention. In November 1861 Captain Charles Wilkes of the U.S.S. *San Jacinto* stopped the British mail and passenger ship *Trent* and forcibly removed Confederate emissaries James M. Mason and John Slidell. News of Wilkes' action brought great rejoicing in the North but outrage in Great Britain, where it was viewed as a violation of Britain's rights on the high seas. Lincoln and Seward, faced with British threats of war at a time when the North could ill afford it, wisely chose to release the envoys and smooth things over with Britain.

The Confederacy was able to obtain some loans and to purchase small amounts of arms, ammunition, and even commerce-raiding ships such as the highly successful C.S.S. *Alabama*. However, Union naval superiority kept such supplies to a minimum.

The War at Sea

The Confederacy's major bid to challenge the Union's naval superiority was based on the employment of a technological innovation, the ironclad ship. The first and most successful of the Confederate ironclads was the C.S.S. *Virginia*. Built on the hull of the abandoned Union frigate *Merrimac*, the *Virginia* was protected from cannon fire by iron plates bolted over her sloping wooden sides. In May 1862 she destroyed two wooden warships of the Union naval force at Hampton Roads, Virginia, and was seriously threatening to destroy the rest of the squadron before being met and fought to a standstill by the Union ironclad U.S.S. *Monitor*.

The Home Front

The war on the home front dealt with the problems of maintaining public morale, supplying the armies of the held, and resolving constitutional questions regarding authority and the ability of the respective governments to deal with crises.

For the general purpose of maintaining public morale but also as items many Republicans had advocated even before the war, Congress in 1862 passed two highly important acts dealing with domestic affairs in the North.

The Homestead Act granted 160 acres of government land free of charge to any person who would farm it for at least five years. Much of the West was eventually settled under the provisions of this act. The Morrill Land Grant Act offered large amounts of the federal government's land to states that would establish "agricultural and mechanical" colleges. Many of the nation's large state universities were founded in later years under the provisions of this act.

Keeping the people relatively satisfied was made more difficult by the necessity, apparent by 1863, of imposing conscription in order to obtain adequate manpower for the huge armies that would be needed to crush the South. Especially hated by many working class Northerners was the provision of the conscription act that allowed a drafted individual to avoid service by hiring a substitute or paying $300. Resistance to the draft led to riots in New York City in which hundreds were killed.

DIDYOU**KNOW?**

With so many men fighting in the war, Southern women faced new challenges. They ran plantations, managed businesses, stretched limited supplies, and helped nurse the wounded and ill soldiers at rudimentary field hospitals.

The Confederacy, with its much smaller manpower pool on which to draw, had instituted conscription in 1862. Here, too, it did not always meet with cooperation. Some Southern governors objected to it on doctrinaire states' rights grounds, doing all they could to obstruct its operation. A provision of the Southern conscription act allowing one man to stay home as overseer for every twenty slaves led the non-slaveholding whites who made up most of the Southern population to grumble that it was a "rich man's war and a poor man's fight." Draft-dodging and desertion became epidemic in the South by the latter part of the war.

Scarcity of food and other consumer goods in the South as well as high prices led to further desertion as soldiers left the ranks to care for their starving families. Discontent also manifested itself in the form of a "bread riot" in Richmond.

Supplying the war placed an enormous strain on both societies, but one the North was better able to bear.

To finance the Northern side of the war, high tariffs and an income tax (the nation's first) were resorted to, yet even more money was needed. The Treasury Department, under Secretary of the Treasury Salmon P. Chase, issued "greenbacks," an unbacked fiat currency that nevertheless fared better than the Southern paper money because of greater confidence in Northern victory. To facilitate the financing of the war through credit expansion, the National Banking Act was passed in 1863.

The South, with its scant financial resources, found it all but impossible to cope with the expense of war. Excise and income taxes were levied and some small loans were obtained in Europe, yet the Southern Congress still felt compelled to issue paper money in such quantities that it became virtually worthless. That, and the scarcity of almost everything created by the war and its disruption of the economy, led to skyrocketing prices.

The Confederate government responded to the inflation it created by imposing taxes-in-kind and impressment, the seizing of produce, livestock, etc., by Confederate agents in return for payment according to an artificially set schedule of prices. Since payment was in worthless inflated currency, this amounted to confiscation and soon resulted in goods of all sorts becoming even scarcer than otherwise when a Confederate impressment agent was known to be in the neighborhood.

Questions of constitutional authority to deal with crises plagued both presidents.

To deal with the emergency of secession, Lincoln stretched the presidential powers to the limit, or perhaps beyond the limit, of the Constitution. To quell the threat of secession in Maryland, Lincoln suspended the writ of *habeas corpus* and imprisoned numerous suspected secessionists without charges or trial, ignoring the insistence of pro-Southern Chief Justice Roger B. Taney in *ex Parte Merryman* (1861) that such action was unconstitutional.

"Copperheads," Northerners such as Clement L. Vallandigham of Ohio who opposed the war, denounced Lincoln as a tyrant and would-be dictator but remained a minority. Though occasionally subject to arrest and/or deportation for their activities, they were generally allowed a considerable degree of latitude.

Davis encountered obstructionism from various state governors, the Confederate Congress, and even his own vice president, who denounced him as a tyrant for assuming too much power and failing to respect states' rights. Hampered by such attitudes, the Confederate government proved less effective than it might have been.

The Emancipation Proclamation

By mid-1862, Lincoln, under pressure from radical elements of his own party and hoping to create a favorable impression on foreign public opinion, determined to issue the Emancipation Proclamation, declaring free, as of January 1, 1863, all slaves in areas still in rebellion. In order that this not appear an act of panic and desperation in view of the string of defeats the North had recently suffered on the battlefields of Virginia, Lincoln, at Seward's recommendation, waited to announce the proclamation until the North should win some sort of victory. This was provided by the Battle of Antietam, September 17, 1862.

Though the Radical Republicans, pre-war abolitionists for the most part, had for some time been urging Lincoln to take such a step, Northern public opinion as a whole was less enthusiastic, as the Republicans suffered major losses in the November 1862 congressional elections.

TEST TIP

Worried about needing to remember the difference between various weapons or interpret battlefield maps? Don't sweat it. The AP U.S. History Exam does not ask you to analyze military strategy or technology. Instead, it will focus on the social, political, or diplomatic aspects and effects of conflicts.

The Turning Point in the East

After his victory of the Second Battle of Bull Run, August 27–30, 1862, Lee moved north and crossed into Maryland, where he hoped to win a decisive victory that would force the North to recognize Southern independence.

He was confronted by the Army of the Potomac, once again under the command of General George B. McClellan. Through a stroke of good fortune early in the campaign, detailed plans for Lee's entire audacious operation fell into McClellan's hands, but the Northern general, by extreme caution and slowness, threw away this incomparable chance to annihilate Lee and win—or at least shorten—the war.

The armies finally met along Antietam Creek, just east of the town of Sharpsburg in western Maryland. In a bloody but inconclusive day-long battle, known as Antietam in the North and as Sharpsburg in the South, McClellan's timidity led him to miss another excellent chance to destroy Lee's cornered and badly outnumbered army. After the battle Lee retreated to Virginia, and Lincoln, besides issuing the Emancipation Proclamation, removed McClellan from command.

To replace him, Lincoln chose General Ambrose E. Burnside, who promptly demonstrated his unfitness for command by blundering into a lopsided defeat at Fredericksburg, Virginia, December 13, 1862.

Lincoln then replaced Burnside with General Joseph "Fighting Joe" Hooker. Handsome and hard-drinking, Hooker had bragged of what he would do to "Bobby Lee" when he got at him; but when he took his army south, "Fighting Joe" quickly lost his nerve. He was out-generaled and soundly beaten at the Battle of Chancellorsville, May 5–6, 1863. At this battle the brilliant Southern General "Stonewall" Jackson was accidentally shot by his own men and died several days later.

Lee, anxious to shift the scene of the fighting out of his beloved Virginia, sought and received permission from President Davis to invade Pennsylvania. He was pursued by the Army of the Potomac, now under the command of General George G. Meade, whom Lincoln had selected to replace the discredited Hooker. They met at Gettysburg, and in a three-day battle (July 1–3, 1863) that was the bloodiest of the entire war, Lee, who sorely missed the services of Jackson and whose cavalry leader, the normally reliable J. E. B. Stuart, failed to provide him with timely reconnaissance, was defeated. However, he was allowed by the victorious Meade to retreat to Virginia with his army intact if battered, much to Lincoln's disgust. Still, Lee would never again have the strength to mount such an invasion.

Lincoln Finds Grant

Meanwhile, Grant undertook to take Vicksburg, one of the two last Confederate bastions on the Mississippi River. In a brilliant campaign, he bottled up the Confederate forces of General John C. Pemberton inside the city and placed them under siege. After six weeks of siege, the defenders surrendered, July 4, 1863. Five days later Port Hudson surrendered as well, giving the Union complete control of the Mississippi.

After Union forces under General William Rosecrans suffered an embarrassing defeat at the Battle of Chickamauga in northwestern Georgia, September 19–20, 1863, Lincoln named Grant overall commander of Union forces in the West.

Grant went to Chattanooga, Tennessee, where Confederate forces under General Braxton Bragg were virtually besieging Rosecrans, and immediately took control of the situation. Gathering Union forces from other portions of the western theater and combining them with reinforcements from the East, Grant won a resounding victory at the Battle of Chattanooga (November 23–25, 1863), in which federal forces stormed seemingly impregnable Confederate positions on Lookout Mountain and Missionary Ridge. This victory put Union forces in position for a drive into Georgia, which began the following spring.

Early in 1864 Lincoln made Grant commander of all Union armies. Grant devised a coordinated plan for constant pressure on the Confederacy. General William T. Sherman would lead a drive toward Atlanta, Georgia, with the goal of destroying the Confederate army under General Joseph E. Johnston (who had replaced Bragg). Grant himself would accompany Meade and the Army of the Potomac in advancing toward Richmond with the goal of destroying Lee's Confederate army.

In a series of bloody battles (the Wilderness, Spotsylvania, Cold Harbor) in May and June of 1864, Grant drove Lee to the outskirts of Richmond. Still unable to take the city or get Lee at a disadvantage, Grant circled around to try to take both by way of the back door, attacking Petersburg, Virginia, an important railroad junction just south of Richmond and the key to that city's—and Lee's—supply lines. Once again turned back by entrenched Confederate troops, Grant settled down to besiege Petersburg and Richmond in a stalemate that lasted some nine months.

Sherman had been advancing simultaneously in Georgia. He maneuvered Johnston back to the outskirts of Atlanta with relatively little fighting. At that point Confederate President Davis lost patience with Johnston and replaced him with the aggressive General John B. Hood. Hood and Sherman fought three fierce but inconclusive battles around Atlanta in late July, then settled down to a siege of their own during the month of August.

TEST TIP

Leave your AP U.S. History textbook and review materials at home or in your locker during the exam. You are not allowed to refer to any potential sources of information during the break period between test sections.

The Election of 1864 and Northern Victory

In the North discontentment grew with the long casualty lists and seeming lack of results. Yet the South could stand the grinding war even less. By late 1864 Jefferson Davis had reached the point of calling for the use of blacks in the Confederate armies, though the war ended before black troops could see action for the Confederacy. The South's best hope was that Northern war-weariness would bring the defeat of Lincoln and the victory of a peace candidate in the election of 1864.

Lincoln ran on the ticket of the National Union Party, essentially the Republican party with loyal or "War" Democrats. His vice-presidential candidate was Andrew Johnson, a loyal Democrat from Tennessee.

The Democratic Party's presidential candidate was General George B. McClellan, who, with some misgivings, ran on a platform labeling the war a failure and calling for a negotiated peace settlement even if that meant Southern independence.

The outlook was bleak for a time, and even Lincoln himself believed that he would be defeated. Then in September 1864 came word that Sherman had taken Atlanta.

As the industrial and political capital of the Confederacy, Richmond, Virginia, found itself caught in the bloody crossfire between two mighty American armies. Here, the Petersburg Railway Depot lies in ruins in 1865. AP/Wide World Photo.

The capture of this vital Southern rail and manufacturing center brought an enormous boost to northern morale. Along with other Northern victories that summer and fall, it insured a resounding election victory for Lincoln and the continuation of the war to complete victory for the North.

To speed that victory, Sherman marched through Georgia from Atlanta to the sea, arriving at Savannah in December 1864 and turning north into the Carolinas, leaving behind a 60-mile-wide swath of destruction. His goal was to impress on southerners that continuation of the war could mean only ruin for all of them. He and Grant planned that his army should press on through the Carolinas and into Virginia to join Grant in finishing off Lee.

Before Sherman's troops could arrive, Lee abandoned Richmond (April 3, 1865) and attempted to escape with what was left of his army. Pursued by Grant, he was cornered and forced to surrender at Appomattox, Virginia, on April 9, 1865. Other Confederate armies still holding out in various parts of the South surrendered over the next few weeks.

Lincoln did not live to receive news of the final surrenders. On April 14, 1865, he was shot in the back of the head while watching a play at Ford's Theater in Washington. His assassin, pro-Southern actor John Wilkes Booth, injured his ankle in making his escape. Hunted down by Union cavalry several days later, he died of a gunshot wound, apparently self-inflicted. Several other individuals were tried, convicted, and hanged by a military tribunal for participating with Booth in a conspiracy to assassinate not only Lincoln, but also Vice President Johnson and Secretary of State Seward.

The Ordeal of Reconstruction

Lincoln's Plan of Reconstruction

Reconstruction began well before the fighting of the Civil War came to an end. It brought a time of difficult adjustments in the South.

Among those who faced such adjustments were the recently freed slaves, who flocked into Union lines, followed advancing Union armies, or whose plantations were part of the growing area of the South that came under Union military control. Some slaves had left their plantations, and thus their only means of livelihood, in order to obtain freedom within Union lines. Many felt they had to leave their plantations in order to be truly free, and some sought to find relatives separated during the days of slavery. Some former slaves also seemed to misunderstand the meaning of freedom, thinking they need never work again.

To ease the adjustment for these recently freed slaves, Congress in 1865 created the Freedman's Bureau, to provide food, clothing, and education, and generally look after the interests of former slaves.

Even before the need to deal with this problem had forced itself on the Northern government's awareness, steps had been taken to deal with another major adjustment of Reconstruction, the restoration of loyal governments to the seceded states. By 1863 substantial portions of several Southern states had come under Northern military control, and Lincoln had set forth a policy for re-establishing governments in those states.

Lincoln's policy, known as the Ten Percent Plan, stipulated that Southerners, except for high-ranking rebel officials, could take an oath promising future loyalty to the Union and acceptance of the end of slavery. When the number of those who had taken this oath within any one state reached ten percent of the number who had been registered to vote in that state in 1860, a loyal state government could be formed. Only those who had taken the oath could vote or participate in the new government.

Tennessee, Arkansas, and Louisiana met the requirements and formed loyal governments but were refused recognition by Congress, which was dominated by Radical Republicans.

The Radical Republicans, such as Thaddeus Stevens of Pennsylvania, believed Lincoln's plan did not adequately punish the South, restructure Southern society, and boost the political prospects of the Republican Party. The loyal southern states were denied representation in Congress and electoral votes in the election of 1864.

Instead, the Radicals in Congress drew up the Wade-Davis Bill. Under its stringent terms a majority of the number who had been alive and registered to vote in 1860 would have to swear an "ironclad" oath stating that they were now loyal and had never been disloyal. This was obviously impossible in any former Confederate state unless blacks were given the vote, something Radical Republicans desired but Southerners definitely did not. Unless the requisite number swore the "ironclad" oath, Congress would not allow the state to have a government.

DID YOU KNOW?

The pocket veto reflects a different era in U.S. government, when Congress typically met for one marathon session before adjourning for several months. Then, Congress gathered again for a shorter second session. Improvements in transportation and a change in the congressional meeting calendar have ended these long intersession breaks, but presidents still have the power of the pocket veto.

Lincoln killed the Wade-Davis bill with a "pocket veto," and the Radicals were furious. When Lincoln was assassinated the Radicals rejoiced, believing Vice President Andrew Johnson would be less generous to the South or at least easier to control.

Johnson's Attempt at Reconstruction

To the dismay of the Radicals, Johnson followed Lincoln's policies very closely, making them only slightly more stringent by requiring ratification of the 13th Amendment (officially abolishing slavery), repudiation of Confederate debts, and renunciation of secession. He also recommended the vote be given to blacks.

Southern states proved reluctant to accept these conditions, some declining to repudiate Confederate debts or ratify the 13th Amendment (it nevertheless received the ratification of the necessary number of states and was declared part of the Constitution in December 1865). No Southern state extended the vote to blacks (at this time no Northern state did, either). Instead the Southern states promulgated Black Codes, imposing various restrictions on the freedom of the former slaves.

Foreign Policy Under Johnson

On coming into office Johnson had inherited a foreign policy problem involving Mexico and France. The French Emperor, Napoleon III, had made Mexico the target of one of his many grandiose foreign adventures. In 1862, while the U.S. was occupied with the Civil War and therefore unable to prevent this violation of the Monroe Doctrine, Napoleon III had Archduke Maximilian of Austria installed as a puppet emperor of Mexico, supported by French troops. The U.S. had protested but for the time could do nothing.

With the war over, Johnson and Secretary of State Seward were able to take more vigorous steps. General Philip Sheridan was sent to the Rio Grande with a military force. At the same time Mexican revolutionary leader Benito Juarez was given the tacit recognition of the U.S. government. Johnson and Seward continued to invoke the Monroe Doctrine and to place quiet pressure on Napoleon III to withdraw his troops. In May 1866, facing difficulties of his own in Europe, the French emperor did so, leaving the unfortunate Maximilian to face a Mexican firing squad.

DIDYOU**KNOW?**

Alaska leads the nations in many geographic respects. It is the largest U.S. state by land area, has a coastline longer than that of all other U.S. states combined, and is home to the nation's highest point, Mount McKinley.

Chapter 7

Industrialism, War, and the Progressive Era (1877–1912)

The New Industrial Era, 1877–1882

The structure of modern American society was erected by democratic, capitalistic and technological forces in the post–Civil War era. Between the 1870s and 1890s, "Gilded Age" America emerged as the world's leading industrial and agricultural producer.

Politics of the Period, 1877–1882

The presidencies of Abraham Lincoln and Theodore Roosevelt mark the boundaries of a half century of relatively weak executive leadership, and legislative domination by Congress and the Republican Party.

The Compromise of 1877

With Southern Democratic acceptance of Rutherford B. Hayes' Republican presidency, the last remaining Union troops were withdrawn from the Old Confederacy (South Carolina, Florida, Louisiana), and the country was at last reunified as a modern nation-state led by corporate and industrial interests. The Hayes election arrangement also marked the government's abandonment of its earlier vague commitment to African-American equality.

Republican Factions

"Stalwarts" led by New York Senator Roscoe Conkling favored the old spoils system of political patronage. "Half-Breeds" headed by Maine Senator James G. Blaine pushed for civil service reform and merit appointments to government posts.

Election of 1880

James A. Garfield of Ohio, a Half-Breed, and his vice presidential running mate, Chester A. Arthur of New York, a Stalwart, defeated the Democratic candidate, General Winfield S. Hancock of Pennsylvania and former Indiana congressman William English. Tragically, the Garfield administration was but an interlude, for the president was assassinated in 1881 by a mentally disturbed patronage seeker, Charles Guiteau. Although without much executive experience, the Stalwart Arthur had the courage to endorse reform of the political spoils system by supporting passage of the Pendleton Act (1883) which established open competitive examinations for civil service positions.

The Greenback-Labor Party

The Greenback-Labor Party movement polled over one million votes in 1878, and elected 14 members to Congress in an effort to promote the inflation of farm prices, and the cooperative marketing of agricultural produce. In 1880, the party's presidential candidate, James Weaver of Iowa, advocated public control and regulation of private enterprises such as railroads in the common interest of more equitable competition. Weaver theorized that because railroads were so essential, they should be treated as a public utility. He polled only 3 percent of the vote.

The Economy, 1877–1882

Industrial expansion and technology assumed mayor proportions in this period. Between 1860 and 1894 the United States moved from the fourth-largest manufacturing nation to the world's leader through capital accumulation, natural resources (especially in iron, oil and coal) an abundance of labor helped by massive immigration, railway transportation and communications (the telephone was introduced by Alexander Graham Bell in 1876), and major technical innovations such as the development of the modern steel industry by Andrew Carnegie, and electrical energy by Thomas Edison. In the petroleum industry, John D. Rockefeller controlled 95 percent of the U.S. oil refineries by 1877.

The New South

By 1880, Northern capital erected the modern textile industry in the New South by bringing factories to the cotton fields. Birmingham, Alabama, emerged as the South's leading steel producer, and the introduction of machine-made cigarettes propelled the Duke family to prominence as tobacco producers.

Standard of Living

An elite class rose during this period which accumulated vast family fortunes, while many Americans, especially immigrants and newly freed slaves, suffered crushing poverty.

Social Darwinism

Many industrial leaders used the doctrines associated with the "Gospel of Wealth" to justify the unequal distribution of national wealth. Self-justification by the wealthy was based on the notion that God had granted wealth as He had given grace for material and spiritual salvation of the select few. These few, according to William Graham Sumner, relied heavily on the survival-of-the-fittest philosophy associated with Charles Darwin.

Labor Unrest

When capital over-expansion and over-speculation led to the economic panic of 1873, massive labor disorders spread through the country leading to the paralyzing railroad strike of 1877. Unemployment and salary reductions caused major class conflict. President Hayes used federal troops to restore order after dozens of workers were killed. Immigrant workers began fighting among themselves in California where Irish and Chinese laborers fought for economic survival.

Labor Unions

The depression of the 1870s undermined national labor organizations. The National Labor Union (1866) had a membership of 600,000 but failed to withstand the impact of economic adversity. The Knights of Labor (1869) managed to open its membership to not only white native American workers, but immigrants, women and African-Americans as well. Although they claimed one million members, they too could not weather the hard times of the 1870s, and eventually went under in 1886 in the wake of the bloody Haymarket Riot in Chicago.

Agricultural Militancy

Agrarian discontent expressed through the activities of the National Grange and the Farmers' Alliances in the West and South showed greater lasting power. During the Civil War, many farmers had over-expanded their operations, purchased more land and machinery, and gone heavily into debt. When the relatively high wartime agricultural prices collapsed in the decades after the war, farmers worked collectively to promote currency inflation, higher farm prices, silver and gold bimetalism, debt relief, cooperative farm marketing ventures, and regulation of monopolies and railroads by the federal and state governments. Although not very successful in the 1870s, farmer militancy continued to be a powerful political and economic force in the decades of the 1880s and 1890s.

Social and Cultural Developments, 1877–1882

Urbanization was the primary social and cultural phenomenon of the period. Both internal and external migrations contributed to an industrial urban state that grew from 40 million people in 1870 to almost 80 million in 1900. New York, Chicago, and Philadelphia emerged as cities of over 1 million people.

Skyscrapers and Immigrants

Cities grew both up and out as the skyscraper made its appearance after the introduction of the mechanical elevator by Elisha Otis. The city also grew outward into a large, impersonal metropolis divided into various business, industrial and residential sectors, usually segregated by ethnic group, social class and race. Slums and tenements sprang up

DIDYOUKNOW?

Ellis Island was the busiest immigration station in the eastern United States. Over 12 million people entered the United States through Ellis Island between 1892 and 1954 (www.nps.gov). On the West Coast, Angel Island served as the main point of entry for many immigrants from China and other Asian nations.

within walking distance of department stores and townhouses. Two million immigrants from northern Europe poured into the U.S. during the 1870s. In the 1880s another 5 million entered the country, but by this time they were coming from southern and eastern Europe.

Lack of Government Policy

There were few programs to deal with the vast influx of humanity other than the prohibition of the criminal and the insane. City governments soon developed the primary responsibility for immigrants—often trading employment, housing and social services for political support.

Social Gospel

In time, advocates of the "social gospel" such as Jane Addams and Washington Gladden urged the creation of settlement houses and better health and education services to accommodate the new immigrants. New religions also appeared, including the Salvation Army, and Mary Baker Eddy's Church of Christian Science in 1879.

Education

Public education continued to expand, especially on the secondary level. Private Catholic parochial schools and teaching colleges grew in number as well. Adult education and English instruction became important functions of both public and private schooling.

African-American Leaders

Booker T. Washington emerged in 1881 as the president of Tuskegee Institute in Alabama, a school devoted to teaching and vocational education for African-Americans with a mission to encourage self-respect and economic equality of the races. It was at Tuskegee that George Washington Carver emerged in subsequent years as an agricultural chemist who did much to find industrial applications for agricultural products.

Feminism

The new urban environment encouraged feminist activism. Millions of women worked outside the home, and continued to demand voting rights. Many women became active in social reform movements such as the prohibitionist Women's Christian Temperance Movement, planned parenthood, humane societies, antiprostitution crusades, and equal rights for all regardless of gender, race, or class.

Literature

Important books appeared such as Henry George's *Progress and Poverty* (1879), a 3-million-copy seller that advocated one single tax on land as the means to redistribute wealth for greater social and economic justice. In fiction Lew Wallace's *Ben Hur* (1880), and the many Horatio Alger stories promoting values such as hard work, honesty, and a touch of good fortune sold many millions of copies. Other famous works of the era included Mark Twain's *The Gilded Age* (1873), and *The Adventures of Tom Sawyer* (1876), Bret Harte's stories of the Old West, William Dean Howell's social commentaries, and Henry James's *Daisy Miller* (1879) and *Portrait of a Lady* (1881).

Foreign Relations, 1877–1882

The United States gradually became involved in the "new imperialism" of the 1870s geared to finding markets for surplus industrial production, access to needed raw materials, and opportunities for overseas investment during a time of domestic economic depression. Unlike European territorial colonialism, however, the United States preferred market expansion without the political liability of military occupation.

Latin America

President Hayes recognized the government of dictator Porfirio Diaz in Mexico, thus encouraging not only trade expansion, but U.S. investment in railroads, mines, agriculture and oil.

Pan Americanism

In 1881 Secretary of State James G. Blaine advocated the creation of an International Bureau of American Republics to promote a customs union of trade and political stability for the Western Hemisphere. The assassination of President Garfield temporarily kept Blaine from forming this organization until 1889. The Bureau subsequently evolved into the Pan American Union in 1910, and the Organization of American States in 1948.

Mediation of Border Disputes

The United States offered its good offices to promote the peaceful resolution of border conflicts between a number of states: in 1876 between Argentina and Paraguay; in 1880 between Colombia and Chile; and in 1881 between Mexico and Guatemala, Argentina and Chile, and Peru and Chile. The United States also worked to bring an end to the War of the Pacific (1879–1884) fought between Chile and the alliance of Peru and Bolivia.

Canal Project

In 1876 the Interoceanic Canal Commission recommended a Nicaraguan route for a canal to link the Atlantic and Pacific oceans. In the 1880s, the U.S. officially took a hostile position against the French Panama Canal project.

The Pacific

In 1878, the United States ratified a treaty with Samoa giving the U.S. trading rights and a naval base at Pago Pago.

Japan

In 1878, the United States was the first country to negotiate a treaty granting tariff autonomy to Japan, and set a precedent for ending the practice by Western nations of controlling customs house collections in Asian states.

Geronimo, Apache leader who rose to prominence in mounting an offensive against U.S. forces' forcible displacement of 4,000 Apaches to a barren wasteland in the Southwest. Undated. AP/Wide World Photo.

Korea

Commodore Robert Wilson Shufeldt opened trade and diplomatic relations with the Hermit Kingdom in 1882. The United States promoted the principles of equal opportunity of trade, and the sovereignty of Korea (later known as open door policies) which had earlier been advocated as desirable in China.

Native Americans

Westward expansion and the discovery of gold in South Dakota in the early 1870s led to the Sioux War, 1876–1877, and George A. Custer's "last stand." In 1877 the Nez Perce War in Idaho resulted from similar causes. The Apache in Arizona and New Mexico fought as well.

Reservations

The Indian tribes were eventually vanquished and compelled to live on isolated reservations. In addition to superior U.S. military force, disease, railway construction, alcoholism, and the virtual extermination of the bison contributed to their defeat. In 1881 Helen Hunt Jackson's *A Century of Dishonor* chronicled the tragic policy pursued against Native Americans.

The Reaction to Corporate Industrialism, 1882–1887

The rise of big business and monopoly capitalism—especially in banking, railroads, mining, and the oil and steel industries—generated a reaction on the part of working class Americans in the form of new labor organizations and collective political action. Most Americans, however, were not opposed to free enterprise economics, but simply wanted an opportunity to share in the profits.

Politics of the Period, 1882–1887

The only Democrat elected president in the half century after the Civil War was Grover Cleveland.

Election of 1884

The Republicans nominated James G. Blaine (Maine) for president and John Logan (Illinois) for vice president. The Democrats chose New York governor Grover Cleveland and Thomas A. Hendricks (Indiana). The defection of Independent Republicans supporting civil service reforms, known as "Mugwumps" (such as E.L. Godkin and Carl Schurz) to the Cleveland camp cost Blaine, the former Speaker of the House, the election. The Democrats held control of the House and the Republicans controlled the Senate.

Presidential Succession Act of 1886

The death of Vice President Hendricks in 1885 led to a decision to change the line of succession (established in 1792) from the president *pro tempore* of the Senate to the Cabinet officers in order of creation of their departments to maintain party leadership. This system lasted until 1947 when the Speaker of the House was declared third in line.

Executive Appointments

President Cleveland insisted that executive appointments and removals were the prerogative of the executive and not the Senate. This was the first time since Andrew Johnson that a president had strengthened the independence of his office.

The Economy, 1882–1887

Large, efficient corporations prospered. Captains of industry, or robber barons, such as John D. Rockefeller in oil, J. P. Morgan in banking, Gustavus Swift in meat processing, Andrew Carnegie in steel, and E. H. Harriman in railroads, put together major industrial empires.

Big Business

The concentration of wealth and power in the hands of a relatively small number of giant firms in many industries led to monopoly capitalism that minimized competition. This process, in turn, led to a demand by smaller businessmen, farmers and laborers for government regulation of the economy in order to promote capital competition for the salvation of free enterprise economics.

The Interstate Commerce Act (1887)

Popular resentment of railroad abuses such as price fixing, kickbacks, and discriminatory freight rates created demands for state regulation of the railway industry. When the Supreme Court ruled individual state laws unconstitutional (*Wabash* case, 1886) because only Congress had the right to control interstate commerce, the Interstate Commerce Act was passed providing that a commission be established to oversee fair and just railway rates, prohibit rebates, end discriminatory practices, and require annual reports and financial statements. The Supreme Court, however, remained a friend of special interests, and often undermined the work of the I.C.C.

Expanding Cultivation

Agrarians and ranchers continued their westward expansion. The amount of land under cultivation between 1870 and 1890 more than doubled from 408 to 840 million acres. Transcontinental railroads, modem farm machinery, and soil conservation practices contributed to national prosperity.

Low Farm Prices

Despite success many farmers were concerned about capital indebtedness, low farm prices resulting from surplus production, railroad rate discrimination, and the lack of sufficient silver currency to promote price inflation. Agrarian groups such as the National Grange and the Farmers' Alliances called for government of the economy to redress their grievances. To a certain extent, however, many of these problems were determined by participation of American agriculture in global markets. Farmers did not completely understand all the risks in an international free market economy.

American Federation of Labor, 1886

Confronted by big business, Samuel Gompers and Adolph Strasser put together a combination of national craft unions to represent the material interests of labor in the matter of wages, hours, and safety conditions. The American Federation of Labor philosophy was pragmatic and not directly influenced by the dogmatic Marxism of some European labor movements. Although militant in its use of the strike and its demand for collective bargaining in labor contracts with large corporations such as those in railroads, mining and manufacturing, the American Federation of Labor did not intend violent revolution or political radicalism.

Scientific Management

Frederick W. Taylor, an engineer credited as the father of scientific management, introduced modern concepts of industrial engineering, plant management, and time and motion studies. This gave rise to efficiency experts and a separate class of managers in industrial manufacturing.

TEST TIP

You may only work on each section of the test during the stated time period. Looking ahead at the essays or trying to go back to check your multiple-choice answers when you should be working on something else can result in having your test scores canceled.

Social and Cultural Developments, 1882–1887

The continued growth of urban America contributed to the dissemination of knowledge and information in many fields.

Newspapers and Magazines

The linotype machine (1886) invented by Otto Mergenthaler cut printing costs dramatically. Press associations flourished and publishing became big business. In 1884, Joseph Pulitzer, a Hungarian-born immigrant, was the first publisher to reach a mass audience selling 100,000 copies of the *New York World*. New magazines such as *Forum* appeared in 1886 with a hard-hitting editorial style that emphasized investigatory journalism and controversial subjects.

Higher Education

Colleges and universities expanded and introduced a more modern curriculum. Graduate study emphasized meticulous research and the seminar method as pioneered in the United States at Johns Hopkins University.

Women's Colleges

Bryn Mawr (1885) was established and soon found a place among such schools as Vassar, Wellesley, and Mount Holyoke in advancing education for women.

Natural Science

Albert Michelson at the University of Chicago, working on measuring the speed of light, contributed in the 1880s to theories which helped prepare the way for Einstein's Theory of Relativity. In 1907, Michelson was the first American to win a Nobel Prize.

The New Social Science

Richard T. Ely studied the ethical implications of economic problems. Henry C. Adams and Simon Patten put forth theories to justify government regulation and planning in the economy. In sociology, Lester Frank Ward's *Dynamic Sociology* (1883) stressed intelligent planning and decision making over genetic determinism as promoted by Social Darwinists such as William Graham Sumner. Woodrow Wilson's *Congressional Government* was a critique of the committee system in Congress and called for a better working relationship between the executive and legislative branches of government. After winning the presidency in 1912, Wilson would be in a position to put his ideas into practice.

Literary Realism

Romanticism declined in favor of a more realistic approach to literature. Novelists explored social problems such as crime and political corruption, urban ghetto life, class conflict, evolution, and the environment. Mark Twain's masterpiece *Huckleberry Finn* appeared in 1884. In 1885, William Dean Howell's *The Rise of Silas Lapham* presented the theme of business ethics in a competitive society. *The Bostonians* (1886) by Henry James attempted a complex psychological study of female behavior.

Art

Realism could also be seen in the artistic works of Thomas Eakins, Mary Cassatt, Winslow Homer, and James Whistler. Museums and art schools expanded. Wealthy patrons spent fortunes on personal art collections.

Foreign Relations, 1882–1887

Contrary to popular belief, the United States was not an isolationist nation in the 1880s. Trade expansion and the protection of markets were primary concerns.

Modern Navy

In 1883 Congress authorized the construction of new steel ships that would take the U.S. Navy in a 20-year period from twelfth to third in world naval ranking. In 1884, the U.S. Naval War College was established in Newport, Rhode Island—the first of its kind.

statements from officials such as Assistant Secretary of the Navy Theodore Roosevelt encouraged popular support for direct American military intervention on behalf of Cuban independence. President McKinley, however, proceeded cautiously through 1897.

Britain and Venezuela (1895)

The dispute over the border of Britain's colony of Guiana threatened war with Venezuela, especially after gold was discovered in the area. Although initially at odds with Britain, the United States eventually came to support British claims against Venezuela when Britain agreed to recognize the Monroe Doctrine in Latin America. Britain also sought U.S. cooperation in its dispute with Germany in South Africa. This rivalry would in time lead to the Boer War. The realignment of the United States and Britain would play a significant role during World War I.

The Sino-Japanese War, 1894–1895

Japan's easy victory over China signaled to the United States and other nations trading in Asia that China's weakness might result in its colonization by industrial powers, and the closing of the China market. The U.S. resolved to seek a naval base in the Pacific to protect its interests. The opportunity to annex the Philippines after the war with Spain was in part motivated by the desire to protect America's trade and future potential in Asia. This concern would also lead the U.S. to announce the Open Door policy with China in 1899 and 1900 designed to protect equal opportunity of trade, and China's political independence.

Latin America

When revolutions broke out in 1894 in both Brazil and Nicaragua, the United States supported the existing governments in power to maintain political stability and favorable trade treaties. Secretaries of State Walter Q. Gresham, Richard Olney and John Sherman continued to support James G. Blaine's Pan American policy.

The Pacific

The United States intervened in the Hawaiian revolution (1893) to overthrow the anti-American government of Queen Liliuokalani. President Cleveland rejected American annexation of Hawaii in 1894, but President McKinley agreed to annex it in 1898.

War and the Americanization of the World, 1897–1902

In 1900 an Englishman named William T. Stead authored a book entitled *The Americanization of the World* in which he predicted that American productivity and economic strength would propel the United States to the forefront of world leadership in the twentieth century. The Spanish-American War and the events following it indicated that the U.S. would be a force in the global balance of power for years to come. Few, however, would have predicted that as early as 1920 the U.S. would achieve the pinnacle of world power as a result of the debilitating policies pursued by European political leaders during World War I (1914–1919). One question remained: Would the American people be prepared to accept the responsibility of world leadership?

Politics of the Period, 1897–1902

President McKinley's wartime leadership and tragic assassination closed one door in American history, but opened another door to the leadership of Theodore Roosevelt, the first "progressive" president.

Election of 1900

The unexpected death of Vice President Garrett Hobart led the Republican Party to choose the war hero and reform governor of New York, Theodore Roosevelt, as President William McKinley's vice presidential running mate. Riding the crest of victory against Spain, the G.O.P. platform called for upholding the gold standard for full economic recovery, promoting economic expansion and power in the Caribbean and the Pacific, and building a canal in Central America. The Democrats once again nominated William Jennings Bryan and Adlai Stevenson on a platform condemning imperialism and the gold standard. McKinley easily won reelection by about 1 million votes (7.2 million to 6.3 million), and the Republicans retained control of both houses of Congress.

Other Parties

The fading Populists nominated Wharton Barker (Pennsylvania) and Ignatius Donnelly (Minnesota) on a pro-inflation platform but only received 50,000 votes. The Socialist Democratic Party nominated Eugene V. Debs (Indiana) and Job Harriman

(California) on a platform urging the nationalization of major industries. Debs received 94,000 votes. The Prohibition Party nominated John Woolley (Illinois) and Henry Metcalf (Rhode Island) and called for a ban on alcohol production and consumption. They received 209,000 votes.

McKinley Assassination (1901)

While attending the Pan American Exposition in Buffalo, New York, the president was shot on September 6 by Leon Czolgosz, an anarchist sworn to destroy all governments. The president died on September 14 after many officials had said they thought he would recover. Theodore Roosevelt became the nation's twenty-fifth president and—at age 42—its youngest to that time.

The Economy, 1897–1902

The war with Spain provided the impetus for economic recovery. President Roosevelt promised a "square deal" for all Americans, farmers, workers, consumers and businessmen. Progressive economic reform was geared to the rejuvenation of free enterprise capitalism following the 1893 depression, and the destruction of illegal monopolies. In this way, radicals would be denied an audience for more revolutionary and violent change.

War with Spain (1898)

The financial cost of the war was $250 million. Eastern and Midwestern industrial cities tended to favor war and benefit from it. Northeastern financial centers were more cautious about war until March 1898, and questioned the financial gains of wartime production at the expense of peacetime expansion and product/market development.

Federal Bankruptcy Act (1898)

This act reformed and standardized procedures for bankruptcy, along with the responsibilities of creditors and debtors.

Erdman Act (1898)

This act provided for mediation by the chair of the Interstate Commerce Commission and the commissioner of the Bureau of Labor in unresolved railroad labor controversies.

Currency Act (1900)

The United States standardized the amount of gold in the dollar at 25.8 grains 9/10 fine. A separate gold reserve was set apart from other general funds, and government bonds were sold to maintain the reserve.

Technology

Between 1860 and 1900 railroad trackage grew from 36,800 miles to 193,350 miles. U.S. Steel Corp. was formed in 1901, Standard Oil Company of New Jersey in 1899.

Social and Cultural Developments, 1897–1902

Debates about the war and territorial acquisitions, and the state of the economy, tended to dominate thought and literature.

Yellow Journalism

Joseph Pulitzer's *New York World* and William Randolph Hearst's *New York Journal* competed fiercely to increase circulation through exaggeration of Spanish atrocities in Cuba. Such stories whipped up popular resentment of Spain, and helped to create a climate of opinion receptive to war.

DeLôme Letter and Sinking of the *Maine*

On February 9, 1898, the newspapers published a letter written by the Spanish minister in Washington, Depuy de Lôme, personally criticizing President McKinley in insulting terms. On February 15, the Battleship U.S.S. *Maine* was blown up in Havana harbor with a loss of 250 Americans. The popular demand for war with Spain grew significantly even though it was likely that the *Maine* was blown up by accident when spontaneous combustion in a coal bunker caused a powder magazine to explode.

U.S. Military

Facing its first war since the Civil War, the U.S. Army was not prepared for a full-scale effort in 1898. Although 245,000 men served in the war (with over 5,000 deaths), the Army at the outset consisted of only 28,000 troops. The volunteers who signed up in the early stages were surprised to be issued winter uniforms to train in the tropics for war in Cuba. Cans of food stockpiled since the Civil War were reissued. After getting past these early problems, the War Department settled down to a more effective organizational procedure. Sadly, more deaths resulted from disease and food poisoning than from battlefield casualties. The U.S. Navy (26,000 men) was far better prepared for war as a result of past years of modernization.

"The Rough Riders" of the U.S. Army's 1st Volunteer Cavalry commanded by Lt. Col. Theodore Roosevelt, atop San Juan Hill. U.S. National Archives and Records Administration.

Territories

After the United States had defeated Spain (see "Foreign Policy"), it was faced with the issue of what to do with such captured territories as the Philippines, Puerto Rico, the Isle of Pines, and Guam. A major public debate ensued with critics of land acquisition forming the Anti-Imperialist League with the support of Mark Twain,

William James, William Jennings Bryan, Grover Cleveland, Charles Francis Adams, Carl Schurz, Charles W. Eliot, David Starr Jordan, Andrew Carnegie and Samuel Gompers among others. Supporters of colonialism included Theodore Roosevelt, Mark Hanna, Alfred Thayer Mahan, Henry Cabot Lodge, Albert Beveridge, President McKinley and many others. Ironically, many individuals in both camps favored U.S. economic expansion, but had difficulty with the idea that a democracy would actually accept colonies and overseas armies of occupations.

One of the most celebrated examples of early skyscrapers, the 21-story Flatiron Building rose in New York in 1902. AP/Wide World Photo.

Literature

Thorstein Veblen's *Theory of the Leisure Class* (1899) attacked the "predatory wealth" and "conspicuous consumption" of the new rich in the gilded age. Veblen added evidence and argument to a critique begun by Jacob Riis in *How the Other Half Lives* (1890), documenting the gnawing poverty, illness, crime and despair of New York's slums. Frank Norris's *McTeague* (1899) chronicled a man's regression to brutish animal behavior in the dog-eat-dog world of unbridled and unregulated capitalist competition. His novel *The Octopus* (1901) condemned monopoly.

U.S.S. *Maine* on February 16, 1898, the day after an explosion sank the battleship in Havana Harbor, killing 266 crew members. AP/Wide World Photo/Key West Art/Historical Society.

Foreign Policy, 1897–1902

The summer war with Spain, and the expansion of American interests in Asia and the Caribbean were dominant factors.

Decision for War (1898)

Loss of markets, threats to Americans in Cuba, and the inability of both Spain and Cuba to resolve the Cuban revolution either by force or diplomacy led to McKinley's request of Congress for a declaration of war. The sinking of the *Maine* in February 1898, and the return of Vermont Senator Redfield Proctor from a fact-finding mission on March 17, 1898, revealed how poor the situation was in Cuba.

McKinley's Ultimatum

On March 27, President McKinley asked Spain to call an armistice, accept American mediation to end the war, and end the use of concentration camps in Cuba. When Spain refused to comply, McKinley requested Congress declare war. On April 21, Congress declared war on Spain with the objective of establishing Cuban independence (Teller Amendment).

Cuba

After the first U.S. forces landed in Cuba on June 22, 1898, the United States proceeded to victories at El Caney and San Juan Hill. By July 17, Admiral Sampson's North Atlantic Squadron destroyed the Spanish fleet, Santiago surrendered, and American troops quickly went on to capture Puerto Rico.

The Philippines

As early as December 1897, Commodore Perry's Asiatic Squadron was alerted to possible war with Spain. On May 1, 1898, the Spanish fleet in the Philippines was destroyed and Manila surrendered on August 13. Spain agreed to a peace conference to be held in Paris in October 1898.

Treaty of Paris

Secretary of State William Day led the American negotiating team, which secured Cuban independence, the ceding of the Philippines, Puerto Rico and Guam to the U.S., and the payment of $20 million to Spain for the Philippines. The treaty was ratified by the Senate February 6, 1900.

Philippines Insurrection

Filipino nationalists under Emilio Aguinaldo rebelled against the United States (February 1899) when they learned the Philippines would not be given independence. The United States used 70,000 men to suppress the revolutionaries by June 1902. A special U.S. commission recommended eventual self-government for the Philippines.

Hawaii and Wake Island

During the war with Spain, the U.S. annexed Hawaii on July 7, 1898. In 1900 the U.S. claimed Wake Island, 2,000 miles west of Hawaii.

China

Fearing the break-up of China into separate spheres of influence, Secretary of State John Hay called for acceptance of the Open Door Notes by all nations trading in the China market to guarantee equal opportunity of trade (1899), and the sovereignty of the Manchu government of China (1900). With Manila as a base of operations, the United States was better able to protect its economic and political concerns in Asia. Such interests included the American China Development Co. (1898), a railway and mining concession in south China, and various oil, timber, and industrial investments in Manchuria.

Boxer Rebellion (1900)

Chinese nationalists ("Boxers") struck at foreign settlements in China, and at the Ch'ing dynasty Manchu government in Beijing for allowing foreign industrial nations such as Britain, Japan, Russia, France, Germany, Italy, Portugal, Belgium, The Netherlands, and the United States large concessions within Chinese borders. An international army helped to put down the rebellion, and aided the Chinese government to remain in power.

Platt Amendment (1901)

Although Cuba was granted its independence, the Platt Amendment provided that Cuba become a virtual protectorate of the United States. Cuba could not 1) make a treaty with a foreign state impairing its independence, or 2) contract an excessive public debt. Cuba was required to 1) allow the U.S. to preserve order on the island, and 2) lease a naval base for 99 years to the U.S. at Guantanamo Bay.

Hay-Pauncefote Treaty (1901)

This treaty between the U.S. and Britain abrogated an earlier agreement (1850, Clayton-Bulwer Treaty) to build jointly an isthmian canal. The United States was free unilaterally to construct, fortify and maintain a canal that would be open to all ships.

Insular Cases (1901–1903)

The Supreme Court decided that constitutional rights did not extend to territorial possessions, thus the Constitution did not follow the flag. Congress had the right to administer each island possession without constitutional restraint. Inhabitants of those possessions did not have the same rights as American citizens.

Theodore Roosevelt and Progressive Reforms, 1902–1907

As a Republican progressive reformer committed to honest and efficient government designed to serve all social classes in America, Theodore Roosevelt restored the presidency to the high eminence it had held through the Civil War era, and redressed the balance of power with old guard leaders in Congress.

Politics of the Period, 1902–1907

President Roosevelt did much to create a bipartisan coalition of liberal reformers whose objective was to restrain corporate monopoly and promote economic competition at home and abroad. Roosevelt won the support of enlightened business leaders, the middle class, consumers, and urban and rural workers with his promise of a "square deal" for all.

Roosevelt's Anti-Trust Policy, 1902

The president pledged strict enforcement of the Sherman Anti-Trust Act (1890) to break up illegal monopolies and regulate large corporations for the public good through honest federal government administration.

Progressive Reform in the States

Taking their cue from Washington, many states enacted laws creating honest and efficient political and economic regulatory standards. Political reforms included enacting laws establishing primary elections (Mississippi, Wisconsin), initiative and referendum (South Dakota, Oregon), and the rooting out of political bosses on the state and municipal levels (especially in New York, Ohio, Michigan, and California).

DIDYOU**KNOW?**

Under the leadership of Progressives like Governor Robert La Follette, Wisconsin became one of the leading places of Progressive reform. Initiatives such as the formation of the first significant U.S. workers' compensation program, creation of a state income tax, limitations on working hours for women and children, and regulations on factory conditions helped earn the state the nickname of "the laboratory of democracy."

Commission Form of Government, 1903

After a hurricane and tidal wave destroyed much of Galveston, Texas, progressive businessmen and Texas state legislators removed the ineffective and corrupt mayor and city council and established a city government of five elected commissioners who were experts in their fields to rebuild Galveston. Numerous other cities adopted the commission form of government to replace the mayor/council format.

State Leaders

Significant state reformers in the period were Robert LaFollette of Wisconsin, Albert Cummins of Iowa, Charles Evans Hughes of New York, James M. Cox of Ohio, Hiram Johnson of California, William S. Wren of Oregon, Albert Beveridge of Indiana, and Woodrow Wilson of New Jersey.

City Reformers

Urban leaders included John Purroy Mitchell of New York City, Tom L. Johnson and Newton Baker of Cleveland, Hazen Pingree of Detroit, Sam Jones of Toledo, and Joseph Folk of St. Louis.

Election of 1904

Having assured Republican Party leaders that he wished to reform corporate monopolies and railroads, but not interfere with monetary policy or tariffs, Roosevelt was nominated for president along with Charles Fairbanks (Indiana) for vice president. The Democratic Party nominated New York judge Alton B. Parker for president and Henry G. Davis (West Virginia) for vice president on a platform that endorsed Roosevelt's "trust-busting," which called for even greater power for such regulatory agencies as the Interstate Commerce Commission, and accepted the conservative gold standard as the basis for monetary policy. Roosevelt easily defeated Parker by about two million votes, and the Republicans retained control of both houses of Congress.

Hepburn Act, 1906

Membership of the Interstate Commerce Commission was increased from five to seven. The I.C.C. could set its own fair freight rates, had its regulatory power extended over pipelines, bridges, and express companies, and was empowered to require a uniform system of accounting by regulated transportation companies. This act and the Elkins Act (1903—reiterated illegality of railroad rebates) gave teeth to the original interstate Commerce Act of 1887.

Pure Food and Drug Act (1906)

Prohibited the manufacture, sale and transportation of adulterated or fraudulently labeled foods and drugs in accordance with consumer demands to which Theodore Roosevelt was especially sensitive.

Meat Inspection Act (1906)

Provided for federal and sanitary regulations and inspections in meat packing facilities. Wartime scandals in 1898 relating to spoiled canned meats were a powerful force for reform.

Immunity of Witness Act (1906)

Corporate officials could no longer make a plea of immunity to avoid testifying in cases dealing with their corporation's illegal activities.

Conservation Laws

From 1902 to 1908 a series of laws and executive actions were enacted to create federal irrigation projects, national parks and forests, develop water power (Internal Waterways Commission), and establish the National Conservation Commission to oversee the nation's resources.

The Economy, 1902–1907

Anti-trust policy and government regulation of the economy gave way to a more lenient enforcement of federal laws after the panic of 1907. Recognition of the rights of labor unions was enhanced.

Anti-Trust Policy (1902)

In order to restore free competition, President Roosevelt ordered the Justice Department to prosecute corporations pursuing monopolistic practices. Attorney General P.C. Knox first brought suit against the Northern Securities Company, a railroad holding corporation put together by J. P. Morgan; then he moved against Rockefeller's Standard Oil Company. By the time he left office in 1909, Roosevelt brought indictments against 25 monopolies.

Department of Commerce and Labor (1903)

A new Cabinet position was created to address the concerns of business and labor. Within the department, the Bureau of Corporations was empowered to investigate and report on the illegal activities of corporations.

Coal Strike (1902)

Roosevelt interceded with government mediation to bring about negotiations between the United Mine Workers union and the anthracite mine owners after a bitter strike over wages, safety conditions and union recognition. This was the first time that the government intervened in a labor dispute without automatically siding with management.

Panic of 1907

A brief economic recession and panic occurred in 1907 as a result, in part, of questionable bank speculations, a lack of flexible monetary and credit policies, and a conservative gold standard. This event called attention to the need for banking reform which would lead to the Federal Reserve System in 1913. Although Roosevelt temporarily eased the pressure on anti-trust activity, he made it clear that reform of the economic system to promote free-enterprise capitalism would continue.

St. Louis World's Fair (1904)

The World's Fair of 1904 celebrated the centennial of the Louisiana Purchase, and brought the participation of Asian nations to promote foreign trade.

Social and Cultural Developments, 1902–1907

Debate and discussion over the expanding role of the federal government commanded the attention of the nation.

Progressive Reforms

There was not one unified progressive movement, but a series of reform causes designed to address specific social, economic, and political problems. Middle-class men and women were especially active in attempting to correct the excessive powers of giant corporations, and the radical extremes of Marxist revolutionaries and radicals among intellectuals and labor activists. However, mainstream of business and labor leaders were moderate in their desire to preserve economic opportunities and the free enterprise system.

Varieties of Reform

Progressive reform goals included not only honest government, economic regulation, environmental conservation, labor recognition, and new political structures. Reformers also called for gender equality for men and women in the work force (Oregon Ten Hour Law), an end to racial segregation (National Association for the Advancement of Colored People), child labor laws, prison reform, regulation of the stock market, direct election of senators, and a more efficient foreign service among other reform activities.

A Chicago stockyard around the time of Upton Sinclair's muckraking book *The Jungle* (1906), which exposed in vivid detail the sordid conditions of the meatpacking industry. Photo courtesy of Dover Publications, Inc.

Muckrakers

Muckrakers (a term coined by Roosevelt) were investigative journalists and authors who were often the publicity agents for reforms. Popular magazines included *McClure's, Collier's, Cosmopolitan*, and *Everybody's*. Famous articles that led to reforms included "The Shame of the Cities" by Lincoln Steffens, "History of Standard Oil Company" by Ida Tarbell, "The Treason of the Senate" by David Phillips, and "Frenzied Finance" by Thomas Lawson.

Literature

Works of literature with a social message included *Following the Color Line* by Ray Stannard Baker, *The Bitter Cry of the Children* by John Spargo, *Poverty* by Robert Hunter, *The Story of Life Insurance* by Burton Hendrick, *The Financier* by Theodore Dreiser, *The Jungle* by Upton Sinclair, *The Boss* by Henry Lewis, *Call of the Wild*, *The Iron Heel* and *The War of the Classes* by Jack London, *A Certain Rich Man* by William Allen White, and *The Promise of American Life* by Herbert Croly.

Inventions

The Wright brothers made the first piloted flight of a heavier-than-air machine at Kitty Hawk, North Carolina, in 1903. News of their feat traveled slowly and was widely doubted.

Foreign Relations, 1902–1907

Theodore Roosevelt's "Big Stick" diplomacy and economic foreign policy were characteristics of the administration.

Panama Canal

Roosevelt used executive power to engineer the separation of Panama from Colombia, and the recognition of Panama as an independent country. The Hay-Bunau-Varilla Treaty of 1903 granted the United States control of the canal zone in Panama for $10 million and an annual fee of $250,000 beginning nine years after ratification of the treaty by both parties. Construction of the canal began in 1904 and was completed in 1914.

Roosevelt Corollary to the Monroe Doctrine

The U.S. reserved the right to intervene in the internal affairs of Latin American nations to keep European powers from using military force to collect debts in the Western Hemisphere. The U.S. eventually intervened in the affairs of Venezuela, Haiti, the Dominican Republic, Nicaragua, and Cuba by 1905 as an international policeman brandishing the "big stick" against Europeans and Latin Americans.

Rio de Janeiro Conference (1906)

Secretary of State Elihu Root attempted to de-emphasize U.S. military and political intervention in order to promote political goodwill, economic development, trade and finances in Latin America. President Roosevelt was actually moving away from "big stick" diplomacy and toward "dollar diplomacy" before he left office. The United States also promoted the Pan American Railway project at this meeting of the International Bureau of American Republics.

China

In pursuit of the Open Door policy of equal opportunity of trade and the guaranteed independence of China, the United States continued to promote its trade interests in Asia. Segregation and restrictions of Chinese immigrants in California and other states led Chinese national leaders to call for a boycott in 1905 of U.S. goods and services in both China and the United States. The boycott ended in 1906 without significant changes in state laws.

Russo-Japanese War (1904–1905)

With American encouragement and financial loans, Japan pursued and won a war against tsarist Russia. Roosevelt negotiated the Treaty of Portsmouth, New Hampshire, which ended the war, and for which the President ironically received the Nobel Peace Prize in 1906. Japan, however, was disappointed at not receiving more territory and financial compensation from Russia and blamed the United States.

Taft-Katsura Memo, 1905

The United States and Japan pledged to maintain the Open Door principles in China. Japan recognized American control over the Philippines and the United States granted a Japanese protectorate over Korea.

Gentleman's Agreement with Japan, 1907

After numerous incidents of racial discrimination against Japanese in California, Japan agreed to restrict the emigration of unskilled Japanese workers to the U.S.

activity and borrowing. Checks on member banks were cleared through the Federal Reserve System.

The Federal Reserve System serviced the financial needs of the federal government. The system was supervised and policy was set by a national Federal Reserve Board composed of the secretary of the Treasury, the comptroller of the currency, and five other members appointed by the president of the United States.

The Clayton Antitrust Act of 1914

This law supplemented and interpreted the Sherman Antitrust Act of 1890. Under its provisions, stock ownership by a corporation in a competing corporation was prohibited. Interlocking directorates of competing corporations were prohibited; that is, the same persons could not manage competing corporations. Price discrimination (charging less in some regions than in others to undercut the competition) and exclusive contracts which reduced competition were prohibited. Officers of corporations could be held personally responsible for violations of antitrust laws. Lastly, labor unions and agricultural organizations were not to be considered "combinations or conspiracies in restraint of trade" as defined by the Sherman Antitrust Act.

The Federal Trade Commission Act of 1914

The law prohibited all unfair trade practices without defining them, and created a commission of Eve members appointed by the president. The commission was empowered to issue cease and desist orders to corporations to stop actions considered to be in restraint of trade, and to bring suit in the courts if the orders were not obeyed. Firms could also contest the orders in court. Under previous antitrust legislation, the government could act against corporations only by bringing suit.

Evaluation

The Underwood-Simmons Tariff, the Federal Reserve Act, and the Clayton Act were clearly in accord with the principles of the New Freedom, but the Federal Trade Commission reflected a move toward the kind of government regulation advocated by Roosevelt in his New Nationalism. Nonetheless, in 1914 and 1915 Wilson continued to oppose federal government action in such matters as loans to farmers, child labor regulation, and woman suffrage.

The Triumph of New Nationalism

Political Background

The Progressive Party dissolved rapidly after the election of 1912. The Republicans made major gains in Congress and in the state governments in the 1914 elections, and their victory in 1916 seemed probable. Early in 1916 Wilson and the Democrats abandoned most of their limited government and states' rights positions in favor of a legislative program of broad economic and social reforms designed to win the support of the former Progressives for the Democratic Party in the election of 1916. The urgency of their concern was increased by the fact that Theodore Roosevelt intended to seek the Republican nomination in 1916.

TEST TIP

As tempting as it may be to talk about the test with your friends, don't do it! Posting information on a social media website or blog about a certain AP Exam test item that gave you trouble may seem harmless, but doing so will result in the cancelation of your score if it's found by the AP Program.

The Brandeis Appointment

Wilson's first action marking the adoption of the new program was the appointment on January 28, 1916, of Louis D. Brandeis, considered by many to be the principal advocate of social justice in the nation, as an associate justice of the Supreme Court.

The Federal Farm Loan Act of 1916

The law divided the country into twelve regions and established a Federal Land Bank in each region. Funded primarily with federal money, the banks made farm mortgage loans at reasonable interest rates. Wilson had threatened to veto similar legislation in 1914.

The Child Labor Act of 1916

This law, earlier opposed by Wilson, forbade shipment in interstate commerce of products whose production had involved the labor of children under fourteen or sixteen, depending on the products. The legislation was especially significant because it was the first time that Congress regulated labor within a state using the interstate commerce power. The law was declared unconstitutional by the Supreme Court in 1918 on the grounds that it interfered with the powers of the states.

The Adamson Act of 1916

This law mandated an eight-hour day for workers on interstate railroads with time and a half for overtime and a maximum of sixteen hours in a shift. Its passage was a major victory for railroad unions, and averted a railroad strike in September 1916.

The Kerr-McGillicuddy Act of 1916

This law initiated a program of workmen's compensation for federal employees.

The Election of 1916

The Democrats

The minority party nationally in terms of voter registration, the Democrats nominated Wilson and adopted his platform calling for continued progressive reforms and neutrality in the European war. "He kept us out of war" became the principal campaign slogan of Democratic politicians.

The Republicans

The convention bypassed Theodore Roosevelt, who had decided not to run as a Progressive and had sought the Republican nomination. On the first ballot it chose Charles Evans Hughes, an associate justice of the Supreme Court and formerly a progressive Republican governor of New York. Hughes, an ineffective campaigner, avoided the neutrality issue because of divisions among the Republicans, and found it difficult to attack the progressive reforms of the Democrats. He emphasized what he considered the inefficiency of the Democrats, and failed to find a popular issue.

Opening game 1916. Bx 112

President Wilson throws out the first pitch on Opening Day, 1916. U.S. Library of Congress.

The Election

Wilson won the election with 277 electoral votes and 9,129,000 popular votes, almost three million more than he received in 1912. Hughes received 254 electoral votes and 8,538,221 popular votes. The Democrats controlled Congress by a narrow margin. While Wilson's victory seemed close, the fact that he had increased his popular vote by almost fifty percent over four years previous was remarkable. It appears that most of his additional votes came from people who had voted for the Progressive or Socialist tickets in 1912.

Social Issues in the First Wilson Administration

Blacks

In 1913 Treasury Secretary William G. McAdoo and Postmaster General Albert S. Burleson segregated workers in some parts of their departments with no objection from Wilson. Many Northern blacks and whites protested, especially black leader W. E. B. DuBois, who had supported Wilson in 1912. William Monroe Trotter, militant editor of the Boston Guardian, led a protest delegation to Washington and clashed verbally with the president. No further segregation in government agencies was initiated, but Wilson had gained a reputation for being inimical to civil rights.

Women

The movement for woman suffrage, led by the National American Woman Suffrage Association, was increasing in momentum at the time Wilson became president, and several states had granted the vote to women. Wilson opposed a federal woman suffrage amendment,

DIDYOU**KNOW?**

The Wyoming territory became the first state to allow women to vote when it joined the Union in 1890. Over the next decade, Utah, Colorado, and Idaho also joined in allowing women's suffrage.

maintaining that the franchise should be controlled by the states. Later he changed his view and supported the 19th Amendment.

Immigration

Wilson opposed immigration restrictions which were proposed by labor unions and some reformers. He vetoed a literacy test for immigrants in 1915, but in 1917 Congress overrode a similar veto.

Wilson's Foreign Policy and the Road to War

Wilson's Basic Premise: New Freedom Policy

Wilson promised a more moral foreign policy than that of his predecessors, denouncing imperialism and dollar diplomacy, and advocating the advancement of democratic capitalist governments throughout the world.

Conciliation Treaties

Secretary Bryan negotiated treaties with 29 nations under which they agreed to submit disputes to international commissions for conciliation, not arbitration. They also included provisions for a cooling-off period, usually one year, before the nations would resort to war. While the treaties probably had no practical effect, they illustrated the idealism of the administration.

Dollar Diplomacy

Wilson signaled his repudiation of Taft's dollar diplomacy by withdrawing American involvement from the six-power loan consortium of China.

Japan

In 1913 Wilson failed to prevent passage of a California law prohibiting land ownership by Japanese aliens. The Japanese government and people were furious, and war seemed possible. Relations were smoothed over, but the issue was unresolved. In 1915 American diplomatic pressure made Japan back off from its 21 demands on China, but in 1917 the Lansing-Ishii Agreement was signed wherein Japan recognized the Open Door in China but the United States recognized Japan's special interest in that nation.

The Caribbean

Like his predecessors, Wilson sought to protect the Panama Canal, which opened in 1914, by maintaining stability in the area. He also wanted to encourage diplomacy and economic growth in the underdeveloped nations of the region. In applying his policy, he became as interventionist as Roosevelt and Taft.

In 1912 American marines had landed in Nicaragua to maintain order, and an American financial expert had taken control of the customs. The Wilson administration kept the marines in Nicaragua, and negotiated the Bryan-Chamorro Treaty of 1914 which gave the United States an option to build a canal through the country. In effect, Nicaragua became an American protectorate, although treaty provisions authorizing such action were not ratified by the Senate.

Claiming that political anarchy existed in Haiti, Wilson sent marines in 1915 and imposed a treaty making the country a protectorate, with American control of its finances and constabulary. The marines remained until 1934.

In 1916 Wilson sent marines to the Dominican Republic to stop a civil war, and established a military government under an American naval commander.

Wilson feared in 1915 that Germany might annex Denmark and its Caribbean possession, the Danish West Indies or Virgin Islands. After extended negotiations, the United States purchased the islands from Denmark by treaty on August 4, 1916 for $25 million, and took possession of them on March 31, 1917.

In 1913 Wilson refused to recognize the government of Mexican military dictator Victoriano Huerta, and offered unsuccessfully to mediate between Huerta and his Constitutionalist opponent, Venustiano Carranza. When the Huerta government arrested several American seamen in Tampico in April 1914, American forces occupied the port of Veracruz, an action condemned by both Mexican political factions. In July 1914 Huerta abdicated his power to Carranza, who was soon opposed by his former general Francisco "Pancho" Villa. Seeking American intervention as a means of undermining Carranza, Villa shot sixteen Americans on a train in northern Mexico in January 1916, and burned the border town of Columbus, New Mexico, in March 1916, killing 19 people. Carranza reluctantly consented to Wilson's request that the United States be allowed to pursue and capture Villa in Mexico, but did not expect the force of about six thousand Army troops under the command of General John J. Pershing which crossed the Rio Grande on March 18. The force advanced over three hundred miles into Mexico, failed to capture Villa, and became, in effect, an army of occupation. The Carranza government demanded an American withdrawal, and several clashes with Mexican troops occurred. War threatened, but in January 1917 Wilson removed the American forces.

Pan American Mediation, 1914

John Barrett, head of the Pan American Union (formerly Blaine's International Bureau of American Republics) called for multilateral mediation to bring about a solution to Mexico's internal problems, and extract the United States from its military presence in Mexico. Although Wilson initially refused, Argentina, Brazil, and Chile did mediate among the Mexican factions and Wilson withdrew American troops. Barrett hoped to replace the unilateral Monroe Doctrine with a multilateral Pan American policy to promote collective responses and mediation to difficult hemispheric problems. Wilson, however, refused to share power with Latin America.

The Road to War in Europe

American Neutrality

When World War I broke out in Europe, Wilson issued a proclamation of American neutrality on August 4, 1914. Despite that action, the United States drifted toward closer ties with the Allies, especially Britain and France. While many Americans were sympathetic to the Central Powers, the majority, including Wilson, hoped for an

Allied victory. Although British naval power effectively prevented American trade with the Central Powers and European neutrals, often in violation of international law, the United States limited itself to formal diplomatic protests. The value of American trade with the Central Powers fell from $169 million in 1914 to almost nothing in 1916, but trade with the Allies rose from $825 million to $3.2 billion during the same period. In addition, the British and French had borrowed about $3.25 billion from American sources by 1917. The United States had become a major supplier of Allied munitions, food, and raw materials.

The Submarine Crisis of 1915

The Germans began the use of submarines in 1915, announced a submarine blockade of the Allies on February 4, and began to attack unarmed British passenger ships in the Atlantic. Wilson insisted to the Germans that Americans had a right as neutrals to travel safely on such ships, and that international law required a war ship to arrange for the safe removal of passengers before attacking such a ship. The sinking of the British liner Lusitania off the coast of Ireland on May 7, 1915, with the loss of 1,198 lives, including 128 Americans, brought strong protests from Wilson. Secretary of State Bryan, who believed Americans should stay off belligerent ships, resigned rather than insist on questionable neutral rights, and was replaced by Robert Lansing. Following the sinking of another liner, the Arabic, on August 19, the Germans gave the "Arabic pledge" to stop attacks on unarmed passenger vessels.

DIDYOU**KNOW?**

Although the British sailed the *Lusitania* as a passenger vessel, the ship was carrying nearly 175 tons of war munitions in its cargo hold. German leaders, who had previously warned that the ship would be sunk, felt that their attack on the *Lusitania* was justified as a measure of war.

The Gore-McLemore Resolution

During the latter part of 1915 the British began to arm their merchant ships. Many Americans thought it in the interest of United States neutrality that Americans not travel on the vessels of belligerents. Early in 1916 the Gore-McLemore Resolution to prohibit American travel on armed ships or on ships carrying munitions was introduced in Congress, but it was defeated in both houses after intensive politicking by Wilson.

The Sussex Pledge

When the unarmed French channel steamer Sussex was torpedoed but not sunk on March 24, 1916, with seven Americans injured, Wilson threatened to sever relations unless Germany ceased all surprise submarine attacks on all shipping, whether belligerent or neutral, armed or unarmed. Germany acceded with the "Sussex pledge" at the beginning of May, but threatened to resume submarine warfare if the British did not stop their violations of international law.

The House-Grey Memorandum

Early in 1915 Wilson sent his friend and adviser, Colonel Edward M. House, on an unsuccessful visit to the capitals of the belligerent nations on both sides to offer American mediation in the war. Late in the year House returned to London to propose that Wilson call a peace conference, and, if Germany refused to attend or was uncooperative at the conference, the United States would probably enter the war on the Allied side. An agreement to that effect, called the House-Grey Memorandum, was signed by the British foreign secretary, Sir Edward Grey, on February 22, 1916.

Preparedness

In November 1915 Wilson proposed a major increase in the Army and the abolition of the National Guard as a preparedness measure. Americans divided on the issue, with organizations like the National Security League proposing stronger military forces, and others like the League to Enforce Peace opposing. After opposition by Southern and Western antipreparedness Democrats, Congress passed a modified National Defense Act in June 1916 which increased the Army from about 90,000 to 220,000, and enlarged the National Guard under federal control. In August over $500 million was appropriated for naval construction. The additional costs were met by increased taxes on the wealthy.

The Election of 1916

Wilson took the leadership on the peace issue, charging that the Republicans were the war party and that the election of Charles Evans Hughes would probably result in war with Germany and Mexico. His position was popular with many Democrats and progressives, and the slogan "He kept us out of war" became the principal theme of Democratic campaign materials, presumably contributing to his election victory.

Wilson's Final Peace Efforts, 1916–1917

On December 12, 1916, the Germans, confident of their strong position, proposed a peace conference, a step which Wilson previously had advocated. When Wilson asked both sides to state their expectations, the British seemed agreeable to reasonable negotiations, but the Germans were evasive and stated that they did not want Wilson at the conference. In an address to Congress on January 22, 1917, Wilson made his last offer to serve as a neutral mediator. He proposed a "peace without victory," based not on a "balance of power" but on a "community of power," alluding to his proposal of May 1916 for an "association of nations."

Unlimited Submarine Warfare

Germany announced on January 31, 1917, that it would sink all ships, belligerent or neutral, without warning in a large war zone off the coasts of the Allied nations in the eastern Atlantic and the Mediterranean. The Germans realized that the United States might declare war, but they believed that, after cutting the flow of supplies to the Allies, they could win the war before the Americans could send any sizable force to Europe. Wilson broke diplomatic relations with Germany on February 3. During February and March several American merchant ships were sunk by submarines.

TEST TIP

Remember that Parts B and C of the free-response section of the AP U.S. History Exam allow you to choose which questions you will answer. Take a few moments to carefully read and consider the two questions in each group. Respond to whichever question in each group you can answer most completely; each question is worth the same possible number of points toward your score.

The Zimmermann Telegram

The British intercepted a secret message from the German foreign secretary, Arthur Zimmermann, to the German minister in Mexico, and turned it over to the United States on February 24, 1917. The Germans proposed that, in the event of a war between the United States and Germany, Mexico attack the United States. After the war, the "lost territories" of Texas, New Mexico, and Arizona would be returned to Mexico. In addition, Japan would be invited to join the alliance against the United States. When the telegram was released to the press on March 1, many Americans became convinced that war with Germany was necessary.

The Declaration of War

Wilson, on March 2, 1917, called Congress to a special session beginning April 2. When Congress convened, he requested a declaration of war against Germany. The declaration was passed by the Senate on April 4 by a vote of 82 to 6, by the House on April 6 by a vote of 373 to 50, and signed by Wilson on April 6.

Wilson's Reasons

Wilson's decision to ask for a declaration of war seems to have been based primarily on four considerations. He believed that the Zimmermann Telegram showed that the Germans were not trustworthy and would eventually go to war against the United States. He also felt that armed neutrality could not adequately protect American shipping. The democratic government established in Russia after the revolution in March 1917 also provided more acceptable as an ally than the Tsarist government. Finally, he was convinced that the United States could hasten the end of the war and insure for itself a major role in designing a lasting peace.

World War I: The Military Campaign

Raising an Army

Despite the enlistment of many volunteers, it was apparent that a draft would be necessary. The Selective Service Act was passed on May 18, 1917, after bitter opposition in the House led by the speaker, "Champ" Clark. Only a compromise outlawing the sale of liquor in or near military camps secured passage. Originally including all males 21 to 30, the limits were later extended to 17 and 46. The first drawing of 500,000 names was made on July 20, 1917. By the end of the war 24,231,021 men had been registered and 2,810,296 had been inducted. In addition, about two million men and women volunteered.

Women and Minorities in the Military

Some women served as clerks in the Navy or in the Signal Corps of the Army. Originally nurses were part of the Red Cross, but eventually some were taken into the Army. About 400,000 black men were drafted or enlisted, despite the objections of Southern political leaders. They were kept in segregated units, usually with white officers, which were used as labor battalions or for other support activities. Some black units did see combat, and a few blacks became officers, but did not command white troops.

The War at Sea

In 1917 German submarines sank 6.5 million tons of Allied and American shipping, while only 2.7 million tons were built. German hopes for victory were based on the destruction of Allied supply lines. The American Navy furnished destroyers to fight the submarines, and, after overcoming great resistance from the British navy, finally began the use of the convoy system in July 1917. Shipping losses fell from almost 900,000 tons in April 1917 to about 400,000 tons in December 1917, and remained below 200,000 tons per month after April 1918. The American Navy transported over 900,000 American soldiers to France, while British transports carried over 1 million. Only two of the well-guarded troop transports were sunk. The Navy had over 2,000 ships and over half a million men by the end of the war.

The American Expeditionary Force

The soldiers and marines sent to France under the command of Major General John J. Pershing were called the American Expeditionary Force, or the AEF. From a small initial force which arrived in France in June 1917, the AEF increased to over two million by November 1918. Pershing resisted efforts by European commanders to amalgamate the Americans with the French and British armies, insisting that he maintain a separate command. American casualties included 112,432 dead, about half of whom died of disease, and 230,024 wounded.

Major Military Engagements

The American force of about 14,500 which had arrived in France by September 1917 was assigned a quiet section of the line near Verdun. As numbers increased, the American role became more significant. When the Germans mounted a major drive toward Paris in the spring of 1918, the Americans experienced their first important engagements. In June they prevented the Germans from crossing the Marne at Chateau-Thierry, and cleared the area of Belleau Woods. In July, eight American divisions aided French troops in attacking the German line between Reims and Soissons. The American First Army with over half a million men under Pershing's immediate command was assembled in August 1918, and began a major offensive at St. Mihiel on the southern part of the front on September 12. Following the successful operation, Pershing began a drive against the German defenses between Verdun and Sedan, an action called the Meuse-Argonne offensive, and reached Sedan on November 7. During the same period the English in the north and the French along the central front also broke through the German lines. The fighting ended with the armistice on November 11, 1918.

Mobilizing the Home Front

Industry

The Council of National Defense, comprised of six cabinet members and a seven-member advisory commission of business and labor leaders, was established in 1916 before American entry into the war to coordinate industrial mobilization, but it had little authority. In July 1917 the council created the War Industries Board to control raw materials, production, prices, and labor relations. The military forces refused to cooperate with the civilian agency in purchasing their supplies, and the domestic war effort seemed on the point of collapse in December 1917 when a Congressional investigation began. In 1918 Wilson took stronger action under his emergency war powers which were reinforced by the Overman Act of May 1918. In March 1918 Wilson appointed Wall Street broker Bernard M. Baruch to head the WIB, assisted by an advisory committee of 100 businessmen. The WIB allocated raw materials, standardized manufactured products, instituted strict production and purchasing controls, and paid high prices to businesses for their products. Even so, American industry was just beginning to produce heavy armaments when the war ended. Most heavy equipment and munitions used by the American troops in France were produced in Britain or France.

> **DID**YOU**KNOW?**
>
> Because so many white men were needed to fight in World War I, factory owners facing labor shortages went South to recruit African-American workers. The massive movement of African Americans north to work in factories began what is now known as the Great Migration.

Food

The United States had to supply not only its own food needs but those of Britain, France, and some of the other Allies as well. The problem was compounded by bad weather in 1916 and 1917 which had an adverse effect on agriculture. The Lever Act of 1917 gave the president broad control over the production, price, and distribution of food and fuel. Herbert Hoover was appointed by Wilson to head a newly-created Food Administration. Hoover fixed high prices to encourage the production of wheat, pork, and other products, and encouraged the conservation of food through such voluntary programs as "Wheatless Mondays" and "Meatless Tuesdays." Despite the bad harvests in 1916 and 1917, food exports by 1919 were almost triple those of the pre-war years, and real farm income was up almost 30 percent.

Fuel

The Fuel Administration under Harry A. Garfield was established in August 1917. It was concerned primarily with coal production and conservation because coal was the predominant fuel of the time and was in short supply during the severe winter of 1917–1918. "Fuelless Mondays" in nonessential industries to conserve coal and "Gasless Sundays" for automobile owners to save gasoline were instituted. Coal production increased about 35 percent from 1914 to 1918.

Railroads

The American railroad system, which provided most of the inter-city transportation in the country, seemed near collapse in December 1917 because of the wartime demands and heavy snows which slowed service. Wilson created the United States Railroad Administration under William G. McAdoo, the secretary of the Treasury, to take over and operate all the railroads in the nation as one system. The government paid the owners rent for the use of their lines, spent over $500 million on improved tracks and equipment, and achieved its objective of an efficient railroad system.

Maritime Shipping

The United States Shipping Board was authorized by Congress in September 1916, and in April 1917 it created a subsidiary, the Emergency Fleet Corporation, to buy, build, lease, and operate merchant ships for the war effort. Edward N. Hurley became the director in July 1917, and the corporation constructed several large shipyards which were just beginning to produce vessels when the war ended. By seizing German and Dutch ships, and by the purchase and requisition of private vessels, the board had accumulated a large fleet by September 1918.

Labor

To prevent strikes and work stoppages in war industries, the War Labor Board was created in April 1918 under the joint chairmanship of former president William Howard Taft and attorney Frank P. Walsh with members from both industry and labor. In hearing labor disputes the WLB in effect prohibited strikes, but it also encouraged higher wages, the eight-hour day, and unionization. Union membership doubled during the war from about 2.5 million to about 5 million.

War Finance and Taxation

The war is estimated to have cost about $33.5 billion by 1920, excluding such future costs as veterans' benefits and debt service. Of that amount at least $7 billion was loaned to the Allies, with most of the money actually spent in the United States for supplies. The government raised about $10.5 billion in taxes, and borrowed the remaining $23 billion. Taxes were raised substantially in 1917, and again in 1918. The Revenue Act of 1918, which did not take effect until 1919, imposed a personal income tax of six percent on incomes up to $4,000, and twelve percent on incomes above that amount. In addition, a graduated surtax went to a maximum of 65 percent on large incomes, for a total of 77 percent. Corporations paid an excess profits tax of 65 percent, and excise taxes were levied on luxury items. Much public, peer, and employer pressure was exerted on citizens to buy Liberty Bonds which covered a major part of the borrowing. An inflation of about one hundred percent from 1915 to 1920 contributed substantially to the cost of the war.

The Committee on Public Information

The committee, headed by journalist George Creel, was formed by Wilson in April 1917. Creel established a successful system of voluntary censorship of the press, and organized about 150,000 paid and volunteer writers, lecturers, artists, and other professionals in a propaganda campaign to build support for the American cause as an idealistic crusade, and to portray the Germans as barbaric and beastial Huns. The CPI set up volunteer Liberty Leagues in every community, and urged their members, and citizens at large, to spy on their neighbors, especially those with foreign names, and to report any suspicious words or actions to the Justice Department.

War Hysteria

A number of volunteer organizations sprang up around the country to search for draft dodgers, enforce the sale of bonds, and report any opinion or conversation considered suspicious. Perhaps the largest such organization was the American Protective League with about 250,000 members, which claimed the approval of the Justice Department. Such groups publicly humiliated people accused of not buying war bonds and persecuted, beat, and sometimes killed people of German descent. As a result of the activities of the CPI and the vigilante groups, German language instruction and German music were banned in many areas, German measles became "liberty measles," pretzels were prohibited in some cities, and the like. The anti-German and anti-subversive war hysteria in the United States far exceeded similar public moods in Britain and France during the war.

The Espionage and Sedition Acts

The Espionage Act of 1917 provided for fines and imprisonment for persons who made false statements which aided the enemy, incited rebellion in the military, or obstructed recruitment or the draft. Printed matter advocating treason or insurrection could be excluded from the mails. The Sedition Act of May 1918 forbade any criticism of the government, flag, or uniform, even if there were not detrimental consequences, and expanded the mail exclusion. The laws sounded reasonable, but they were applied in ways which trampled on civil liberties. Eugene V. Debs, the perennial Socialist candidate for president, was given a ten-year prison sentence for a speech at his party's convention in which he was critical of American policy in entering the war and warned of the dangers of militarism. Movie producer Robert Goldstein released the movie *The Spirit of '76* about the Revolutionary War. It naturally showed the British fighting the Americans. Goldstein was fined $10,000 and sentenced to ten years in prison because the film depicted the British, who were now fighting on the same side as the United States, in an unfavorable light. The Espionage Act was upheld by the Supreme Court in the case of *Shenk v. United States* in 1919. The opinion, written by Justice Oliver Wendell Holmes Jr., stated that Congress could limit free speech when the words represented a "clear and present danger," and that, in effect, a person cannot cry "fire" in a crowded theater. The Sedition Act was similarly upheld in *Abrams v. United States* a few months later. Ultimately 2,168 persons were prosecuted under the laws, and 1,055 were convicted, of whom only ten were charged with actual sabotage.

TEST TIP

Keep an eye on the clock as you work on your responses. Setting your watch to 12:00 at the beginning of each section can help you quickly see how much time you have used without having to remember your actual start time.

Wartime Social Trends

Women

With approximately 16 percent of the normal labor force in uniform and demand for goods at a peak, large numbers of women, mostly white, were hired by factories and other enterprises in jobs never before open to them. They were often resented and ridiculed by male workers. When the war ended, almost all returned to traditional "women's jobs" or to homemaking. Returning veterans replaced them in the labor market. Women continued to campaign for woman suffrage. In 1917 six states, including the large and influential states of New York, Ohio, Indiana, and Michigan, gave the vote to women. Wilson changed his position in 1918 to advocate woman suffrage as a war measure. In January 1918 the House of Representatives adopted a suffrage amendment to the constitution which was defeated later in the year by Southern forces in the Senate. The way was paved for the victory of the suffragists after the war.

Racial Minorities

The labor shortage opened industrial jobs to Mexican-Americans and to blacks. W. E. B. DuBois, among the most prominent black leaders of the time, supported the war effort in the hope that a war to make the world safe for democracy would bring a better life for blacks in the United States. About half a million rural Southern blacks migrated to cities, mainly in the North and Midwest, to obtain employment in war and other industries, especially in steel and meatpacking. Some white Southerners, fearing the loss of labor when cotton prices were high, tried forceably to prevent their departure. Some white Northerners, fearing job competition and encroachment on white neighborhoods, resented their arrival. In 1917 there were race riots in twenty-six cities North and South, with the worst in East St. Louis, Illinois. Despite the opposition and their concentration in entry-level positions, there is evidence that the blacks who migrated generally improved themselves economically.

Prohibition

Proponents of prohibition stressed the need for military personnel to be sober and the need to conserve grain for food, and depicted the hated Germans as disgusting beer drinkers. In December 1917 a constitutional amendment to prohibit the manufacture and sale of alcoholic beverages in the United States was passed by Congress and submitted to the states for ratification. While alcohol consumption was being attacked, cigarette consumption climbed from 26 billion in 1916 to 48 billion in 1918.

Peacemaking and Domestic Problems, 1918–1920

The Fourteen Points

From the time of the American entry into the war, Wilson had maintained that the war would make the world safe for democracy. He insisted that there should be peace without victory, meaning that the victors would not be vindictive toward the losers, so that a fair and stable international situation in the postwar world would insure lasting peace. In an address to Congress on January 8, 1918, he presented his specific peace plan in the form of the Fourteen Points. The first five points called for open rather than secret peace treaties, freedom of the seas, free trade, arms reduction, and a fair adjustment of colonial claims. The next eight points were concerned with the national aspirations of various European peoples and the adjustment of boundaries, as, for example, in the creation of an independent Poland. The fourteenth point, which he considered the most important and had espoused as early as 1916, called for a "general association of nations" to preserve the peace. The reception of the Fourteen Points was mixed in Europe, as there was a great desire to punish Germany. In the United States, however, many people opposed a peace plan that risked American involvement in another European war.

The Election of 1918

On October 25, 1918, a few days before the congressional elections, Wilson appealed to the voters to elect a Democratic Congress, saying that to do otherwise would be a repudiation of his leadership in European affairs. Republicans, who had loyally supported his war programs, were affronted. The voters, probably influenced more by domestic and local issues than by foreign policy, gave the Republicans a slim margin in both houses in the election. Wilson's statement had undermined his political support at home and his stature in the eyes of world leaders.

The Armistice

The German Chancellor, Prince Max of Baden, on October 3, 1918, asked Wilson to begin peace negotiations based on his concepts of a just peace and the Fourteen Points. Wilson insisted that the Germans must evacuate Belgium and France and form a civilian government. By early November the Allied and American armies were advancing rapidly and Germany was on the verge of collapse. The German Emperor fled to the Netherlands and abdicated. Representatives of the new German republic signed the armistice on November 11, 1918, to be effective at 11:00 a.m. that day, and agreed to withdraw German forces to the Rhine and to surrender military equipment, including 150 submarines.

The Versailles or Paris Peace Conference

Wilson decided that he would lead the American delegation to the peace conference which opened in Paris on January 12, 1919. In doing so he became the first president to leave the country during his term of office. The other members of the delegation were Secretary of State Robert Lansing, General Tasker Bliss, Colonel Edward M. House, and attorney Henry White. Wilson made a serious mistake in not appointing any leading Republicans to the commission and in not consulting the Republican leadership in the Senate about the negotiations. In Paris, Wilson joined Prime Minister David Lloyd George of Great Britain, Premier Georges Clemenceau of France, and Prime Minister Vittorio Orlando of Italy to form the "Big Four" which dominated the conference. In the negotiations, which continued until May 1919, Wilson found it necessary to make many compromises in forging the text of the treaty.

The Soviet Influence

Russia was the only major participant in the war which was not represented at the peace conference. Following the Communist Revolution of 1917, Russia had made a separate peace with Germany in March 1918. Wilson had resisted Allied plans to send major military forces to Russia to oust the Communists and bring Russia back into the war. An American force of about five thousand was sent to Murmansk in the summer of 1918 in association with British and French troops to prevent the Germans from taking military supplies, and was soon active in assisting Russian anti-Bolsheviks. It remained in the area until June 1919. In July 1918 Wilson also sent about ten thousand soldiers to Siberia where they took over the operation of the railroads to assist a Czech army which was escaping from the Germans by crossing Russia. They were also to counterbalance a larger Japanese force in the area, and remained until April 1920. Wilson believed that the spread of communism was the greatest threat to peace and international order. His concern made him reluctant to dispute too much with the other leaders at the Versailles Conference, and more agreeable to compromise, because he believed it imperative that the democracies remain united in the face of the communist threat.

Important Provisions of the Versailles Treaty

In the drafting of the treaty Wilson achieved some of the goals in the Fourteen Points, compromised on others, and failed to secure freedom of the seas, free trade, reduction of armaments, or the return of Russia to the society of free nations. Some major decisions were as follows:

1) The League of Nations was formed, implementing the point which Wilson considered the most important. Article X of the Covenant, or charter, of the League called on all members to protect the "territorial integrity" and "political independence" of all other members.

2) Germany was held responsible for causing the war, and required to agree to pay the Allies for all civilian damage and veterans' costs, which eventually were calculated at $33 billion; the German army and navy were limited to tiny defensive forces; and the west bank of the Rhine was declared a military-free zone forever and occupied by the French for fifteen years. These decisions were clearly contrary to the idea of peace without victory.

3) New nations of Yugoslavia, Austria, Hungary, Czechoslovakia, Poland, Lithuania, Latvia, Estonia, and Finland partially fulfilled the idea of self-determination for all nationalities, but the boundaries drawn at the conference left many people under the control of other nationalities.

4) German colonies were made mandates of the League of Nations, and given in trusteeship to France, Japan, and Britain and its Dominions.

Germany and the Signing of the Treaty

The German delegates were allowed to come to Versailles in May 1919 after the completion of the treaty document. They expected to negotiate on the basis of the draft, but were told to sign it "or else," probably meaning an economic boycott of Germany. They protested, but signed the Versailles Treaty on June 28, 1919.

The Senate and the Treaty

Following a protest by 39 senators in February 1919, Wilson obtained some changes in the League structure to exempt the Monroe Doctrine and domestic matters from League jurisdiction. Then, on July 26, 1919, he presented the treaty with the League within it to the Senate for ratification. Almost all of the 47 Democrats supported Wilson and the treaty, but the 49 Republicans were divided. About a dozen were "irreconcilables" who thought that the United States should not be a member of the League under any circumstances. The remainder included 25 "strong" and 12 "mild" reservationists who would accept the treaty with some changes. The main objection centered on Article X of the League Covenant, where the reservationists wanted it understood that the United States would not go to war to defend a League member without the approval of Congress. The leader of the reservationists was Henry Cabot Lodge of Massachusetts, the chairman of the Foreign Relations Committee. More senators than the two-thirds necessary for ratification favored the treaty either as written or with reservations.

Wilson and the Senate

On September 3, 1919, Wilson set out on a national speaking tour to appeal to the people to support the treaty and the League, and to influence their senators. He collapsed after a speech in Pueblo, Colorado, on September 25, and returned to Washington where he suffered a severe stroke on October 2 which paralyzed his left side. He was seriously ill for several months, and never fully recovered. In a letter to the Senate Democrats on November 18, Wilson urged them to oppose the treaty with the Lodge reservations. In votes the next day, the treaty failed to get a two-thirds majority either with or without the reservations.

> **DID YOU KNOW?**
>
> As a result of Wilson's stroke, his wife Edith handled many of the administrative duties of the White House. Critics argued that she served as a de facto president—and not a very good one—but there is little historical evidence to support this claim.

The Final Vote

Many people, including British and French leaders, urged Wilson to compromise with Lodge on reservations, including the issue of Article X. Wilson, instead, wrote an open letter to Democrats on January 8, 1920, urging them to make the election of a

Democratic president in 1920 a "great and solemn referendum" on the treaty as written. Such partisanship only acerbated the situation. Many historians think that Wilson's ill health impaired his judgment, and that he would have worked out a compromise had he not had the stroke. The Senate took up the treaty again in February 1920, and on March 19 it was again defeated both with and without the reservations. The United States officially ended the war with Germany by a resolution of Congress signed on July 2, 1921, and a separate peace treaty was ratified on July 25. The United States did not join the League.

Consequences of War

The impact of the war was far-reaching in the twentieth century. The United States emerged as the economic and political leader of the world—even if the American people were not prepared to accept the responsibility. The Russian revolution overthrew the tsar and inaugurated a communist dictatorship. Britain, France, Austria, and Turkey went into various states of decline. Germany was devastated at the Versailles Peace Conference. Revenge and bitterness would contribute to the rise of Adolf Hitler and the Nazi movement. The European industrial nations would never recover from the cost of the war. Lingering economic problems would contribute to the Crash of 1929 and the Great Depression of the 1930s. The seeds of World War II had been planted.

Domestic Problems and the End of the Wilson Administration

Demobilization

The AEF was brought home as quickly as possible in early 1919, and members of the armed forces were rapidly discharged. Congress provided for wounded veterans through a system of veteran's hospitals under the Veteran's Bureau, and funded relief, especially food supplies, for war-torn Europe. The wartime agencies for the control of the economy, such as the War Industries Board, were soon disbanded. During 1919 Congress considered various plans to nationalize the railroads or continue their public operation, but then passed the Esch-Cummings or Transportation Act of 1920 which returned them to private ownership and operation. It did extend Interstate Commerce Commission control over their rates and financial affairs, and allowed supervised pooling. The fleet of ships accumulated by the Shipping Board during the war was sold to private owners at attractive prices.

Final Reforms of the Progressive Era

In January 1919 the 18th Amendment to the Constitution prohibiting the manufacture, sale, transportation, or importation of intoxicating liquors was ratified by the states, and it became effective in January 1920. The 19th Amendment providing for woman suffrage, which had been defeated in the Senate in 1918, was approved by Congress in 1919. It was ratified by the states in time for the election of 1920.

The Postwar Economy

Despite fear of unemployment with the return of veterans to the labor force and the end of war purchases, the American economy boomed during 1919 and the first half of 1920. Consumers had money from high wages during the war, and the European demand for American food and manufactured products continued for some months after the war. The demand for goods resulted in a rapid inflation. Prices in 1919 were 77 percent above the prewar level, and in 1920 they were 105 percent above that level.

Strikes

The great increase in prices prompted 2,655 strikes in 1919 involving about four million workers or twenty percent of the labor force. Unions were encouraged by the gains they had made during the war and thought they had the support of public opinion. However, the Communist Revolution in Russia in 1917 soon inspired in many Americans, including government officials, a fear of violence and revolution by workers. While most of the strikes in early 1919 were successful, the tide of opinion gradually shifted against the workers.

Four major strikes received particular attention. In January 1919 all unions in Seattle declared a general strike in support of a strike for higher pay by shipyard workers. The action was widely condemned, the federal government sent marines, and the strike was soon abandoned.

In September 1919 Boston police struck for the right to unionize. Governor Calvin Coolidge called out the National Guard and stated that there was "no right to strike against the public safety by anybody, anywhere, anytime." The police were fired and a new force was recruited.

The American Federation of Labor attempted to organize the steel industry in 1919. When Judge Elbert H. Gary, the head of U.S. Steel, refused to negotiate, the workers struck in September. After much violence and the use of federal and state troops, the strike was broken by January 1920.

The United Mine Workers of America under John L. Lewis struck for shorter hours and higher wages on November 1, 1919. Attorney General A. Mitchell Palmer obtained injunctions and the union called off the strike. An arbitration board later awarded the miners a wage increase.

The Red Scare

Americans feared the spread of the Russian Communist Revolution to the United States, and many interpreted the widespread strikes of 1919 as communist-inspired and the beginning of the revolution. Bombs sent through the mail to prominent government and business leaders in April 1919 seemed to confirm their fears, although the ori-

> **DID**YOU**KNOW?**
>
> The Wobblies often used song to spread their labor messages, once proclaiming: "Sing and fight! Right was the tyrant king who said: 'Beware of a movement that sings'" in a leaflet. Some Wobbly songs include "Hallelujah, I'm a Bum," "The Rebel Girl," and "Solidarity Forever" (www.folkways.si.edu).

gin of the bombs has never been determined. The membership of the two communist parties founded in the United States in 1919 was less than one hundred thousand, but many Americans were sure that many workers, all foreign-born persons, radicals, and members of the International Workers of the World (also known as "Wobblies"), a radical union in the western states, were communists. The anti-German hysteria of the war years was transformed into the anti-communist and anti-foreign hysteria of 1919 and 1920, and continued in various forms through the twenties.

The Palmer Raids

Attorney General A. Mitchell Palmer was one of the targets of the anonymous bombers in the spring of 1919. He was also an aspirant for the Democratic nomination for president in 1920, and he realized that many Americans saw the threat of a communist revolution as a grave danger. In August 1919 he named J. Edgar Hoover to head a new Intelligence Division in the Justice Department to collect information about radicals. In November 1919 Palmer's agents arrested almost seven hundred persons, mostly anarchists, and deported forty-three of them as undesirable aliens. On January 2, 1920, Justice Department agents, local police, and vigilantes in thirty-three cities arrested about four thousand people accused of being communists. It appears that many people caught in the sweep were neither communists nor aliens. Eventually 556 were shown to be communists and aliens, and were deported. Palmer then announced that huge communist riots were planned for major cities on May Day, May 1, 1920. Police and troops were alerted, but the day passed with no radical activity. Palmer was discredited and the Red Scare subsided.

The Race Riots of 1919

During the war about half a million blacks had migrated from the South to industrial cities, mostly in the North and Midwest, to find employment. After the war, white hostility based on competition for lower-paid jobs and black encroachment into neighborhoods led to race riots in twenty-five cities with hundreds killed or wounded and millions of dollars in property damage. Beginning in Longview, Texas, the riots spread, among other places, to Washington, D.C., and Chicago. The Chicago riot in July was the worst, lasting 13 days and leaving 38 dead, 520 wounded, and 1,000 families homeless. Fear of resuming black veterans in the South lead to an increase of lynchings from 34 in 1917 to 60 in 1918 and 70 in 1919. Some of the victims were veterans still in uniform.

(Before taking the quiz noted below, please review the summary timeline for this chapter on the following pages.)

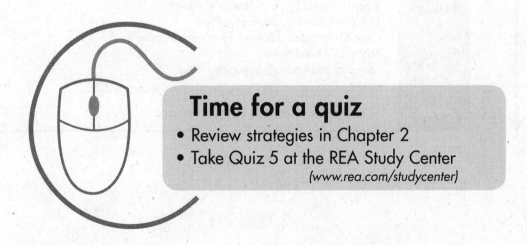

Time for a quiz
- Review strategies in Chapter 2
- Take Quiz 5 at the REA Study Center
  (www.rea.com/studycenter)

Wilson and World War I (1912–1920)

Historical Timeline (1912–1920)

1912	Wilson elected president
1913	Underwood Tariff Federal Reserve Act 16th Amendment (income tax) ratified 17th Amendment (direct senator election) ratified
1914	Clayton Antitrust Act Panama Canal opens World War I begins
1915	Germans sink *Lusitania*
1916	Margaret Sanger organizes New York Birth Control League Gen. Pershing pursues Pancho Villa in Mexico
1917	Germany resumes unrestricted submarine warfare U.S. declares war on Germany War Industries Board established Espionage Act passed Russian Revolution Committee on Public Information established
1918	Wilson proposes Fourteen Points Armistice ends war U.S. troops intervene in Russia
1919	Treaty of Versailles Red Scare and Palmer raids Senate rejects U.S. role in League of Nations 18th Amendment (Prohibition) ratified Over 20 percent of U.S. labor force goes on strike *Schenck v. United States* Race riots and lynchings throughout U.S.
1920	19th Amendment (women's suffrage) ratified

Chapter 13

The Roaring Twenties and Economic Collapse (1920–1929)

The Election of 1920

The Political Climate

It seemed to many political observers in 1920 that the Republicans had an excellent chance of victory. The Wilson administration was blamed by many for the wartime civil liberties abuses, the League of Nations controversy, and the strikes and inflation of the postwar period.

The Republican Convention

The principal contenders for the nomination were General Leonard Wood, who had the support of the followers of the deceased Theodore Roosevelt, and Governor Frank O. Lowden of Illinois, the pick of many of the party bosses. When the convention seemed to deadlock, Henry Cabot Lodge, the convention chairman, and several other leaders arranged for the name of Senator Warren G. Harding of Ohio to be introduced as a dark-horse candidate. Harding was nominated on the tenth ballot, and Governor Calvin Coolidge of Massachusetts was chosen as the vice presidential nominee. The platform opposed the League, and promised low taxes, high tariffs, immigration restriction, and aid to farmers.

DIDYOU**KNOW?**

The results of the 1920 presidential election were the first to be broadcast on the radio as the subject of the nation's first-ever commercial radio programming on Pittsburgh's KDKA.

despite prohibition. He was accused of keeping a mistress, Nan Britton. His economic philosophy was conservative.

The Cabinet and Government Appointments

Harding appointed some outstanding persons to his Cabinet, including Secretary of State Charles Evans Hughes, a former Supreme Court justice and presidential candidate; Secretary of the Treasury Andrew Mellon, a Pittsburgh aluminum and banking magnate and reportedly the richest man in America; and Secretary of Commerce Herbert Hoover, a dynamic multimillionaire mine owner who was famous for wartime relief efforts. Less impressive was his appointment of his cronies Albert B. Fall as Secretary of the Interior and Harry M. Daugherty as Attorney General. Other cronies, some dishonest, were appointed to other government posts.

guilty. After all, all but one of the jurors were church members. The town was firmly in opposition to Scopes, Darrow, and Darwin. Darrow's early strategy was to minimize the difference between evolution and the creation account in Genesis, using the written testimony of evolution experts.

As the trial progressed, however, the focus turned to Bryan. Defense counsel Darrow asked to crossexamine prosecution counsel Bryan, a very unorthodox procedure. Darrow's purpose was to suggest that belief in the historical accuracy and the miracles of the Bible was unreasonable in an age of modern science. Darrow questioned the story of Jonah and the whale, Joshua causing the earth to stand still, and Bishop Ussher's contention that creation occurred in 4004 B.C. Darrow accused Bryan of insulting "every man of science and learning in the world because he does not believe in your fool religion." Bryan shot back that the purpose of the defense attack was "to cast ridicule on anyone who believed in the Bible." The questioning of Bryan by Darrow lasted for two hours on the trial's seventh day. On the next morning the judge ruled the entire examination of Bryan irrelevant to the case and that it would be removed from the trial's records. Darrow then changed Scopes's plea to guilty, thus preventing Bryan from delivering a closing statement, which would amount to a speech opposing evolution. Scopes was found guilty after nine minutes of jury deliberation and fined $100. The defense team appealed the decision and the Tennessee Supreme Court overturned the conviction on a technicality, though it supported the constitutionality of the Butler Act, which remained on the books in Tennessee until 1967.

The Scopes trial was the first legal challenge to the teaching of evolution in public schools. Despite the Butler Act, evolution continued to be taught in biology classes in Tennessee. Scopes abandoned teaching after the trial and studied geology at the University of Chicago. While the Scopes trial was a 1925 Tennessee event, the evolution versus-creation argument still rages across the nation. In 1968 the U.S. Supreme Court ruled in *Epperson v. Arkansas* that evolution can be taught in public schools because it is a science, but creationism cannot be taught, because it constitutes religious teaching. Bryan and Darrow provided the first major confrontation in a debate that continues today.

Tax Reduction

Mellon believed in low taxes and government economy to free the rich from "oppressive" taxes and thus encourage investment. The farm bloc of Midwestern Republicans and Southern Democrats in Congress prevented cuts in the higher tax brackets as great as Mellon recommended. The Revenue Acts of 1921 and 1924 cut the maximum tax rates to 50 percent and then to 40 percent. Taxes in lower brackets were also reduced, but inheritance and corporate income taxes were retained. Despite the cuts, Mellon was able to reduce the federal debt by an average of $500 million a year.

The Fordney-McCumber Tariff

Mellon sought substantial increases in the tariffs, but again there was a compromise with the farm bloc. The Fordney-McCumber Tariff of September 1922 imposed high rates on farm products and protected such infant industries as rayon, china, toys, and chemicals. Most other items received moderate protection, and a few items including farm equipment, were duty-free. The president could raise or lower rates to a limit of 50 percent on recommendation of the Tariff Commission. The average rate was about 33 percent, compared with about 26 percent under the previous tariff.

The Budget

As a result of the Budget and Accounting Act of 1921, the federal government had a unified budget for the first time. The law also provided for a director of the budget to assist in its preparation, and a comptroller general to audit government accounts.

The Harding Scandals

Harding apparently was completely honest, but several of his friends whom he appointed to office became involved in major financial scandals. Most of the information about the scandals did not become public knowledge until after Harding's death.

The "Teapot Dome" Scandal began when Secretary of the Interior Albert B. Fall in 1921 secured the transfer of several naval oil reserves to his jurisdiction. In 1922 he secretly leased reserves at Teapot Dome in Wyoming to Harry F. Sinclair of Monmouth Oil and at Elk Hills in California to Edward Doheny of Pan-American Petroleum. A Senate investigation later revealed that Sinclair had given Fall $305,000 in cash and bonds and a herd of cattle, while Doheny had given him a $100,000 unsecured loan. Sinclair and Doheny were acquitted in 1927 of charges of defrauding the government, but in 1929 Fall was convicted, fined, and imprisoned for bribery.

Another scandal involved Charles R. Forbes, appointed by Harding to head the new Veterans' Bureau. He seemed energetic and efficient in operating the new hospitals and services for veterans. It was later estimated that he had stolen or squandered about $250 million in bureau funds.

Scandal also tainted Attorney General Daugherty who, through his intimate friend Jesse Smith, took bribes from bootleggers, income tax evaders, and others in return for protection from prosecution. When the scandal began to come to light, Smith committed suicide in Daugherty's Washington apartment in May 1923. There was also evidence that Daugherty received money for using his influence in returning the American Metal Company, seized by the government during the war, to its German owners.

> **DIDYOUKNOW?**
>
> Scholars routinely rank Warren G. Harding as one of the nation's very worst presidents, alongside such dismal leaders as James Buchanan—widely considered the president who failed to prevent the Civil War—and Andrew Johnson, the first president to undergo the impeachment process.

Harding's Death

Depressed by the first news of the scandals, Harding left in June 1923 for an extended trip that included a tour of Alaska. On his return to California, he died suddenly in San Francisco on August 2, 1923, apparently of a heart attack. Rumors of foul play or suicide persisted for years.

Coolidge Becomes President

Vice President Calvin Coolidge became president to complete Harding's term. As the scandals of the deceased president's administration came to light, Coolidge was able to avoid responsibility for them. He had a reputation for honesty, although he did not remove Daugherty from the Cabinet until March 1924.

The Election of 1924

The Republicans

Progressive insurgents failed to capture the convention. Calvin Coolidge was nominated on the first ballot with Charles G. Dawes as his running mate. The platform endorsed business development, low taxes, and rigid economy in government. The party stood on its record of economic growth and prosperity since 1922.

The Democrats

The party had an opportunity to draw farmers and labor into a new progressive coalition. An attractive Democratic candidate would have had a good chance against the bland Coolidge and the Harding scandals. Instead, two wings of the party battled to exhaustion at the convention. The Eastern wing, led by Governor Alfred E. Smith of New York, wanted the platform to favor repeal of prohibition and to condemn the Ku Klux Klan. Southern and Western delegates, led by William G. McAdoo and William Jennings Bryan, narrowly defeated both proposals. Smith and McAdoo contested for 103 ballots with neither receiving the two-thirds necessary for nomination. John W. Davis, a conservative Wall Street lawyer, was finally chosen as a dark horse with Charles W. Bryan, brother of William Jennings, as the vice presidential candidate. The platform favored a lower tariff, but otherwise was similar to the Republican document.

The Progressives

Robert M. LaFollette, after failing in a bid for the Republican nomination, formed a new Progressive Party with support from Midwest farm groups, socialists, and the American Federation of Labor. The platform attacked monopolies and called for the nationalization of railroads, the direct election of the president, and other reforms.

The Campaign

Neither Coolidge nor Davis were active or effective campaigners. Republican publicity concentrated on attacking LaFollette as a communist. LaFollette campaigned vigorously, but he lacked money and was disliked by many for his 1917 opposition to entrance into World War I.

The Election

Coolidge received 15,725,016 votes and 382 electoral votes, more than his two opponents combined. Davis received 8,385,586 votes and 136 electoral votes, while LaFollette had 4,822,856 votes and 13 electoral votes from his home state of Wisconsin.

The Coolidge Administration

Calvin Coolidge

Coolidge was a dour and taciturn man. Born in Vermont, his adult life and political career were spent in Massachusetts. "The business of the United States is business," he proclaimed, and "the man who builds a factory builds a temple." His philosophy of life was stated in the remark that "four-fifths of all our troubles in this world would disappear if only we would sit down and keep still." Liberal political commentator Walter Lippmann wrote that "Mr. Coolidge's genius for inactivity is developed to a very high point." He intentionally provided no presidential leadership.

DIDYOU**KNOW?**

Coolidge's personal brevity earned him the nickname "Silent Cal." Nevertheless, over the years he has become known for a certain dry wit. One Coolidge comment: When asked about the burdens of the presidency, he once famously replied, "Oh, I don't know. There are only so many hours in the day, and one can do the best he can in the time he's got. When I was mayor of Northampton I was pretty busy most of the time, and I don't seem to be much busier here" (www.heritage.org).

The McNary-Haugen Bill

In 1921 George Peek and Hugh S. Johnson, farm machinery manufacturers in Illinois, developed a plan to raise prices for basic farm products. The government would buy and resell in the domestic market a commodity such as wheat at the world price plus the tariff. The surplus would be sold abroad at the world price, and the difference made up by an equalization fee on all farmers in proportion to the amount of the commodity they had sold. When farm conditions did not improve, the idea was incorporated in the McNary-Haugen Bill, which passed Congress in 1927 and 1928, but was vetoed both times by Coolidge. The plan was a forerunner of the agricultural programs of the 1930s.

Muscle Shoals

During World War I the government had constructed a dam and two nitrate plants on the Tennessee River at Muscle Shoals, Alabama. In 1925 Senator George W. Norris of Nebraska led the defeat of a plan to lease the property to private business, but his proposal for government operation was vetoed by Coolidge in 1928. The facility was to become the nucleus of the Tennessee Valley Authority in the 1930s.

Veterans' Bonus

Legislation to give veterans of World War I 20-year endowment policies with values based on their length of service was passed over Coolidge's veto in 1924.

The Revenue Act of 1926

Mellon's tax policies were finally implemented by the Revenue Act of 1926, which reduced the basic income tax, cut the surtax to a maximum of 20 percent, abolished the gift tax, and cut the estate tax in half.

The Election of 1928

The Republicans

Coolidge did not seek another term, and the convention quickly nominated Herbert Hoover, the secretary of commerce, for president, and Charles Curtis as his running mate. The platform endorsed the policies of the Harding and Coolidge administrations.

The Democrats

Governor Alfred E. Smith of New York, a Catholic and an anti-prohibitionist, controlled most of the non-Southern delegations. Southerners supported his nomination with the understanding that the platform would not advocate repeal of prohibition. Senator Joseph T. Robinson of Arkansas, a Protestant and a prohibitionist, was the vice presidential candidate. The platform differed little from that of the Republicans, except in advocating lower tariffs.

The Campaign

Hoover asserted that Republican policies would end poverty in the country. Smith was also economically conservative, but he attacked prohibition and bigotry. He was met in the South by a massive campaign headed by Bishop James Cannon Jr. of the Methodist Episcopal Church South, attacking him as a Catholic and a wet.

The Election

Hoover received 21,392,190 votes and 444 electoral votes, carrying all of the North except Massachusetts and Rhode Island, and seven states in the Solid South. Smith had 15,016,443 votes for 87 electoral votes in eight states.

Foreign Policy in the Twenties

The Washington Conference

At the invitation of Secretary of State Charles Evans Hughes, representatives of the United States, Great Britain, France, Japan, Italy, China, the Netherlands, Belgium, and Portugal met in Washington in August 1921 to discuss naval limitations and Asian affairs. Three treaties resulted from the conference.

The Five Power Pact or Treaty, signed in February 1922, committed the United States, Britain, Japan, France, and Italy to end new construction of capital naval vessels, to scrap some ships, and to maintain a ratio of 5:5:3:1.67:1.67 for tonnage of capital or major ships in order of the nations listed. Hughes did not realize that the treaty gave Japan naval supremacy in the Pacific.

The Nine Power Pact or Treaty was signed by all of the participants at the conference. It upheld the Open Door in China by binding the nations to respect the sovereignty, independence, and integrity of China.

The Four Power Pact or Treaty bound the United States, Great Britain, Japan, and France to respect each other's possessions in the Pacific, and to confer in the event of disputes or aggression in the area.

War Debts, Reparations, and International Finance

The United States had lent the Allies about $7 billion during World War I and about $3.25 billion in the postwar period, and insisted on full payment of the debts. Meanwhile, Germany was to pay reparations to the Allies, but by 1923 Germany was bankrupt. The Dawes Plan, proposed by American banker Charles G. Dawes, was accepted in 1924. Under it, American banks made loans of $2.5 billion to Germany by 1930. Germany paid reparations of over $2 billion to the Allies during the same period, and the Allies paid about $2.6 billion to the United States on their war debts. The whole cycle was based on loans from American banks.

The Kellogg-Briand Pact

A group of American citizens campaigned during the 1920s for a treaty which would outlaw war. In 1927 the French foreign minister, Aristide Briand, proposed such a treaty with the United States. Frank B. Kellogg, Coolidge's secretary of state, countered by proposing that other nations be invited to sign. At Paris, in August 1928, almost all major nations signed the treaty, which renounced war as an instrument of national policy. It outlawed only aggression, not self-defense, and had no enforcement provisions.

Latin America

American investment in Latin America almost doubled during the 1920s to $5.4 billion, and relations with most nations in the region improved. Coolidge removed the Marines from Nicaragua in 1925, but a revolution erupted and the Marines were returned. Revolutionary General Augusto Sandino fought against the marines until they were replaced by an American-trained national guard under Anastasio Somoza. The Somoza family ruled Nicaragua until 1979 when they were overthrown by revolutionaries called the Sandinistas.

The Great Depression: The Crash

Hoover Becomes President

Herbert Hoover, an Iowa farm boy and an orphan, graduated from Stanford University with a degree in mining engineering. He became a multimillionaire from mining and other investments around the world. After serving as the director of the

Food Administration under Wilson, be became secretary of commerce under Harding and Coolidge. He believed that an associative economic system with voluntary cooperation of business and government would enable the United States to abolish poverty through continued economic growth.

The Stock Market Boom

Stock prices increased throughout the decade. The boom in prices and volume of sales was especially active after 1925, and was intensive during 1928–29. The Dow Jones Industrial Average finished the year 1924 at 120; for the month of September 1929 it was 381; and for the year 1932 it dropped to 41.

DIDYOU**KNOW?**

Much of the meteoric rise of the stock market during the 1920s was fueled by intense stock speculation. When the stock market crashed, even famed movie star Groucho Marx was wiped out because of these risky investing practices.

Stocks were selling for more than 16 times their earnings in 1929, well above the rule of thumb at the time of ten times their earnings.

The Stock Market Crash

Careful investors, realizing that stocks were overpriced, began to sell to take their profits. During October 1929 prices declined as more stock was sold. On "Black Thursday," October 24, 1929, almost 13 million shares were traded, a large number for that time, and prices fell precipitously. Investment banks tried to boost the market by buying, but on October 29, "Black Tuesday," the market fell about 40 points, with 16.5 million shares traded. A long decline followed until early 1933, and with it, depression.

The Roaring Twenties and Economic Collapse (1920–1929)

Historical Timeline (1920–1929)

Year	Events
1920	Sacco and Vanzetti arrested Harding elected president First commercial radio broadcast
1921	Washington Naval Conference Emergency Quota Act restricts immigration
1923	Teapot Dome scandal Marcus Garvey claims 6 million followers Ku Klux Klan claims 5 million members
1924	National Origins Act sets 2 percent quotas for immigration
1925	*Scopes* Tennessee evolution trial Model T Ford drops to cost of $290 (three months' wages)
1927	Lindbergh's solo flight across the Atlantic Sacco and Vanzetti executed Babe Ruth hits 60 home runs for the Yankees Al Jolson stars in *The Jazz Singer*, the first talking film
1928	Hoover elected president Fifty-two nations sign Kellogg-Briand Pact renouncing war
1929	Stock market crashes in October

The Great Depression and the New Deal (1929–1941)

Reasons for the Depression

A stock market crash does not mean that a depression must follow. A similar crash in October 1987, for example, did not lead to depression. In 1929 a complex interaction of many factors caused the decline of the economy.

Many people had bought stock on a margin of ten percent, meaning that they had borrowed ninety percent of the purchase through a broker's loan, and put up the stock as collateral. Broker's loans totaled $8.5 billion in 1929, compared with $3.5 billion in 1926. When the price of a stock fell more than ten percent, the lender sold the stock for whatever it would bring and thus further depressed prices. The forced sales brought great losses to the banks and businesses which had financed the broker's loans, as well as to the investors.

There were already signs of recession before the market crash in 1929. Because the gathering and processing of statistics was not as advanced then as it is now, some factors were not so obvious to people at the time. The farm economy, which involved almost twenty-five percent of the population, had been depressed throughout the decade. Coal, railroads, and New England textiles had not been prosperous. After 1927 new construction declined and auto sales began to sag. Many workers had been laid off before the crash of 1929.

Many scholars believe that there was a problem of underconsumption, meaning that ordinary workers and farmers, after using their consumer credit, did not have enough money to keep buying the products which were being produced. One estimate says that the income of the top one percent of the population increased at least 75 percent during the decade, while that of the bottom 93 percent increased only 6 percent. The process continued after the depression began. After the stock market crash, people were conservative and saved their money, thus reducing the demand for goods. As demand decreased, workers were laid off or had wage reductions, further reducing their purchasing power and bringing another decrease in demand.

With the decline in the economy, Americans had less money for foreign loans and bought fewer imported products. That meant that foreign governments and individuals were not able to pay their debts in the United States. The whole reparations and war debts structure collapsed. American exports dropped, further hurting the domestic economy. The depression eventually spread throughout the world.

Economic Effects of the Depression

During the early months of the depression most people thought it was just an adjustment in the business cycle which would soon be over. Hoover repeatedly assured the public that prosperity was just around the corner. As time went on, the worst depression in American history set in, reaching its bottom point in early 1932. The gross national product fell from $104.6 billion in 1929 to $56.1 billion in 1933. Unemployment reached about 13 million in 1933, or about 25 percent of the labor force excluding farmers. National income dropped 54 percent from $87.8 billion to $40.2 billion. Labor income fell about 41 percent, while farm income dropped 55 percent from $11.9 billion to $5.3 billion. Industrial production dropped about 51 percent. The banking system suffered as 5,761 banks, over 22 percent of the total, failed by the end of 1932.

The Human Dimension of the Depression

As the depression grew worse, more and more people lost their jobs or had their wages reduced. Many were unable to continue credit payments on homes, automobiles, and other possessions, and lost them. Families doubled up in houses and apartments. Both the marriage rate and the birth rate declined as people put off family formation. Hundreds of thousands became homeless and lived in groups of makeshift shacks

DIDYOUKNOW?

During the Depression, the wandering unemployed men known as hobos developed their own unique subculture. This included a system of simple glyphs representing concepts ranging from helpful directions, to safe places to sleep, to tips on how to get a homeowner to give out food, to warnings about potential dangers (www.worldpath.net).

called Hoovervilles in empty spaces around cities. Others traveled the country by foot and boxcar seeking food and work. State and local government agencies and private charities were overwhelmed in their attempts to care for those in need, although public and private soup kitchens and soup lines were set up throughout the nation. Malnutrition was widespread but few died of starvation, perhaps because malnourished people are susceptible to many fatal diseases.

Hoover's Depression Policies

The Agricultural Marketing Act

Passed in June 1929 before the market crash, the Agricultural Marketing Act, proposed by the president, created the Federal Farm Board with a revolving fund of $500 million to lend the agricultural cooperatives to buy commodities such as wheat and cotton, and hold them for higher prices. Until 1931 it did keep agricultural prices above the world level. Then world prices plummeted, the board's funds ran out, and there was no period of higher prices in which the cooperatives could sell their stored commodities.

The Hawley-Smoot Tariff

The Hawley-Smoot Tariff, passed in June 1930, raised duties on both agricultural and manufactured imports. It did nothing of significance to improve the economy, and historians argue over whether or not it contributed to the spread of the international depression.

Voluntarism

Hoover believed that voluntary cooperation would enable the country to weather the depression. He held meetings with business leaders at which he urged them to avoid lay-offs of workers and wage cuts, and he secured no-strike pledges from labor leaders. He urged all citizens to contribute to charities to help alleviate the suffering. While people were generous, private charity could not begin to meet the needs.

Public Works

In 1930 Congress appropriated $750 million for public buildings, river and harbor improvements, and highway construction in an effort to stimulate employment.

The Reconstruction Finance Corporation

Chartered by Congress in 1932, the RFC had an appropriation of $500 million and authority to borrow $1.5 billion for loans to railroads, banks, and other financial institutions. It prevented the failure of basic firms on which many other elements of the economy depended, but was criticized by some as relief for the rich.

The Federal Home Loan Bank Act

The Federal Home Loan Bank Act, passed in July 1932, injected $125 million of capital into newly created home loan banks so that loans could be made to building and loan associations, savings banks, and insurance companies to help them avoid foreclosures on homes.

A shantytown, or "Hooverville," in Seattle, Wash., March 20, 1933. AP/Wide World Photo

Relief

Hoover staunchly opposed the use of federal funds for relief for the needy. In July 1932 he vetoed the Garner-Wagner Bill, which would have appropriated funds for relief. He did compromise by approving legislation authorizing the RFC to lend $300 million to the states for relief, and to make loans to states and cities for self-liquidating public works.

The Bonus Army

The Bonus Expeditionary Force, which took its name from the American Expeditionary Force of World War I, was a group of about fourteen thousand unemployed veterans who went to Washington in the summer of 1932 to lobby Congress for immediate payment of the bonus which had been approved in 1926 for payment in 1945. At Hoover's insistence, the Senate did not pass the bonus bill, and about half of the BEF accepted a congressional offer of transportation home. The remaining five or six thousand, many with wives and children, continued to live in shanties along the Anacostia River and to lobby for their cause. After two veterans were killed in a clash with the police, Hoover, calling them insurrectionists and communists, ordered the Army to remove them. On July 28, 1932, General Douglas MacArthur, the Army chief of staff, assisted by Majors Dwight D. Eisenhower and George S. Patton, personally commanded the removal operation. With machine guns, tanks, cavalry, infantry with fixed bayonets, and tear gas, MacArthur drove the veterans from Washington and burned their camp.

The Farm Holiday Association

Centered in Iowa, the Farm Holiday Association, headed by Milo Reno and others, called a farm strike in August 1932. They urged farmers not to take their products to market in an effort to raise farm prices. The picketing of markets led to violence, and the strike collapsed.

The Election of 1932

The Republicans

At the Republican convention in Chicago, Hoover was nominated on the first ballot. The platform called for a continuation of his depression policies.

The Democrats

Franklin D. Roosevelt, the popular governor of New York, gained the support of many Southern and Western delegates through the efforts of his managers, Louis

Howe and James Farley. When the Democratic convention opened in Chicago, he had a majority of delegates, but not the necessary two-thirds for nomination. House speaker John Nance Garner, a favorite son candidate from Texas, threw support to Roosevelt, who was nominated on the fourth ballot. Garner then became the vice presidential candidate. Roosevelt took the unprecedented step of flying to the convention to accept the nomination in person, declaring that he pledged a "new deal" for the American people. The platform called for the repeal of prohibition, government aid for the unemployed, and a twenty five percent cut in government spending.

The Campaign

Hoover declared that he would lead the nation to prosperity with higher tariffs and the maintenance of the gold standard. He warned that the election of Roosevelt would lead to grass growing in the streets of the cities and towns of America. Roosevelt called for "bold, persistent experimentation," and expressed his concern for the "forgotten man" at the bottom of the economic heap, but he did not give a clear picture of what he intended to do. Roosevelt had a broad smile and amiable disposition which attracted many people, while Hoover was aloof and cold in his personal style.

The Election

Roosevelt received 22,809,638 votes for 57.3 percent of the total, and 472 electoral votes, carrying all but six Northeastern states. Hoover had 15,758,901 votes and 59 electoral votes. Despite the hard times, Norman Thomas, the Socialist candidate, received only 881,951 votes. The Democrats also captured the Senate, and increased their majority in the House.

The First New Deal

Franklin D. Roosevelt

The heir of a wealthy family and a fifth cousin of Theodore Roosevelt, Franklin was born in 1882 on the family estate at Hyde Park, New York. He graduated from Harvard and the Columbia Law School, married his distant cousin Anna Eleanor Roosevelt in 1905, and practiced law in New York City. He entered state politics, then served as assistant secretary of the Navy under Wilson, and was the Democratic vice-presidential candidate in 1920. In 1921 he suffered an attack of polio which left him paralyzed for several years and on crutches or in a wheelchair for the rest of his life. In 1928 he was elected governor of New York to succeed Al Smith, and was reelected in 1930. As governor, his depression programs for the unemployed, public works, aid to farmers, and conservation attracted national attention.

DIDYOU**KNOW?**

Although most Americans were not aware of FDR's lameness, the president worked diligently in support of polio research. He helped found the March of Dimes to seek a cure for polio, and the institution put millions of dollars into research by the time a vaccine was developed in the mid-1950s. FDR's contributions forever tied him to the dime in a unique way; his portrait now appears on that U.S. coin.

The Cabinet

Important Cabinet appointments included Senator Cordell Hull of Tennessee as secretary of state; Henry A. Wallace as secretary of agriculture; Harold L. Ickes as secretary of the interior; Frances Perkins, a New York social worker, as secretary of labor and the first woman appointed to a Cabinet post; and James A. Farley, Roosevelt's political manager, as postmaster general.

The Brain Trust

Roosevelt's inner circle of unofficial advisors, first assembled during the campaign, was more influential than the Cabinet. Prominent in it were agricultural economist Rexford G. Tugwell, political scientist Raymond Moley, lawyer Adolph A. Berle Jr., the originators of the McNary-Haugen Bill—Hugh S. Johnson and George Peek—and Roosevelt's personal political advisor, Louis Howe.

The New Deal Program

Roosevelt did not have a developed plan of action when he took office. He intended to experiment and to find that which worked. As a result, many programs overlapped or contradicted others, and were changed or dropped if they did not work.

Repeal of Prohibition

In February 1933, before Roosevelt took office, Congress passed the 21st Amendment to repeal prohibition, and sent it to the states. In March the new Congress

Mexican Americans and the New Deal

Mexican Americans benefitted the least from the New Deal, for few programs covered them. Farm owners turned against them as farm workers after they attempted to form a union between 1933 and 1936. By 1940 most had been replaced by whites dispossessed by the depression. Many returned to Mexico, and the Mexican American population dropped almost forty percent from 1930 to 1940.

Women During the New Deal

The burden of the depression fell on women as much or more as it did on men. Wives and mothers found themselves responsible for stretching meager budgets by preparing inexpensive meals, patching old clothing, and the like. "Making do" became a slogan of the period. In addition, more women had to supplement or provide the family income by going to work. In 1930 there were 10.5 million working women comprising 29 percent of the work force. By 1940 the figures had grown to over 13 million and 35 percent. There was much criticism of working women based on the idea that they deprived men of jobs. Male job losses were greatest in heavy industry such as factories and mills, while areas of female employment such as retail sales were not hit as hard. Unemployed men seldom sought jobs in the traditional women's fields.

Labor Unions

Unions During the First New Deal

Labor unions had lost members and influence during the twenties, and slipped further during the economic decline of 1929 to 1933. The National Industrial Recovery Act gave them new hope when Section 7a guaranteed the right to unionize, and during 1933 about 1.5 million new members joined unions. It soon became clear that enforcement of the industrial codes by the NRA was ineffective, and labor leaders began to call it the "National Run Around." As a result in 1934 there were many strikes, sometimes violent, including a general strike in San Francisco involving about 125,000 workers.

Craft Versus Industrial Unions

The passage of the National Labor Relations, or Wagner, Act in 1935 resulted in a massive growth of union membership, but only at the expense of bitter conflict within the labor movement. The American Federation of Labor was made up primarily of craft unions. Some leaders, especially John L. Lewis, the dynamic president of the United Mine Workers, wanted to unionize the mass production industries, such as automobiles and rubber, with industrial unions. In 1934 the AFL convention authorized such unions, but the older unions continued to try to organize workers in those industries by crafts. In November 1935 Lewis and others established the Committee for Industrial Organization to unionize basic industries, presumably within the AFL. President William Green of the AFL ordered the CIO to disband in January 1936. When the rebels refused, they were expelled by the AFL executive council in March 1937. The insurgents then reorganized the CIO as the independent Congress of Industrial Organizations to be composed of industrial unions.

The Growth of the CIO

During its organizational period the CIO sought to initiate several industrial unions, particularly in the steel, auto, rubber, and radio industries. In late 1936 and early 1937 it used a tactic called the sit-down strike, with the strikers occupying the workplace to prevent any production. There were 477 sit-down strikes involving about 400,000 workers. The largest was in the General Motors plant in Flint, Michigan, as the union sought recognition by that firm. In February 1937 General Motors recognized the United Auto Workers as the bargaining agent for its 400,000 workers. When the CIO established its independence in March 1937, it already had 1.8 million members, and it reached a membership of 3.75 million six months later. The AFL had about 3.4 million members at that time. By the end of 1941 the CIO had about 5 million members, the AFL about 4.6 million, and other unions about one million. Union members comprised about 11.5 percent of the work force in 1933, and 28.2 percent in 1941.

Cultural Trends of the 1930s
Literary Developments

The writers and intellectuals who had expressed disdain for the middle class materialism of the 1920s found it even more difficult to deal with the meaning of the crushing poverty in America and the rise of fascism in Europe during the 1930s. Some turned to communism, including the fifty-three writers who signed an open letter endorsing the Communist presidential candidate in 1932. Some turned to proletarian novels, such as Jack Conroy in *The Disinherited* (1933) and Robert Cantwell in *The Land of Plenty* (1934). Ernest Hemingway seemed to have lost his direction in *Winner Take All*

(1933) and *The Green Hills of Africa* (1935), but in *To Have and Have Not* (1937), a strike novel, he turned to social realism, and *For Whom the Bell Tolls* (1941) expressed his concern about fascism. Sinclair Lewis also dealt with fascism in *It Can't Happen Here* (1935), but did not show the power of his works of the 1920s. John Dos Passos depicted what he saw as the disintegration of American life from 1900 to 1929 in his trilogy *U.S.A.* (1930–1936). William Faulkner sought values in Southern life in *Light in August* (1932), *Absalom! Absalom!* (1936), and *The Unvanquished* (1938). The endurance of the human spirit and personal survival were depicted in James T. Farrell's trilogy *Studs Lonigan* (1936) about the struggles of lower-middle-class Irish Catholics in Chicago, while Erskine Caldwell's *Tobacco Road* (1932) dealt with impoverished Georgia share-croppers, and John Steinbeck's *The Grapes of Wrath* (1939) depicted "Okies" migrating from the dust bowl to California in the midst of the depression.

New Deal-era poster shows a man with a WPA shovel attacking a wolf called Rumor

Popular Culture

The depression greatly reduced the amount of money available for recreation and entertainment. There was an increase in games and sports among family groups and friends. The WPA and the CCC constructed thousands of playgrounds, playing fields, picnic areas, and the like for public use. Roosevelt and Harry Hopkins, the director of the WPA, hoped to develop a mass appreciation of culture through the WPA murals in public buildings, with traveling plays, concerts, and exhibits, and with community arts centers. Beyond some revival of handicrafts, it is doubtful that the program had much effect. There were, however, several popular forms of entertainment.

Radio was the favorite form of daily entertainment during the depression because, after the initial cost of the instrument, it was free. There were about forty million radios in the United States by 1938. It provided comedy and mystery shows, music, sports and news. A study at the time indicated that radio tended to make Americans more uniform in their attitudes, taste, speech, and humor.

DIDYOU**KNOW?**

Among the most popular radio programs of the 1930s were the ongoing serial dramas known as "soap operas," so called because they were usually sponsored by household cleaning products. By 1940, soap operas made up as much as 90 percent of daytime sponsored radio programming (www.soapcentral.com).

While radio was the form of entertainment most used, the movies were the most popular. By 1939 about 65 percent of the people went to the movies at least once a week. The movie industry was one of the few which did not suffer financially from the depression. Movies were the great means of escape, providing release from the pressures of the depression by transporting people to a make-believe world of beauty, mystery, or excitement. Spectacular musicals with dozens of dancers and singers, such as *Broadway Melody of 1936*, were popular. The dance team of Fred Astaire and Ginger Rogers thrilled millions in *Flying Down to Rio* and *Shall We Dance?* Shirley Temple charmed the public as their favorite child star. Judy Garland rose to stardom in *The Wizard of Oz*, while animated films like *Snow White* appealed to children of all ages. People enjoyed the triumph of justice and decency in *Mr. Smith Goes to Washington* and *You Can't Take It with You* with Jimmy Stewart. Dozens of light comedies starred such favorites as Cary Grant, Katharine Hepburn, Clark Gable, and Rosalind Russell, while Errol Flynn played in such larger-than-life roles as Robin Hood. A different kind of escape was found in gangster movies with Edward G. Robinson, James Cagney, or George Raft. Near the end of the decade *Gone with the Wind*, released in 1939 starring Clark

Gable and Vivien Leigh, became a timeless classic, while *The Grapes of Wrath* in 1940 commented on the depression itself.

The popular music of the decade was swing, and the big bands of Duke Ellington, Benny Goodman, Glenn Miller, Tommy Dorsey, and Harry James vied for public favor. The leading popular singer was Bing Crosby. City African Americans refined the country blues to city blues, and interracial audiences enjoyed both city blues and jazz. African American musicians were increasingly accepted by white audiences.

Comic strips existed before the thirties, but they became a standard newspaper feature as well as a source of comic books during the decade. "Dick Tracy" began his war on crime in 1931, and was assisted by "Superman" after 1938. "Tarzan" began to swing through the cartoon jungles in 1929, and "Buck Rogers" began the exploration of space in 1930.

New Deal Diplomacy and the Road to War

The Good Neighbor Policy

Roosevelt and Secretary of State Cordell Hull continued the policies of their predecessors in endeavoring to improve relations with Latin American nations, and formalized their position by calling it the Good Neighbor Policy.

Nonintervention

At the Montevideo Conference of American Nations in December of 1933 the United States renounced the right of intervention in the internal affairs of Latin American countries. In 1936, in the Buenos Aires Convention, the United States further agreed to submit all American disputes to arbitration. Accordingly, the Marines were removed from Haiti, Nicaragua, and the Dominican Republic by 1934. The Haitian protectorate treaty was allowed to expire in 1936, the right of intervention in Panama was ended by treaty in 1936, and the receivership of the finances of the Dominican Republic ended in 1941.

Cuba

The United States did not intervene in the Cuban revolution in the spring of 1933, but it did back a coup by Fulgencio Batista to overthrow the liberal regime of Ramon Grau San Martin in 1934. Batista was given a favorable sugar import status for Cuba in return for establishing a conservative administration. In May 1934 the United States abrogated its Platt Amendment rights in Cuba except for control of the Guantanamo Naval Base.

Mexico

The Mexican government of Lazaro Cardenas began to expropriate American property, including oil holdings, in 1934. Despite calls for intervention, Roosevelt insisted only on compensation. A joint commission worked out a settlement which was formally concluded on November 19, 1941.

The London Economic Conference

An international conference in London in June 1933 tried to obtain tariff reduction and currency stabilization for the industrialized nations. Roosevelt would not agree to peg the value of the dollar to other currencies because he feared that it might impede his recovery efforts. The conference failed for lack of American cooperation.

Recognition of Russia

The United States had not had diplomatic relations with the Union of Soviet Socialist Republics since it was established after the 1917 revolution. In an effort to open trade with Russia, mutual recognition was negotiated in November 1933. The financial results were disappointing.

Philippine Independence

The Tydings-McDuffie Act of March 1934 forced the Philippines to become independent on July 4, 1946, rather than granting the dominion status which the Filipinos had requested.

The Reciprocal Trade Agreement Act

The Reciprocal Trade Agreement, the idea of Cordell Hull, was passed in June 1934. It allowed the president to negotiate agreements which could vary from the rates of the Hawley-Smoot Tariff up to 50 percent. By 1936 lower rates had been negotiated with 13 nations, and by 1941 almost two-thirds of all American foreign trade was covered by agreements.

United States Neutrality Legislation

Isolationism

Belief that the United States should stay out of foreign wars and problems began in the 1920s and grew in the 1930s. It was fed by House and Senate investigations of arms traffic and the munitions industry in 1933 and 1934, especially an examination of profiteering by bankers and munitions makers in drawing the United States into World War I by Senator Gerald Nye of North Dakota. Books of revisionist history which asserted that Germany had not been responsible for World War I and that the United States had been misled were also influential during the 1930s. A Gallup poll in April 1937 showed that almost two-thirds of those responding thought that American entry into World War I had been a mistake. Such feelings were strongest in the Midwest and among Republicans, but were found in all areas and across the political spectrum. Leading isolationists included Congressman Hamilton Fish of New York, Senator William Borah of Idaho, and Senator George Norris of Nebraska, all Republicans. Pacifist movements, such as the Fellowship of Christian Reconciliation, were influential among college and high school students and the clergy.

The Johnson Act of 1934

When European nations stopped payment on World War I debts to the United States, the Johnson Act of 1934 prohibited any nation in default from selling securities to any American citizen or corporation.

The Neutrality Acts of 1935

Isolationist sentiment prompted Senator Key Pittman, a Nevada Democrat, to propose these laws. Roosevelt would have preferred more presidential flexibility, but Congress wanted to avoid flexibility and the mistakes of World War I. The laws provided that, on outbreak of war between foreign nations, all exports of American arms and munitions to them would be embargoed for six months. In addition, American ships were prohibited from carrying arms to any belligerent, and the president was to warn American citizens not to travel on belligerent ships.

The Neutrality Acts of 1936

The Neutrality Acts of 1936 gave the president authority to determine when a state of war existed, and prohibited any loans or credits to belligerents.

The Neutrality Acts of 1937

The Neutrality Acts of 1937 gave the president authority to determine if a civil war was a threat to world peace and covered by the Neutrality Acts, prohibited all arms sales to belligerents, and allowed the cash and carry sale of nonmilitary goods to belligerents.

TEST TIP

Try to leave a few minutes at the end of the time allotted for each essay to reread your work. This will help you ensure that you didn't accidentally skip an important word or idea as you were writing.

Threats to World Order

The Manchurian Crisis

In September 1931 the Japanese army invaded and seized the Chinese province of Manchuria. The action violated the Nine Power Pact and the Kellogg-Briand Pact. When the League of Nations sought consideration of some action against Japan, Hoover refused to consider either economic or military sanctions. The only American action was to refuse recognition of the action or the puppet state of Manchukuo which the Japanese created.

Ethiopia

Following a border skirmish between Italian and Ethiopian troops, the Italian army of Fascist dictator Benito Mussolini invaded Ethiopia from neighboring Italian colonies in October 1935. The League of Nations failed to take effective action, the United States looked on, and Ethiopia fell in May 1936.

Occupation of the Rhineland

In defiance of the Versailles Treaty, Nazi dictator Adolf Hitler sent his German army into the demilitarized Rhineland in March 1936.

The Rome-Berlin Axis

Germany and Italy, under Hitler and Mussolini, formed an alliance called the Rome-Berlin Axis on October 25, 1936.

The Sino-Japanese War

The Japanese launched a full-scale invasion of China in July 1937. When Japanese planes sank the American Gunboat *Panay* and three Standard Oil tankers on the Yangtze River in December 1937, the United States accepted a Japanese apology and damage payments while the American public called for the withdrawal of all American forces from China.

The "Quarantine the Aggressor" Speech

In a speech in Chicago in October 1937 Roosevelt proposed that the democracies unite to quarantine the aggressor nations. When public opinion did not pick up on the idea, he did not press the issue.

German Expansion

Hitler brought about a union of Germany and Austria in March 1938, took the German-speaking Sudetenland from Czechoslovakia in September 1938, and occupied the rest of Czechoslovakia in March 1939.

The Invasion of Poland and the Beginning of World War II

On August 24, 1939, Germany signed a nonaggression pact with Russia which contained a secret provision to divide Poland between them. German forces then invaded Poland on September 1, 1939. Britain and France declared war on Germany on September 3 because of their treaties with Poland. By the end of September Poland had been dismembered by Germany and Russia, but the war continued in the west along the French-German border.

The American Response to the War in Europe

Preparedness

Even before the outbreak of World War II, Roosevelt began a preparedness program to improve American defenses. In May 1938 he requested and received a naval construction appropriation of about one billion dollars. In October, Congress provided an additional $300 million for defense, and in January 1939 a regular defense appropriation of $1.3 billion with an added $525 million for equipment, especially airplanes. Defense spending increased after the outbreak of war. In August 1939 Roosevelt created the War Resources Board to develop a plan for industrial mobilization in the event of war. The next month he established the Office of Emergency Management in the White House to centralize mobilization activities.

The Neutrality Act of 1939

Roosevelt officially proclaimed the neutrality of the United States on September 5, 1939. He then called Congress into special session on September 21 and urged it to allow the cash-and-carry sale of arms. Despite opposition from isolationists, the Democratic Congress, in a vote that followed party lines, passed a new Neutrality Act in November. It allowed the cash-and-carry sale of arms and short-term loans to belligerents, but forbade American ships to trade with belligerents or Americans to travel on belligerent ships. The new law was helpful to the Allies because they controlled the Atlantic.

Changing American Attitudes

Hitler's armies invaded and quickly conquered Denmark and Norway in April 1940. In May, German forces swept through the Netherlands, Belgium, Luxembourg, and France. The British were driven from the continent, and France surrendered on June 22. Almost all Americans recognized Germany as a threat. They divided on whether to aid Britain or to concentrate on the defense of America. The Committee to Defend America by Aiding the Allies was formed in May 1940, and the America First Committee, which opposed involvement, was incorporated in September 1940.

Greenland

In April 1940 Roosevelt declared that Greenland, a possession of conquered Denmark, was covered by the Monroe Doctrine, and he supplied military assistance to set up a coastal patrol there.

Defense Mobilization

In May 1940 Roosevelt appointed a Council of National Defense chaired by William S. Knudson, the president of General Motors, to direct defense production and especially to build fifty thousand planes. The Council was soon awarding defense contracts at the rate of $1.5 billion a month. The Office of Production Management was created to allocate scarce materials, and the Office of Price Administration was established to prevent inflation and protect consumers. In June, Roosevelt made Republicans Henry L. Stimson and Frank Knox secretaries of war and the Navy, respectively, partly as an attempt to secure bipartisan support.

Selective Service

Congress approved the nation's first peacetime draft, the Selective Service and Training Act, in September 1940. Men ages 21 to 35 were registered, and many were called for one year of military training.

Destroyers for Bases

Roosevelt had determined that to aid Britain in every way possible was the best way to avoid war with Germany. He ordered the army and navy to turn over all available weapons and munitions to private dealers for resale to Britain. In September 1940 he signed an agreement to give Britain fifty American destroyers in return for a 99-year lease on air and naval bases in British territories in Newfoundland, Bermuda, and the Caribbean.

The Election of 1940

The Republicans

Passing over their isolationist front-runners, Senator Robert A. Taft of Ohio and New York attorney Thomas E. Dewey, the Republicans nominated Wendell L. Willkie of Indiana, a dark horse candidate. Willkie was a liberal Republican who had been a Democrat most of his life, and the head of an electric utility holding company which had fought against the TVA. The platform supported a strong defense program, but severely criticized the New Deal domestic policies.

The Democrats

Roosevelt did not reveal his intentions regarding a third term, but he neither endorsed another candidate nor discouraged his supporters. When the convention came in July, he sent a message to the Democratic National Committee implying that he would accept the nomination for a third time if it were offered. He was then nominated on the first ballot, breaking a tradition which had existed since the time of Washington. Only with difficulty did Roosevelt's managers persuade the delegates to accept his choice of vice president, Secretary of Agriculture Henry A. Wallace, to succeed Garner. The platform endorsed the foreign and domestic policies of the administration.

The Campaign

Willkie's basic agreement with Roosevelt's foreign policy made it difficult for him to campaign. Willkie had a folksy approach which appealed to many voters, but he first attacked Roosevelt for the slowness of the defense program, and then, late in the campaign, called him a warmonger. Roosevelt, who lost the support of many Democrats, including his adviser James Farley, over the third term issue, campaigned very little. When Willkie began to gain on the warmongering issue, Roosevelt declared on October 30 that "your boys are not going to be sent into any foreign wars."

The Election

Roosevelt won by a much narrower margin than in 1936, with 27,243,466 votes, 54.7 percent, and 449 electoral votes. Willkie received 22,304,755 votes and 82 electoral votes. Socialist Norman Thomas had 100,264 votes, and Communist Earl Browder received 48,579.

DIDYOUKNOW?

FDR is the only U.S. president to be elected to more than two terms in office, but he is not the only U.S. president to have won the popular vote more than twice. Both Andrew Jackson and Grover Cleveland carried the popular vote three times, but each failed to generate the necessary electoral college votes to win office.

American Involvement with the European War

The Lend-Lease Act

The British were rapidly exhausting their cash reserves with which to buy American goods. In January 1941 Roosevelt proposed that the United States provide supplies to be paid for in goods and services after the war. The Lend-Lease Act was passed by Congress and signed on March 11, 1941, and the first appropriation of $7 billion was provided. In effect, the law changed the United States from a neutral to a nonbelligerent on the Allied side.

The Patrol of the Western Atlantic

The Germans stepped up their submarine warfare in the Atlantic to prevent the flow of American supplies to Britain. In April 1941 Roosevelt started the American Neutrality Patrol. The American navy would search out but not attack German submarines in the western half of the Atlantic, and warn British vessels of their location.

Greenland

In April 1941, United States forces occupied Greenland and in May the president declared a state of unlimited national emergency.

Occupation of Iceland

American Marines occupied Iceland, a Danish possession, in July 1941 to protect it from seizure by Germany. The American Navy began to convoy American and Icelandic ships between the United States and Iceland.

The Atlantic Charter

On August 9, 1941, Roosevelt and Winston Churchill, the British prime minister, met for the first time on a British battleship off Newfoundland. They issued the Atlantic Charter, which described a postwar world based on self-determination for all nations. It also endorsed the principles of freedom of speech and religion and freedom from want and fear, which Roosevelt had proposed as the Four Freedoms earlier that year.

Aid to Russia

Germany invaded Russia in June 1941, and in November the United States extended lend-lease assistance to the Russians.

The Shoot-on-Sight Order

The American destroyer *Greer* was attacked by a German submarine near Iceland on September 4, 1941. Roosevelt ordered the American military forces to shoot on sight at any German or Italian vessel in the patrol zone. An undeclared naval war had begun. The American destroyer *Kearny* was attacked by a submarine on October 16, and the destroyer *Reuben James* was sunk on October 30, with 115 lives lost. In November, Congress authorized the arming of merchant ships.

The Road to Pearl Harbor

A Japanese Empire

Following their invasion of China in 1937, the Japanese began to speak of the Greater East Asia Co-Prosperity Sphere, a Japanese empire of undefined boundaries in east Asia and the western Pacific. Accordingly, they forced out American and other business interests from occupied China, declaring that the Open Door policy had ended. Roosevelt responded by lending money to China and requesting American aircraft manufacturers not to sell to Japan.

The Embargo of 1940

Following the fall of France, a new and more militant Japanese government in July 1940 obtained from the German-controlled Vichy French government the right to build air bases and to station troops in northern French Indochina. The United States, fearing that the step would lead to further expansion, responded in late July by placing an embargo on the export of aviation gasoline, lubricants, and scrap iron and steel to Japan, and by granting an additional loan to China. In December the embargo was extended to include iron ore and pig iron, some chemicals, machine tools, and other products.

The Tripartite Pact

Japan joined with Germany and Italy to form the Rome-Berlin-Tokyo Axis on September 27, 1940, when it signed the Tripartite Pact or Triple Alliance with the other Axis powers.

The Embargo of 1941

In July 1941 Japan extracted a new concession from Vichy France by obtaining military control of southern Indochina. Roosevelt reacted by freezing Japanese funds in the United States, closing the Panama Canal to Japan, activating the Philippine militia, and placing an embargo on the export of oil and other vital products to Japan.

Japanese-American Negotiations

Negotiations to end the impasse between the United States and Japan were conducted in Washington between Secretary Hull and Japanese Ambassador Kichisaburo

Nomura. Hull demanded that Japan withdraw from Indochina and China, promise not to attack any other area in the western Pacific, and withdraw from the Tripartite Pact in return for the reopening of American trade. The Japanese offered to withdraw from Indochina when the Chinese war was satisfactorily settled, to promise no further expansion, and to agree to ignore any obligation under the Tripartite Pact to go to war if the United States entered a defensive war with Germany. Hull refused to compromise.

TEST TIP

No peeking! Wait until the test proctor tells you to begin work on your AP Exam before opening your test booklet. Starting too soon can cause the proctor to disqualify you to take the exam.

A Summit Conference Proposed

The Japanese proposed in August 1941 that Roosevelt meet personally with the Japanese prime minister, Prince Konoye, in an effort to resolve their differences. Such an action might have strengthened the position of Japanese moderates, but Roosevelt replied in September that he would do so only if Japan agreed to leave China. No meeting was held.

Final Negotiations

In October 1941 a new military cabinet headed by General Hideki Tojo took control of Japan. The Japanese secretly decided to make a final effort to negotiate, and to go to war if no solution was found by November 25. A new round of talks followed in Washington, but neither side would make a substantive change in its position, and on November 26, Hull repeated the American demand that the Japanese remove all their forces from China and Indochina immediately. The Japanese gave final approval on December 1 for an attack on the United States.

Japanese Attack Plans

The Japanese planned a major offensive to take the Dutch East Indies, Malaya, and the Philippines in order to obtain the oil, metals, and other raw materials which they needed. At the same time they would attack Pearl Harbor in Hawaii to destroy the American Pacific fleet to keep it from interfering with their plans.

American Awareness of Japanese Plans

The United States had broken the Japanese diplomatic codes, and knew that trouble was imminent. Between December 1 and December 6, 1941, it became clear to administration leaders that Japanese task forces were being ordered into battle. American commanders in the Pacific were warned of possible aggressive action there, but not forcefully. Apparently most American leaders thought that Japan would attack the Dutch East Indies and Malaya, but would avoid American territory so as not to provoke action by the United States. Some argue that Roosevelt wanted to let the Japanese attack so that the American people would be squarely behind the war.

The attack on Pearl Harbor by the Japanese pushed the United States into World War II.
U.S. Naval Historical Center Photo

The Pearl Harbor Attack

At 7:55 a.m. on Sunday December 7, 1941, the first wave of Japanese carrier-based planes attacked the American fleet in Pearl Harbor. A second wave followed at 8:50 a.m. American defensive action was almost nil, but by the second wave a few anti-aircraft batteries were operating and a few Army planes from another base in Hawaii engaged the enemy. The United States suffered the loss of two battleships sunk, six damaged and out of action, three cruisers and three destroyers sunk or damaged, and a number of lesser vessels destroyed or damaged. All of the 150 aircraft at Pearl Harbor were destroyed on the ground. Worst of all, 2,323 American servicemen were killed and about 1,100 wounded. The Japanese lost 29 planes, five midget submarines, and one fleet submarine.

The Declaration of War

On December 8, 1941, Roosevelt told a joint session of Congress that the day before had been a "date that would live in infamy." Congress declared war on Japan with one dissenting vote. On December 11, Germany and Italy declared war on the United States.

(Before taking the quiz noted below, please review the summary timeline for this chapter on the following pages.)

Time for a quiz
- Review strategies in Chapter 2
- Take Quiz 6 at the REA Study Center
  (www.rea.com/studycenter)

The Great Depression and the New Deal (1929–1941)

Historical Timeline (1929–1941)

Year	Events
1929	Agricultural Marketing Act attempts to support farm prices
1930	Hawley-Smoot Tariff raises duties on farm products and manufactured goods
1931	Japan invades Manchuria
1932	Reconstruction Finance Corporation attempts to support industry Bonus Expeditionary Force marches on Washington, D.C. Franklin Roosevelt wins presidency
1933	Prohibition repealed Hundred Days of legislation follows FDR's inauguration Banks closed after over 6,000 fail FDIC established by Glass-Steagall Act Agricultural Adjustment Act passed National Industrial Recovery Act passed Tennessee Valley Authority established Civilian Conservation Corps enrolls 250,000 young men Hitler becomes chancellor of Germany
1934	Securities and Exchange Commission established Huey Long begins Share Our Wealth clubs Dr. Francis Townsend promotes Old Age Revolving Pension Plan Nye Committee probes World War I profiteering by American industrialists
1935	*Schecter v. United States* rules NIRA unconstitutional Works Progress Administration established National Labor Relations (Wagner) Act protects workers' rights Social Security Act passed Congress passes first of annual Neutrality Acts
1936	FDR defeats Republican Landon and third-party Union Party for president General Motors sitdown strike Germany occupies the Rhineland Spanish Civil War begins Ethiopia falls to Italy
1937	FDR proposes court-packing plan, which fails Japan invades China U.S. gunship *Panay* sunk by Japanese in Yangtze River

(continued)

retaliation" and "liberation" rather than containment. He wished to emphasize nuclear deterrents rather than conventional armed forces. Dulles served as secretary of state until ill health forced him to resign in April 1959. Christian A. Herter took his place.

Hydrogen Bomb

The U.S. exploded its first hydrogen bomb in November 1952 while the Soviets followed with theirs in August 1953.

Soviet Change of Power

Josef Stalin died in March 1953. After an internal power struggle that lasted until 1955, Nikita Khrushchev emerged as the Soviet leader. He talked of both "burying" capitalism and "peaceful coexistence."

Asia

In 1954 the French asked the U.S. to commit air forces to rescue French forces at Dien Bien Phu, Vietnam, as they were besieged by the nationalist forces led by Ho Chi Minh, but Eisenhower refused. In May 1954 Dien Bien Phu surrendered.

Geneva Accords

France, Great Britain, the Soviet Union, and China signed the Geneva Accords in July 1954, dividing Vietnam along the 17th parallel. The North would be under Ho Chi Minh and the South under Emperor Bao Dai. Elections were scheduled for 1956 to unify the country, but Ngo Dinh Diem overthrew Bao Dai and prevented the elections from taking place. The United States supplied economic aid to South Vietnam.

Southeast Asia Treaty Organization

Dulles attempted to establish a Southeast Asia Treaty Organization parallel to NATO but was able to obtain only the Philippine Republic, Thailand, and Pakistan as signatories in September 1954.

Quemoy and Matsu

The small islands of Quemoy and Matsu off the coast of China were occupied by the Nationalist Chinese under Chiang Kai-shek but claimed by the People's Republic of China. In 1955, after the mainland Chinese began shelling these islands, Eisenhower obtained authorization from Congress to defend Formosa (Taiwan) and related areas.

Middle East—The Suez Canal Crisis

The United States had agreed to lend money to Egypt, under the leadership of Colonel Gamal Abdul Nasser, to build the Aswan Dam but refused to give arms. Nasser then drifted toward the Soviet Union and in 1956 established diplomatic relations with the People's Republic of China. In July 1956 the U.S. withdrew its loan to Egypt. In response, Nasser nationalized the Suez Canal. France, Great Britain, and Israel then attacked Egypt but Eisenhower demanded that they pull out. On November 6 a cease-fire was announced.

Eisenhower Doctrine

President Eisenhower announced in January 1957 that the U.S. was prepared to use armed force in the Middle East against communist aggression. Under this doctrine, U.S. marines entered Beirut, Lebanon in July 1958 to promote political stability during a change of governments. The Marines left in October.

Summit Conference with the Soviet Union

In July 1955 President Eisenhower met in Geneva with Anthony Eden, prime minister of Great Britain, Edgar Faure, premier of France, and Nikita Khrushchev and Nikolai Bulganin, at the time co-leaders of the Soviet Union. They discussed disarmament and reunification of Germany but made no agreements.

Atomic Weapons Test Suspension

Eisenhower and Khrushchev voluntarily suspended in October 1958 atmospheric tests of atomic weapons.

Soviet-American Visitations

Vice President Richard M. Nixon visited the Soviet Union and Soviet Vice-Premier Anastas I. Mikoyan came to the United States in the summer of 1959. In September Premier Khrushchev toured the United States and agreed to another summit meeting.

U-2 Incident

On May 1, 1960, an American U-2 spy plane was shot down over the Soviet Union and pilot Francis Gary Powers was captured. Eisenhower ultimately took responsibility for the spy plane and Khrushchev angrily called off the Paris summit conference which was to take place in a few days.

Latin America

The U.S. supported the overthrow of President Jacobo Arbenz Guzman of Guatemala in 1954 because he began accepting arms from the Soviet Union.

Vice President Nixon had to call off an eight nation goodwill tour of Latin America after meeting hostile mobs in Venezuela and Peru in 1958.

In January 1959 Fidel Castro overthrew Fulgencio Batista, dictator of Cuba. Castro soon began criticizing the United States and moved closer to the Soviet Union, signing a trade agreement with the Soviets in February 1960. The United States prohibited the importation of Cuban sugar in October 1960 and broke off diplomatic relations in January 1961.

TEST TIP

Worried about whether your essay responses are scored fairly? Don't be. AP Exam essay graders are experienced college professors and high school teachers who are specially trained in the subject they're scoring. Scores are checked to ensure that different graders score essays in a consistent, fair manner.

The Politics of Affluence: Demobilization and Domestic Policy

Truman Becomes President

Harry S. Truman, formerly a senator from Missouri and vice president of the United States, became president on April 12, 1945. In September 1945 he proposed a liberal legislative program, including expansion of unemployment insurance, extension of the Employment Service, a higher minimum wage, a permanent Fair Employment Practices Commission, slum clearance, low-rent housing, regional TVA-type programs, and a public works program, but was unable to put it through Congress.

Employment Act of 1946

This act established a three member Council of Economic Advisors to evaluate the economy, advise the president, and set up a Congressional Joint Committee on the Economic Report. The act declared that the government was committed to maintaining maximum employment.

Atomic Energy

Congress created the Atomic Energy Commission in 1946, establishing civilian control over nuclear development and giving the president sole authority over the use of atomic weapons in warfare.

Price Controls

Truman vetoed a weak price control bill passed by Congress, thereby ending the wartime price control program. When prices quickly increased about 6 percent, Congress passed another bill in July 1946. Although Truman signed this bill, he used its powers inconsistently, especially when—bowing to pressure—he ended price controls on beef. In late 1946, he lifted controls on all items except rents, sugar, and rice.

Labor

In early 1946, the United Auto Workers, under Walter Reuther, struck General Motors, and steelworkers, under Philip Murray, struck U.S. Steel, demanding wage increases. Truman suggested an 18 cent-per-hour wage increase and in February allowed

U.S. Steel to raise prices to cover the increase. This formula became the basis for settlements in other industries. After John L. Lewis's United Mine Workers struck in April 1946, Truman ordered the government to take over the mines and then accepted the union's demands, which included safety and health and welfare benefits. The president averted a railway strike by seizing the railroads and threatening to draft strikers into the Army.

Demobilization

By 1947 the total armed forces had been cut to 1.5 million. The Army fell to 600,000 from a WWII peak of 8 million. The Serviceman's Readjustment Act (G.I. Bill of Rights) of 1944, provided $13 billion in aid ranging from education to housing.

Taft-Hartley Act

The Republicans, who had gained control of Congress as a result of the 1946 elections, sought to control the power of the unions through the Taft-Hartley Act, passed in 1947. This act made the "closed-shop" illegal; labor unions could no longer force employers to hire only union members although it allowed the "union shop" in which newly hired employees were required to join the union. It established an 80 day cooling-off period for strikers in key industries; ended the practice of employers collecting dues for unions; forbade such actions as secondary boycotts, jurisdictional strikes, featherbedding, and contributing to political campaigns; and required an anti-communist oath of union officials. The act slowed down efforts to unionize the South and by 1954, 15 states had passed "right to work" laws, forbidding the "union shop."

Reorganization of Armed Forces

In 1947 Congress passed the National Security Act creating a National Military Establishment, National Security Council, Joint Chiefs of Staff, and Central Intelligence Agency (CIA). Together these organizations were intended to coordinate the armed forces and intelligence services.

Government Reorganization

Truman in 1947 appointed former President Herbert Hoover to head a Commission on Organization of the Executive Branch. The Commission's 1949 report led to the

Organization Act of 1949 which allowed the president to make organizational changes subject to congressional veto.

Civil Rights

In 1946 Truman appointed the President's Committee on Civil Rights, which a year later produced its report *To Secure These Rights*. The report called for the elimination of all aspects of segregation. In 1948 the president banned racial discrimination in federal hiring practices and ordered desegregation of the armed forces.

Presidential Succession

The Presidential Succession Act of 1947 placed the speaker of the House and the president pro tempore of the Senate ahead of the secretary of state and after the vice president in the line of succession. The 22nd Amendment to the Constitution, ratified in 1951, limited the president to two terms.

Election of 1948

Truman was the Democratic nominee but the Democrats were split by the States' Rights Democratic Party (Dixiecrats) which nominated Governor Strom Thurmond of South Carolina and the Progressive Party which nominated former Vice-President Henry Wallace. The Republicans nominated Governor Thomas E. Dewey of New York. After traveling widely and attacking the "do-nothing Congress," Truman won a surprise victory.

The Fair Deal

The Fair Deal Program

Truman sought to enlarge and extend the New Deal. He proposed increasing the minimum wage, extending Social Security to more people, maintaining rent controls, clearing slums and building public housing, and providing more money to TVA, rural electrification, and farm housing. He also introduced bills dealing with civil rights, national health insurance, federal aid to education, and repeal of the Taft-Hartley Act. A coalition of Republicans and Southern Democrats prevented little more than the maintenance of existing programs.

Farm Policy

Because of improvements in agriculture, overproduction continued to be a problem. Secretary of Agriculture Charles F. Brannan proposed a program of continued price supports for storable crops and guaranteed minimum incomes to farmers of perishable crops. It was defeated in Congress and surpluses continued to pile up.

Anticommunism

Smith Act

The Smith Act of 1940, which made it illegal to advocate the overthrow of the government by force or to belong to an organization advocating such a position, was used by the Truman administration to jail leaders of the American Communist Party.

Loyalty Review Board

In response to criticism, particularly from the House Committee on Un-American Activities, that his administration was "soft on communism," Truman established this board in 1947 to review government employees.

The Hiss Case

In 1948 Whittaker Chambers, formerly a communist and then an editor of *Time*, charged Alger Hiss, a former State Department official and then president of the Carnegie Endowment for International Peace, with having been a communist who supplied classified American documents to the Soviet Union. In 1950 Hiss was convicted of perjury, the statute of limitations on his alleged spying having run out.

McCarran Internal Security Act

Passed in 1950, this act required communist-front organizations to register with the attorney general and prevented their members from defense work and travel abroad. It was passed over Truman's veto.

Rosenberg Case

In 1950 Julius and Ethel Rosenberg, as well as Harry Gold, were charged with giving atomic secrets to the Soviet Union. The Rosenbergs were convicted and executed in 1953.

Joseph McCarthy

On February 9, 1950, Senator Joseph R. McCarthy of Wisconsin stated that he had a list of known communists who were working in the State Department. He later expanded his attacks to diplomats and scholars and contributed to the electoral defeat of two senators. After making charges against the army, he was censured and discredited by the Senate in 1954 and died in 1957.

TEST TIP

Nothing will hurt your essay score more than failing to directly answer the free-response question. Be sure to clearly state your thesis at both the beginning and the end of your essay, to ensure that your writing adequately conveys that you have responded to the question asked.

Eisenhower's Dynamic Conservatism

1952 Election

The Republicans nominated Dwight D. Eisenhower, most recently NATO commander, for the presidency and Richard M. Nixon, senator from California, for the vice-presidency. The Democrats nominated Governor Adlai E. Stevenson of Illinois for president. Eisenhower won by a landslide; for the first time since Reconstruction the Republicans won some Southern states.

Conservatism

Eisenhower sought to balance the budget and lower taxes but did not attempt to roll back existing social and economic legislation. Eisenhower first described his policy as "dynamic conservatism" and then as "progressive moderation." The administration abolished the Reconstruction Finance Corporation, ended wage and price controls, and reduced farm price supports. It cut the budget and in 1954 lowered tax rates for corporations and individuals with high incomes; an economic slump, however, made balancing the budget difficult.

Social Legislation

Social Security was extended in 1954 and 1956 to an additional 10 million people, including professionals, domestic and clerical workers, farm workers, and members of the armed services. In 1959 benefits were increased 7 percent. In 1955 the minimum wage was raised from 75 cents to $1.00 an hour.

Public Power

Opposed to the expansion of TVA, the Eisenhower administration supported a plan to have a privately owned power plant (called Dixon-Yates) built to supply electricity to Memphis, Tennessee. After two years of controversy and discovery that the government consultant would financially benefit from Dixon-Yates, the administration turned to a municipally owned power plant. The Idaho Power Company won the right to build three small dams on the Snake River rather than the federal government establishing a single large dam at Hell's Canyon. The Atomic Energy Act of 1954 allowed the construction of private nuclear power plants under Atomic Energy Commission license and oversight.

Farm Policy

The Rural Electrification Administration announced in 1960 that 97 percent of American farms had electricity. In 1954 the government began financing the export of farm surpluses in exchange for foreign currencies and later provided surpluses free to needy nations, including milk to school children and to the poor in exchange for governmentally issued food stamps.

Public Works

In 1954 Eisenhower obtained congressional approval for joint Canadian-U.S. construction of the St. Lawrence Seaway, giving ocean-going vessels access to the Great Lakes. In 1956 Congress authorized construction of the Interstate Highway System, with the federal government covering 90 percent of the cost and the states 10 percent. The program further undermined the American railroad system.

Supreme Court

Eisenhower appointed Earl Warren, formerly governor of California, chief justice of the Supreme Court in 1953. That same year he appointed William J. Brennan associate justice. Although originally perceived as conservatives, both justices used the court as an agency of social and political change.

Election of 1956

The 1956 election once again pitted Eisenhower against Stevenson. The president won easily, carrying all but seven states.

Space and Technology

The launching of the Soviet space satellite Sputnik on October 4, 1957, created fear that America was falling behind technologically. Although the U.S. launched Explorer I on January 31, 1958, the concern continued. In 1958 Congress established the National Aeronautics and Space Administration (NASA) to coordinate research and development and passed the National Defense Education Act to provide grants and loans for education.

Sherman Adams Scandal

In 1958 the White House chief of staff, Sherman Adams, resigned after it was revealed that he had received a fur coat and an oriental rug in return for helping a Boston industrialist deal with the federal bureaucracy. This became known as the Sherman Adams Scandal.

Labor

The Landrum-Griffen Labor-Management Act of 1959 sought to control unfair union practices by establishing rules such as penalties for misuse of funds.

New States

On January 3, 1959, Alaska became the forty-ninth state and on August 21, 1959, Hawaii became the fiftieth.

Civil Rights

Initial Eisenhower Actions

Eisenhower completed the formal integration of the armed forces, desegregated public services in Washington, D.C., naval yards, and veteran's hospitals, and appointed a Civil Rights Commission.

Legal Background to *Brown*

In *Ada Lois Sipuel v. Board of Regents* (1948) and *Sweatt v. Painter* (1950) the Supreme Court ruled that African Americans must be allowed to attend integrated law schools in Oklahoma and Texas.

Brown v. Board of Education of Topeka

In *Brown v. Board of Education of Topeka*, a 1954 case, NAACP lawyer Thurgood Marshall challenged the doctrine of "separate but equal" (*Plessy v. Ferguson*, 1896). The Court declared that separate educational facilities were inherently unequal. In 1955 the Court ordered states to integrate "with all deliberate speed."

Southern Reaction

Although at first the South reacted cautiously, by 1955 there were calls for "massive resistance" and White Citizens Councils emerged to spearhead the resistance. State legislatures used a number of tactics to get around Brown. By the end of 1956 desegregation of the schools had advanced very little.

Little Rock

Although he did not personally support the Supreme Court decision, Eisenhower sent 10,000 National Guardsmen and 1,000 paratroopers to Little Rock, Arkansas, to control mobs and enable blacks to enroll at Central High in September 1957. A small force of soldiers was stationed at the school throughout the year.

Emergence of Non-Violence

On December 1, 1955, in Montgomery, Alabama, Rosa Parks, a black woman, refused to give up her seat on a city bus to a white passenger and was arrested. Under the leadership of Martin Luther King Jr., a black pastor, blacks of Montgomery organized a bus boycott that lasted for a year, until in December 1956 the Supreme Court refused to review a lower court ruling that stated that separate but equal was no longer legal.

Civil Rights Acts

Eisenhower proposed the Civil Rights Act of 1957, that established a permanent Civil Rights Commission and a Civil Rights Division of the Justice Department which was empowered to prevent interference with the right to vote. The Civil Rights Act of 1960 gave the federal courts power to register African American voters.

Ending "Massive Resistance"

In 1959 state and federal courts nullified Virginia laws which prevented state funds from going to integrated schools. This proved to be the beginning of the end for "massive resistance."

Sit-Ins

In February 1960 four black students who had been denied service staged a sit-in at a segregated Woolworth lunch counter in Greensboro, North Carolina. This inspired sit-ins elsewhere in the South and led to the formation of the Student Nonviolent Coordinating Committee (SNCC). SNCC's primary aims included the end of segregation in public accommodations and winning voting rights.

The Election of 1960

The Nominations

Vice President Richard M. Nixon won the Republican presidential nomination while the Democrats nominated Senator John F. Kennedy for the presidency with Lyndon B. Johnson, majority leader of the Senate, as his running mate.

Catholicism

Kennedy's Catholicism was a major issue until, on September 12, he told a gathering of Protestant ministers that he accepted the separation of church and state and that he would not allow Catholic leaders to tell him how to act as president.

Debates

A series of televised debates between Kennedy and Nixon helped create a positive image for Kennedy and may have been a turning point in the election.

Kennedy's Victory

Kennedy won the election by slightly over 100,000 popular votes and 94 electoral votes, based on majorities in New England, the Middle Atlantic, and the South.

Society and Culture

Gross National Product

The GNP almost doubled between 1945 and 1960, growing at an annual rate of 3.2 percent from 1950 to 1960. Inflation meanwhile remained under 2 percent annually throughout the 1950s. Defense spending was the most important stimulant, and military-related research helped create or expand the new industries of chemicals, electronics, and aviation. The U.S. had a virtual monopoly over international trade, because of the devastation of the World War. Technological innovations contributed to productivity, which jumped 35 percent between 1945 and 1955. After depression and war, Americans had a great desire to consume. Between 1945 and 1960 the American population grew by nearly 30 percent, which contributed greatly to consumer demand.

Consumption Patterns

Home ownership grew by 50 percent between 1945 and 1960. These new homes required such appliances as refrigerators and washing machines, but the most popular product was television, which increased from 7,000 sets in 1946 to 50 million sets in 1960. *TV Guide* became the fastest-growing magazine and advertising found the TV medium especially powerful. Consumer credit increased 800 percent between 1945 and 1957 while the rate of savings dropped to about

DIDYOU**KNOW?**

Elvis Presley is the highest-selling music artist of all time. During his career, Presley released 40 top ten songs and starred in over 30 movies, including 1957's *Jailhouse Rock* (www.elvis.com).

5 percent of income. The number of shopping centers rose from 8 in 1945 to 3,840 in 1960. Teenagers became an increasingly important consumer group, making—among other things—a major industry of rock 'n' roll music, with Elvis Presley as its first star, by the mid-1950s.

Demographic Trends

Population Growth

In the 1950s population grew by over 28 million, 97 percent of which was in urban and suburban areas. The average life expectancy increased from 66 in 1955 to 71 in 1970. Dr. Benjamin Spock's *The Commonsense Book of Baby and Child Care* sold an average of 1 million copies a year between 1946 and 1960.

The Sun Belt

Aided by use of air conditioning, Florida, the Southwest, and California grew rapidly, with California becoming the most populous state by 1963. The Northeast, however, remained the most densely populated area.

Suburbs

The suburbs grew six times faster than the cities in the 1950s. William Levitt pioneered the mass-produced housing development when he built 10,600 houses (Levittown) on Long Island in 1947, a pattern followed

DIDYOU**KNOW?**

In 1950, the average U.S. home was 983 square feet and was valued at $7,354 (U.S. Census Bureau).

widely elsewhere in the country. The Federal Housing Administration helped builders by insuring up to 95 percent of a loan and buyers by insuring their mortgages. Thanks in part to the development of the interstate highway system during the Eisenhower administration, auto production increased from 2 million in 1946 to 8 million in 1955, which further encouraged the development of suburbia. As increasing numbers of African Americans moved into the Northern and Midwestern cities, whites moved to the suburbs, a process dubbed "white flight." About 20 percent of the population moved their residence each year.

Middle Class

The number of American families that were classified as middle class changed from 5.7 million in 1947 to more than 12 million by the early 1960s.

Jobs

The number of farm workers dropped from 9 million to 5.2 million between 1940 and 1960. By 1960 more Americans held white-collar than blue-collar jobs.

Conformity and Security

Corporate Employment

Employees tended to work for larger organizations. By 1960, 38 percent of the workforce was employed by organizations with over 500 employees. Such environments encouraged the managerial personality and corporate cooperation rather than individualism.

Homogeneity

Observers found the expansion of the middle class an explanation for emphasis on conformity. David Riesman argued in *The Lonely Crowd* (1950) that American were moving from an inner-directed to an outer-directed orientation. William Whyte's *The Organization Man* (1956) saw corporate culture as emphasizing the group rather than the individual. Sloan Wilson's *The Man in the Grey Flannel Suit* (1955) expressed similar concerns in fictional form.

Leisure

The standard work week shrank from six to five days. Television became the dominant cultural medium, with over 530 stations by 1961. Sales of books, especially paperbacks, increased annually.

Women

A cult of feminine domesticity re-emerged after World War II. Marynia Farnham and Ferdinand Lundberg published *Modern Woman: The Lost Sex* in 1947; Farnham suggested that science supported the idea that women could find fulfillment only in domesticity. Countless magazine articles also promoted the notion that a woman's place was in the home.

Religion

From 1940, when less than half the population belonged to a church, membership rose to more than 65 percent by 1960. Catholic Bishop Fulton J. Sheen had a popular weekly television show, "Life Worth Living," while Baptist evangelist Billy Graham held huge crusades. Norman Vincent Peale best represented the tendency of religion to emphasize reassurance with his best-seller *The Power of Positive Thinking* (1952). Critics noted the shallowness of this religion. Will Herberg in *Protestant-Catholic-Jew* (1955) said that popular religiosity lacked conviction and commitment. Reinhold Niebuhr, the leading neo-orthodox theologian, criticized the self-centeredness of popular religion and its failure to recognize the reality of sin.

Seeds of Rebellion

Intellectuals

Intellectuals became increasingly critical of American life. John Kenneth Galbraith in *The Affluent Society* (1958) argued that the public sector was underfunded. John Keats's *The Crack in the Picture Window* (1956) criticized the homogeneity of suburban life in the new mass-produced communities. The adequacy of American education was questioned by James B. Conant in *The American High School Today* (1959).

Theatre and Fiction

Arthur Miller's *Death of a Salesman* (1949) explored the theme of the loneliness of the other-directed person. Novels also took up the conflict between the individual and mass society. Notable works included J.D. Salinger's *The Catcher in the Rye* (1951), James Jones's *From Here to Eternity* (1951), Joseph Heller's *Catch-22* (1955), Saul Bellow's *The Adventures of Augie March* (1953), and John Updike's *Rabbit, Run* (1960).

Art

Painter Edward Hopper portrayed isolated, anonymous individuals. Jackson Pollock, Robert Motherwell, Willem de Kooning, Arshile Gorky, and Mark Rothko were among the leaders in abstract expressionism, in which they attempted spontaneous expression of their subjectivity.

The Beats

The Beats were a group of young men alienated by twentieth-century life. Their movement began in Greenwich Village, New York, with the friendship of Allen Ginsburg, Jack Kerouac, William Burroughs, and Neal Cassady. They emphasized alcohol, drugs, sex, jazz, Buddhism, and a restless vagabond life, all of which were vehicles for their subjectivity. Ginsberg's long poem *Howl* (1956) and Kerouac's novel *On the Road* (1957) were among the more important literary works to emerge from the Beat movement.

World War II and the Postwar Era (1941–1960)

Historical Timeline (1941–1960)

Year	Events
1941	Axis Powers declare war on the U.S. three days after Pearl Harbor
1942	Japan captures Philippine Islands as Bataan and Corregidor fall War Production Board established U.S. begins interning Japanese-American citizens Germany sinks 400 American ships Battle of Coral Sea Battle of Midway U.S. attacks Vichy forces and Germans in North Africa Manhattan Project begins
1943	Casablanca Conference Americans seize Guadalcanal Island Soviets defeat Germans at Stalingrad Allies invade Italy Teheran Conference
1944	Allies invade France at Normandy (D-Day) June 6 Battle of Leyte Gulf Roosevelt elected president for fourth term Island-hopping campaign retakes Guam Island Battle of the Bulge
1945	Yalta Conference U.S. bombing raids destroy 250,000 buildings in Tokyo 50 nations approve United Nations Charter in San Francisco Conference Hitler commits suicide in Berlin bunker V-E Day Americans recapture the Philippine Islands Potsdam Conference Bomb dropped on Hiroshima Soviets declare war on Japan Bomb dropped on Nagasaki V-J Day
1946	Churchill gives "Iron Curtain" speech George Kennan proposes containment policy
1947	Truman Doctrine aids nations resisting communism Marshall Plan provides economic aid to Europe House Un-American Activities Committee investigates Hollywood Jackie Robinson breaks color line in baseball Taft-Hartley Act slows growth of labor unions

World War II and the Postwar Era (1941–1960)

(*continued*)

Historical Timeline
(1941–1960)

Year	Events
1948	Soviets block access to West Berlin in Berlin Airlift Alger Hiss case begins Truman signs armed forces desegregation order Israel becomes a nation Truman defeats Dewey in presidential election
1949	NATO formed Soviet Union explodes atomic bomb Mao leads communist takeover in China
1950	Korean War begins U.S. troops invade North Korea Chinese troops enter war Rosenberg spy trial begins McCarthy begins anti-communist campaign U.S. begins hydrogen bomb program
1951	Gen. MacArthur relieved of command in Korea Peace negotiations begin in Panmunjon, Korea
1952	U.S. ends Japan occupation Eisenhower elected president
1953	Korean War ends with truce and demilitarized zone Stalin dies
1954	*Brown v. Topeka Board of Education* Army-McCarthy hearings French surrender at Dienbienphu in Vietnam Sen. McCarthy censured by Senate
1955	Martin Luther King Jr. begins Montgomery Bus Boycott
1956	Suez crisis Soviets crush Hungarian revolt
1957	Soviets launch Sputnik Eisenhower Doctrine commits economic aid to Middle East Little Rock school desegregation crisis
1959	Castro takes over in Cuba Soviet Premier Khrushchev visits U.S.

The New Frontier, Vietnam, and Social Upheaval (1960–1972)

Kennedy's "New Frontier" and the Liberal Revival

Legislative Failures

Kennedy was unable to get much of his program through Congress because of an alliance of Republicans and southern Democrats. He proposed plans for federal aid to education, urban renewal, medical care for the aged, reductions in personal and corporate income taxes, and the creation of a Department of Urban Affairs. None of these proposals passed.

Kennedy did, however, gain congressional approval for raising the minimum wage from $1.00 to $1.25 an hour and extending it to 3 million more workers.

Housing Act

The 1961 Housing Act provided nearly $5 billion over four years for the preservation of open urban spaces, development of mass transit, and the construction of middle-class housing.

Civil Rights

Freedom Riders

In May 1961, blacks and whites, sponsored by the Congress on Racial Equality, boarded buses in Washington, D.C., and traveled across the South to New Orleans to test federal enforcement of regulations prohibiting discrimination. They met violence in Alabama but continued to New Orleans. Others came into the South to test the segregation laws.

Justice Department

The Justice Department, under Attorney General Robert F. Kennedy (1925–1968), the president's brother, began to push for civil rights, including desegregation of interstate transportation in the South, integration of schools, and supervision of elections.

Mississippi

In the fall of 1962, President Kennedy called the Mississippi National Guard to federal duty to enable an African American, James Meredith, to enroll at the University of Mississippi.

Dr. Martin Luther King Jr. and Rev. Ralph Abernathy leave Birmingham, Alabama, prison April 19, 1963, after having been arrested eight days earlier, during a Good Friday pilgrimage to City Hall. AP/Wide World Photo.

March on Washington

Kennedy presented a comprehensive civil rights bill to Congress in 1963. It banned racial discrimination in public accommodations, gave the attorney general power to bring suits on behalf of individuals for school integration, and withheld federal funds from state-administered programs that practiced discrimination. While the bill was held up in Congress, 200,000 people marched on August 28, 1963, in Washington, D.C. During their demonstration, Martin Luther King Jr. gave his seminal "I Have a Dream" speech.

The Cold War Continues

Bay of Pigs

Under Eisenhower, the Central Intelligence Agency had begun training some 2,000 men for an invasion of Cuba to overthrow Fidel Castro, the left-leaning revolutionary who had taken power in 1959. On April 19, 1961, this force invaded at the Bay of Pigs, but was pinned down and forced to surrender. Some 1,200 men were captured.

Berlin Wall

After a confrontation between Kennedy and Khrushchev in Berlin, Kennedy called up reserve and National Guard units and asked for an increase in defense funds. In August 1961, Khrushchev responded by closing the border between East and West Berlin and ordering the erection of the Berlin Wall.

Nuclear Testing

The Soviet Union began the testing of nuclear weapons in September 1961. Kennedy then authorized resumption of underground testing by the United States.

Cuban Missile Crisis

On October 14, 1962, a U-2 reconnaissance plane brought photographic evidence that missile sites were being built in Cuba. Kennedy, on October 22, announced a blockade of Cuba and called on Khrushchev to dismantle the missile bases and remove from Cuba all weapons capable of attacking the United States. Six days later, Khrushchev backed down, withdrew the missiles, and Kennedy lifted the blockade. The United States promised not to invade Cuba, and removed missiles from bases in Turkey, claiming they had planned to do so anyway.

Afterwards, a "hot line" telephone connection was established between the White House and the Kremlin to effect quick communication in threatening situations.

Nuclear Test Ban

In July 1963, a treaty banning the atmospheric testing of nuclear weapons was signed by all the major powers except France and China.

Alliance for Progress

In 1961, Kennedy announced the Alliance for Progress, which would provide $20 million in aid to Latin America.

Peace Corps

The Peace Corps, established in 1961, sent young volunteers to third-world countries to contribute their skills in locally sponsored projects.

> **DIDYOUKNOW?**
>
> Since 1961, the Peace Corps has placed over 200,000 volunteers to work in 137 countries (www.peacecorps.gov).

Johnson and the Great Society

Kennedy Assassination

On November 22, 1963, Kennedy was assassinated by Lee Harvey Oswald in Dallas, Texas. Jack Ruby, a nightclub owner, killed Oswald two days later. Conspiracy theories emerged. Chief Justice Earl Warren led an investigation of the murder and concluded that Oswald had acted alone, but questions remain.

Lyndon Johnson

Succeeding Kennedy, Johnson had extensive experience in both the House and Senate, and as a Texan, was the first southerner to serve as president since Woodrow Wilson. He pushed hard for Kennedy's programs, which were languishing in Congress.

A tax cut of more than $10 billion passed Congress in 1964, and an economic boom resulted.

Civil Rights Act

The 1964 Civil Rights Act outlawed racial discrimination by employers and unions, created the Equal Employment Opportunity Commission to enforce the law, and eliminated the remaining restrictions on African-American voting.

Following President Kennedy's assassination, Lyndon Johnson takes the oath of office aboard Air Force One at Love Field, Dallas, Texas. Photo by Cecil Stoughton, New York World-Telegram and the Sun Newspaper Photograph Collection. U.S. Library of Congress.

Fulfilling JFK's pledge eight years earlier to send an American to the moon before the end of the decade, Apollo 11's Buzz Aldrin walks on the lunar surface July 20, 1969. Aldrin followed Neil Armstrong in setting foot on the moon. Photo by Neil Armstrong, NASA.

Election of 1964

Lyndon Johnson was nominated for president by the Democrats, with Senator Hubert H. Humphrey of Minnesota for vice-president. The Republicans nominated Senator Barry Goldwater, a conservative from Arizona. Johnson won more than 61 percent of the popular vote and could now launch his own "Great Society" program.

Health Care

The Medicare Act of 1965 combined hospital insurance for retired people with a voluntary plan to cover physician's bills. Medicaid provided grants to states to help the poor below retirement age.

Education

In 1965, the Elementary and Secondary Education Act provided $1.5 billion to school districts to improve the education of poor people. Head Start prepared educationally disadvantaged children for elementary school.

Immigration

The Immigration Act of 1965 discontinued the national origin system, basing immigration instead on such things as skills and the need for political asylum.

Cities

The 1965 Housing and Urban Development Act provided 240,000 housing units and $2.9 billion for urban renewal. The Department of Housing and Urban Affairs was established in 1966, and rent supplements for low-income families also became available.

Space

Fulfilling a goal established by Kennedy, Neil Armstrong and Edwin "Buzz" Aldrin became the first humans to walk on the moon, on July 20, 1969.

Emergence of Black Power

Voting Rights

In 1965, Martin Luther King Jr. announced a voter registration drive. With help from the federal courts, he dramatized his effort by leading a march from Selma to Montgomery, Alabama, between March 21 and 25. The Voting Rights Act of 1965 authorized the attorney general to appoint officials to register voters.

Racial Riots

Seventy percent of African-Americans lived in city ghettos across the country. It did not appear that the tactics used in the South would help them. Frustration built up. In August 1965, Watts, an area of Los Angeles, erupted in riot. More than 15,000 National Guardsmen were brought in; 34 people were killed, 850 wounded, and 3,100 arrested. Property damage reached nearly $200 million. In 1966, New York and Chicago experienced riots, and the following year there were riots in Newark and Detroit. The Kerner Commission, appointed to investigate the riots, concluded that they were directed at a social system that prevented African Americans from getting good jobs and crowded them into ghettos.

Black Power

Stokely Carmichael, chairman of SNCC, was by 1964 unwilling to work with white civil-rights activists. In 1966, he called for the civil rights movements to be "black-staffed, black-controlled, and black-financed." Later, he moved on to the Black Panthers, self-styled urban revolutionaries based in Oakland, California. Other leaders such as H. Rap Brown also called for Black Power.

DIDYOU**KNOW?**

Although the Black Panthers are widely remembered for their militant actions, the Panthers also initiated a number of community service programs. These programs included a free breakfast for schoolchildren, free medical clinics in black neighborhoods, and free afterschool classes teaching black history.

King Assassination

On April 4, 1968, Martin Luther King Jr. was assassinated in Memphis. James Earl Ray pleaded guilty and was convicted of the murder. Riots in more than 100 cities followed. Ray died in prison in 1998.

Civil rights march from Selma to Montgomery, Alabama, March 23, 1965. AP/Wide World Photo.

Black Officials

Despite the rising tide of violence, the number of African-Americans achieving elected and appointed office increased. Among the more prominent were Associate Justice of the Supreme Court Thurgood Marshall, Secretary of Housing and Urban Affairs Robert Weaver, and Senator Edward W. Brooke.

Ethnic Activism

United Farm Workers

Cesar Chavez founded the United Farm Workers' Organizing Committee to unionize Mexican-American farm laborers. He turned a grape pickers strike in Delano,

California, into a national campaign by attacking the structure of the migrant labor system through a boycott of grapes.

Native Americans

The American Indian Movement (AIM) was founded in 1968. At first it staged sit-ins to bring attention to Native American demands. By the early 1970s, it was turning to the courts.

The New Left

Demographic Origins

By the mid-1960s, the majority of Americans were under age 30. College enrollments increased fourfold between 1945 and 1970.

Students for a Democratic Society

Students for a Democratic Society was organized by Tom Hayden and Al Haber of the University of Michigan in 1960. Hayden's Port Huron Statement (1962) called for "participatory democracy." SDS drew much of its ideology from the writings of C. Wright Mills, Paul Goodman, and Herbert Marcuse.

Free-Speech Movement

Students at the University of California, Berkeley, staged sit-ins in 1964 to protest the prohibition of political canvassing on campus. Led by Mario Savio, the movement changed from emphasizing student rights to criticizing the bureaucracy of American society. In December, police broke up a sit-in; protests spread to other campuses around the nation.

Vietnam

Student protests began focusing on the Vietnam War. In the spring of 1967, 500,000 gathered in Central Park in New York City to protest the war, many burning their draft cards. SDS became more militant and willing to use violence. It turned to Lenin for its ideology.

1968

More than 200 large campus demonstrations took place in the spring, culminating in the occupation of buildings at Columbia University to protest the university's involvement in military research and its poor relations with minority groups. Police wielding clubs eventually broke up the demonstration. In August, thousands gathered in Chicago to protest the war during the Democratic convention. Although police violence against the demonstrators aroused anger, the antiwar movement began to split between those favoring violence and those opposed to it.

Decline

Beginning in 1968, SDS began breaking up into rival factions. After the more radical factions began using bombs, Tom Hayden left the group. By the early 1970s, the New Left had lost political influence, having abandoned its original commitment to democracy and nonviolence.

The Counterculture

Origins

Like the New Left, the founders of the counterculture were alienated by bureaucracy, materialism, and the Vietnam War, but they turned away from politics in favor of an alternative society. In many respects, they were heirs of the Beats.

Counterculture Expression

Many young people formed communes in such places as San Francisco's Haight-Ashbury district or in rural areas. "Hippies," as they were called, experimented with Eastern religions, drugs, and sex, but most were unable to establish a self-sustaining lifestyle. Leading spokesmen included Timothy Leary, Theodore Roszak, and Charles Reich.

DIDYOUKNOW?

In 1969, over 500,000 young people gathered in upstate New York, to attend what became one of the most famous music festivals of all time—Woodstock. Performers included Jimi Hendrix, Janis Joplin, the Who, and Jefferson Airplane (www.woodstock.com).

Women's Liberation

Betty Friedan

In *The Feminine Mystique* (1963), Betty Friedan argued that middle-class society stifled women and did not allow them to use their individual talents. She attacked the cult of domesticity.

National Organization for Women

Friedan and other feminists founded the National Organization for Women (NOW) in 1966, calling for equal employment opportunities and equal pay.

DIDYOU**KNOW?**

The number of U.S. women in the civilian labor force climbed from 11,970,000 in 1940 to 25,952,000 in 1965 (U.S. Census Bureau).

Problems

The women's movement was largely limited to the middle class. The Equal Rights Amendment failed to pass. Abortion rights stirred up a counter "right-to-life" movement.

Vietnam

Background

After the French defeat in 1954, the United States sent military advisors to South Vietnam to aid the government of Ngo Dinh Diem. The pro-Communist Vietcong forces gradually grew in strength, partly because Diem failed to follow through on promised reforms. They received support from North Vietnam, the Soviet Union, and China. The U.S. government supported a successful military coup against Diem in the fall of 1963.

Escalation

In August 1964—after claiming that North Vietnamese gunboats had fired on American destroyers in the Gulf of Tonkin—Lyndon Johnson pushed the Gulf of Tonkin resolution through Congress, authorizing him to use military force in Vietnam. After a February 1965 attack by the Vietcong on Pleiku, Johnson ordered operation "Rolling

Thunder," the first sustained bombing of North Vietnam. Johnson then sent combat troops to South Vietnam; under the leadership of General William C. Westmoreland, they conducted search and destroy operations. The number of troops increased to 184,000 in 1965, 385,000 in 1966, 485,000 in 1967, and 538,000 in 1968.

Defense of American Policy

"Hawks" defended the president's policy and, drawing on containment theory, said that the nation had the responsibility to resist aggression. Secretary of State Dean Rusk became a major spokesman for the domino theory, which justified government policy by analogy with England's and France's failure to stop Hitler prior to 1939. If Vietnam should fall, it was said, all Southeast Asia would eventually go. The administration stressed its willingness to negotiate the withdrawal of all "foreign" forces from the war.

Tet Offensive

On January 31, 1968, the first day of the Vietnamese new year (Tet), the Vietcong attacked numerous cities and towns, American bases, and even Saigon. Although they suffered large losses, the Vietcong won a psychological victory, as American opinion began turning against the war.

TEST TIP

Remember that you need to sign up for the AP Exam at least several weeks before the test date, so be sure to talk to your AP teacher or your school's AP coordinator about taking the exam well before the scheduled exam time. If you are homeschooled or if your school does not offer AP programs, you can still take the exam. However, you will need to contact AP Services directly to learn how to register. Usually, you need to do this by the beginning of March to take the exam in mid-May.

Election of 1968

Eugene McCarthy

In November 1967, Senator Eugene McCarthy of Minnesota announced his candidacy for the 1968 Democratic presidential nomination, running on the issue of opposition to the war.

New Hampshire

In February, McCarthy won 42 percent of the Democratic vote in the New Hampshire primary, compared with Johnson's 48 percent. Robert F. Kennedy then announced his candidacy for the Democratic presidential nomination.

Johnson's Withdrawal

Lyndon Johnson withdrew his candidacy on March 31, 1968, and Vice-President Hubert H. Humphrey took his place as a candidate for the Democratic nomination.

Kennedy Assassination

After winning the California primary over McCarthy, Robert Kennedy was assassinated by Sirhan Sirhan, a young Palestinian. This event assured Humphrey's nomination.

The Nominees

The Republicans nominated Richard M. Nixon, who chose Spiro T. Agnew, governor of Maryland, as his running mate in order to appeal to southern voters. Governor George C. Wallace of Alabama ran for the presidency under the banner of the American Independent party, appealing to fears generated by left-wing protestors and big government.

Nixon's Victory

Johnson suspended air attacks on North Vietnam shortly before the election. Nonetheless, Nixon, who emphasized stability and order, defeated Humphrey by a margin of 1 percent. Wallace's 13.5 percent was the best showing by a third-party candidate since 1924.

DIDYOU**KNOW?**

Nixon's 1968 campaign strove to appeal to conservative white voters in the South who were unhappy with the recent changes wrought by the civil rights movement and Johnson's Great Society. This "Southern strategy" helped change the South from a reliably Democratic region to firmly Republican stronghold, reshaping U.S. politics for decades to come.

The Nixon Conservative Reaction

Civil Rights

The Nixon administration sought to block renewal of the Voting Rights Act and delay implementation of court-ordered school desegregation in Mississippi. After the Supreme Court ordered busing of students in 1971 to achieve school desegregation, the administration proposed an antibusing bill, which was blocked in Congress.

Supreme Court

In 1969, Nixon appointed Warren E. Burger, a conservative, as chief justice, but ran into opposition with the nomination of southerners Clement F. Haynesworth, Jr., and G. Harrold Carswell. After these nominations were defeated, he nominated Harry A. Blackmun, who received Senate approval. He later appointed Lewis F. Powell Jr. and William Rehnquist as associate justices. Although more conservative than the Warren court, the Burger court did declare the death penalty, as used at the time, unconstitutional in 1972, and struck down state anti-abortion legislation in 1973.

Revenue Sharing

The heart of Nixon's "New Federalism," passed by Congress in 1972, was a five-year plan to distribute $30 billion of federal revenues to the states.

Congressional Legislation

Congress passed bills giving 18-year-olds the right to vote (1970), increasing Social Security benefits and funding for food stamps (1970), as well as establishing the Occupational Safety and Health Act (1970), the Clean Air Act (1970), laws to control water pollution (1970, 1972), and the Federal Election Campaign Act (1972). None was supported by the Nixon administration.

Economic Problems and Policy

Unemployment climbed to 6 percent in 1970, real gross national product declined in 1970, and in 1971 the United States experienced a trade deficit. Inflation reached

12 percent by 1974. These problems resulted from federal deficits in the 1960s, growing international competition, and rising energy costs.

In 1969, Nixon cut spending and raised taxes. He encouraged the Federal Reserve Board to raise interest rates. The economy worsened. In 1970, Congress gave the president the power to regulate prices and wages. Nixon used this power in August 1971 by declaring a 90-day price and wage freeze and taking the United States off the gold standard. At the end of the 90 days he established mandatory guidelines for wage and price increases. Finally, in 1973, he turned to voluntary wage and price controls, except on health care, food, and construction. When inflation increased rapidly, Nixon cut back on government expenditures, impounding funds already appropriated by Congress.

Vietnamization

Nixon proposed that all non-South Vietnamese troops be withdrawn in phases, and that an internationally supervised election be held in South Vietnam. The North Vietnamese rejected this plan.

The president then turned to "Vietnamization," the effort to build up South Vietnamese forces while withdrawing American troops. In 1969, Nixon reduced American troop strength by 60,000, but at the same time ordered the bombing of Cambodia, a neutral country, in the interests of flushing out Vietcong.

Protests

Two Moratorium Days in 1969 brought out several hundred thousand protesters, and reports of an American massacre of Vietnamese at My Lai reignited controversy over the nature of the war, but Nixon continued to defend his policy. Troop withdrawals continued, and a lottery system was instituted in 1970 to make the draft more equitable. In 1973, Nixon abolished the draft and established an all-volunteer army.

Cambodia

In April 1970, Nixon announced that Vietnamization was succeeding and that another 150,000 American troops would be out of Vietnam by the end of the year. A few days later, he sent troops into Cambodia to clear out Vietcong sanctuaries and resumed bombing of North Vietnam.

Kent State

Protests against escalation of the war were especially strong on college campuses. During a May 1970 demonstration at Kent State University in Ohio, National Guardsmen opened fire on protestors, killing four students. Soon after, two black students were killed by a Mississippi state policeman at Jackson State University. Several hundred colleges were soon closed down by student strikes, as moderates joined the radicals. Congress repealed the Gulf of Tonkin Resolution.

TEST TIP

Don't worry about including everything you ever learned about a particular topic in your essays. Scorers look for a strong thesis supported by a clear, logical argument and relevant evidence, not a laundry list of names, dates, and facts.

Pentagon Papers

The publication in 1971 of "the Pentagon Papers," classified Defense Department documents that were leaked to the press, revealed that the government had misled the Congress and the American people about its intentions in Vietnam during the mid-1960s.

End of U.S. Involvement

In the summer of 1972, negotiations between the United States and North Vietnam began in Paris. By October, a draft agreement was developed which included provisions for a cease-fire, the return of American prisoners of war, and the withdrawal of U.S. forces from Vietnam. A few days before the 1972 presidential election, Henry Kissinger, the president's national security advisor, declared that "peace was at hand."

Resumption of Bombing

Nixon resumed bombing of North Vietnam in December 1972, claiming that the North Vietnamese were not bargaining in good faith. In January 1973, the opponents reached a settlement in which the North Vietnamese retained control over large areas of the South and agreed to release American prisoners of war within 60 days. After the prisoners were released, the United States would withdraw its remaining troops. On

March 29, 1973, the last American combat troops left South Vietnam. Nearly 60,000 Americans had been killed and 300,000 more wounded; the war's financial cost to the United States was $109 billion.

War Powers Act

Later in 1973, the War Powers Act was passed. It required congressional approval of any commitment of combat troops beyond 90 days.

Foreign Policy

China

With his national security advisor, Henry Kissinger, Nixon took some bold diplomatic initiatives. Kissinger traveled to China and the Soviet Union for secret sessions to plan summit meetings with the Communists. In February 1972, Nixon and Kissinger went to China to meet with Mao Tse-tung and his associates. The United States agreed to support China's admission to the United Nations and to pursue economic and cultural exchanges.

Soviet Union

At a May 1972 meeting with the Soviets, the Strategic Arms Limitation Treaty (SALT) was signed. The signatories agreed to stop making nuclear ballistic missiles and to reduce the number of anti-ballistic missiles to 200 for each power.

DIDYOU**KNOW?**

Richard Nixon was the first U.S. president to attempt to normalize relations with communist countries such as the Soviet Union and China. This policy is known as *détente*.

Middle East

Following the Arab-Israeli war of 1973, Arab states staged an oil boycott to push the Western nations into forcing Israel to withdraw from lands controlled since the Six-Day War of 1967. Kissinger, now secretary of state, negotiated the withdrawal of Israel from some of the lands and the Arabs lifted their boycott. The five-member Organization of Petroleum Exporting Countries (OPEC)—composed of Venezuela, Saudi Arabia, Kuwait, Iraq, and Iran—then raised the price of oil from about $3.00 to $11.65 a barrel. U.S. gas prices doubled and inflation shot above 10 percent.

Election of 1972

George McGovern

The Democrats nominated Senator George McGovern of South Dakota for president and Senator Thomas Eagleton for vice president. After the press revealed that Eagleton had been treated for psychological problems, McGovern eventually forced him off the ticket, replacing him with Sargent Shriver.

George Wallace

George Wallace, a longtime segregationist, ran once again as the American Independent party candidate. While campaigning at a Maryland shopping center on May 15, 1972, he became the victim of an assassination attempt that left him paralyzed below the waist. Arthur Bremer, 21, was sentenced to 63 years for shooting Wallace and three others.

Richard M. Nixon

Richard M. Nixon and Spiro T. Agnew, who had been renominated by the Republicans, won a landslide victory, receiving 521 electoral votes to McGovern's 17.

(Before taking the quiz noted below, please review the summary
timeline for this chapter on the following pages.)

Time for a quiz
- Review strategies in Chapter 2
- Take Quiz 7 at the REA Study Center
  (www.rea.com/studycenter)

The New Frontier, Vietnam, and Social Upheaval (1960–1972)

Historical Timeline (1960–1972)

1960	Kennedy and Nixon participate in first televised presidential debates Greensboro sit-in protests Kennedy defeats Nixon
1961	Bay of Pigs invasion fails Freedom rides Berlin Wall built Peace Corps established Alliance for Progress established
1962	Cuban Missile Crisis Students for a Democratic Society formed
1963	Rev. King begins Birmingham desegregation efforts University of Alabama admits first black student Civil Rights March on Washington Premier Diem of South Vietnam toppled by U.S.-approved coup President Kennedy assassinated
1964	President Johnson announces war on poverty Freedom summer vote registration campaign in Mississippi Civil Rights Act passed VISTA established Berkeley Free Speech Movement Gulf of Tonkin Resolution passed U.S. begins bombing of North Vietnam Johnson elected president
1965	Medicare funding begins Race riots in Watts Malcolm X assassinated American combat troops sent to Vietnam
1966	National Organization for Women (NOW) formed Stokely Carmichael leads black power movement
1967	Race riots in Detroit and Newark Massive antiwar protest in Washington, D.C. Israel, Arab neighbors fight Six-Day War

The Roaring Twenties and Economic Collapse (1920–1929)

(continued)

Historical Timeline (1920–1929)

Year	Events
1968	Viet Cong launch Tet Offensive Johnson withdraws from presidential race Dr. Martin Luther King Jr. assassinated Robert Kennedy assassinated Protests at Chicago Democratic Convention Nixon elected president
1969	Woodstock festival Apollo 11 crew lands on moon Stonewall Riots launch gay liberation movement
1970	U.S. invades Cambodia Kent State Massacre
1972	Nixon visits People's Republic of China Détente begins with Soviet Union SALT I Treaty signed with Soviet Union

Watergate, Conservatism's Rise, and Post–Cold War Challenges (1972–2008)

The Watergate Scandal

The Break-In

What became known as the Watergate crisis began during the 1972 presidential campaign. Early on the morning of June 17, James McCord, a security officer for the Committee for the Re-election of the President, and four other men broke into Democratic headquarters at the Watergate apartment complex in Washington, D.C., and were caught while going through files and installing electronic eavesdropping devices. On June 22, Nixon announced that the administration was in no way involved in the burglary attempt.

James McCord

The trial of the burglars began in early 1973, with all but McCord (who was convicted) pleading guilty. Before sentencing, McCord wrote a letter to U.S. District Court Judge John J. Sirica arguing that high Republican officials had known in advance about the burglary and that perjury had been committed at the trial.

Further Revelations

Soon Jeb Stuart Magruder, head of the Nixon re-election committee, and John W. Dean, Nixon's attorney, revealed that they had been involved. Dean testified before a Senate Watergate committee that Nixon had been involved in covering up the incident.

Over the next several months, extensive involvement of the White House administration, including payment of "hush" money to the burglars, destruction of FBI records, forgery of documents, and wiretapping, was revealed. Dean was fired and H. R. Haldeman and John Ehrlichman,

who headed the White House staff, and Attorney General Richard Kleindienst, resigned. Nixon claimed that he had not personally been involved in the cover-up but refused, on the grounds of executive privilege, to allow investigation of White House documents.

White House Tapes

Under considerable pressure, Nixon agreed to the appointment of a special prosecutor, Archibald Cox of Harvard Law School. When Cox obtained a subpoena for tape recordings of White House conversations (whose existence had been revealed in testimony during the Senate hearings)—and the administration lost an appeal in the appellate court—Nixon ordered Elliot Richardson, the attorney general, to fire Cox. Both Richardson and his subordinate, William Ruckelshaus, resigned, leaving Robert Bork, the solicitor general, to carry out the order. This "Saturday Night Massacre," which took place on October 20, 1973, caused a storm of controversy. The House Judiciary Committee, headed by Peter Rodino of New Jersey, began looking into the possibility of impeachment. Nixon agreed to turn the tapes over to Judge Sirica and named Leon Jaworski as the new special prosecutor. But it soon became known that some of the tapes were missing and that a portion of another had been erased.

The Vice-Presidency

Vice-President Spiro Agnew was accused of income tax fraud and having accepted bribes while a local official in Maryland. He resigned the vice-presidency in October 1973 and was replaced by Congressman Gerald R. Ford of Michigan under provisions of the new 25th Amendment.

Nixon's Taxes

Nixon was accused of paying almost no income taxes between 1969 and 1972, and of using public funds for improvements to his private residences in California and Florida. The IRS reviewed the president's tax return and assessed him nearly $500,000 in back taxes and interest.

Indictments

In March 1974 a grand jury indicted Haldeman, Ehrlichman, former Attorney General John Mitchell, and four other White House aides, and named Nixon as an unindicted coconspirator.

Calls for Resignation

In April, Nixon released edited transcripts of the White House tapes, the contents of which led to further calls for his resignation. Jaworski subpoenaed 64 additional tapes, which Nixon refused to turn over, and the case went to the Supreme Court.

President Nixon departing from the White House following his resignation on Aug. 9, 1974.
Richard Nixon Presidential Materials Project.

Impeachment Debate

Meanwhile, the House Judiciary Committee televised its debate over impeachment, adopting three articles of impeachment. It charged the president with obstructing justice, misusing presidential power, and failing to obey the committee's subpoenas.

Resignation

Before the House began to debate impeachment, the Supreme Court ordered the president to release the subpoenaed tapes to the special prosecutor. On August 5, Nixon, under pressure from his advisors, made public the tape of June 23, 1972. This tape, recorded less than a week after the break-in, revealed that Nixon had used the CIA to keep the FBI from investigating the case. Nixon announced his resignation on August 8, 1974, to take effect at noon the following day. Gerald Ford then became president.

Legislative Response

Congress responded to the Vietnam War and Watergate by enacting legislation intended to prevent such situations. In 1974 Congress limited the amounts of contributions and expenditures in presidential campaigns. It also strengthened the 1966 Freedom of Information Act by requiring the government to act promptly when asked for information and to prove its case for classification when attempting to withhold information on grounds of national security.

The Ford Presidency

Gerald Ford

Gerald Ford was in many respects the opposite of Nixon. Although a partisan Republican, he was well liked and free from any hint of scandal. Ford almost immediately encountered controversy when, in September 1974, he offered to pardon Nixon. Nixon accepted the offer, although he admitted no wrongdoing and had not yet been charged with a crime.

The Economy

Ford also faced major economic problems, which he approached somewhat inconsistently. Saying that inflation was the major problem, he called for voluntary restraints and asked citizens to wear "Whip Inflation Now," or WIN, buttons. The economy went into decline. Ford asked for tax cuts to stimulate business and argued against spending for social programs.

When New York City teetered on the verge of bankruptcy in 1975, Ford at first opposed federal aid but changed his mind when the Senate and House Banking Committees guaranteed the loans.

Vietnam

As North Vietnamese forces pushed back the South Vietnamese, Ford asked Congress to provide more arms for the South. Congress rejected the request, and in April 1975 Saigon fell to the North Vietnamese.

Election of 1976

Ronald Reagan, formerly a movie actor and governor of California, opposed Ford for the Republican nomination, but Ford won by a slim margin. The Democrats nominated James Earl Carter, formerly governor of Georgia, who ran on the basis of his integrity and lack of Washington connections. Carter, with Senator Walter Mondale of Minnesota as his vice-presidential candidate, narrowly defeated Ford.

TEST TIP

Multiple-choice questions on the AP U.S. History Exam do not typically appear in chronological order. Don't be surprised if the first question asks you about the 1970s, and the second question about the 1870s!

Carter's Moderate Liberalism

Policy Orientation in the Carter Administration

Carter sought to conduct the presidency on democratic and moral principles. The former peanut farmer, however, often misread political sentiment on Capitol Hill: the administration typically proposed complex programs but failed to support them through the legislative process.

The Economy

Carter approached economic problems inconsistently. In 1978, he proposed voluntary wage and price guidelines. Although somewhat successful, the guidelines did not apply to oil, housing, and food. Carter then named Paul A. Volcker as chairman of the Federal Reserve Board. Volcker tightened the money supply in order to reduce inflation, but this action caused interest rates to go even higher. High interest rates depressed sales of automobiles and houses, which in turn increased unemployment. By 1980, unemployment stood at 7.5 percent, interest at 20 percent, and inflation at 12 percent.

Domestic Achievements

Carter offered amnesty to Americans who had fled the draft and gone to other countries during the Vietnam War. He established the Departments of Energy and Education and placed the civil service on a merit basis. He created a "superfund" for cleanup of chemical waste dumps, established controls over strip mining, and protected 100 million acres of Alaskan wilderness from development.

Carter's Foreign Policy

Human Rights

Carter sought to base foreign policy on human rights, but was criticized for inconsistency and lack of attention to American interests.

Panama Canal

Carter negotiated a controversial treaty with Panama, affirmed by the Senate in 1978, that provided for the transfer of ownership of the canal to Panama in 1999 and guaranteed its neutrality.

China

Carter ended official recognition of Taiwan and in 1979 recognized the People's Republic of China. Conservatives called the decision a "sell-out."

next five years. In a straight party vote—Republicans voting against and Democrats voting in favor— Congress in December gave the power to decide whether new tax and spending proposals violated the deficit-cutting agreement to the Congressional Budget office. This power had been in the hands of the White House Office of Management and Budget.

Savings and Loan Debacle

With the savings and loan industry in financial trouble in February 1989, largely because of bad real-estate loans, Bush proposed to close or sell 350 institutions, to be paid for by the sale of government bonds. In July he signed a bill that created the Resolution Trust Corporation to oversee the closure and merging of savings and loans, and which provided $166 billion over 10 years to cover the bad debts. Estimates of the total cost of the debacle ran to upward of $300 billion.

Scandals in the Financial Markets

Charges of insider trading, stock manipulation, and falsification of records resulted in Drexel Burnham Lambert, a major securities firm, pleading guilty in December 1988 to six violations of federal law. The company filed for bankruptcy and Michael Milken, its "junk bond king" (junk bonds are bonds below an investment grade of BB or Bb, which because of their risk carry a two- to three-point interest advantage), pleaded guilty to conspiracy, among other charges, in 1990. Meanwhile, in July 1989, 46 futures traders at the Chicago Mercantile Exchange were charged with racketeering.

Economic Slowdown

The gross national product slowed from 4.4 percent in 1988 to 2.9 percent in 1989. Unemployment gradually began to increase, reaching 6.8 percent in March 1991, a three-year high. Every sector of the economy except for medical services and all geographical areas experienced the slowdown. The "Big Three" automakers posted record losses and Pan American World Airways and Eastern Airlines entered bankruptcy proceedings. In September 1991, the Federal Reserve lowered the interest rate.

Other Domestic Issues Under Bush

Exxon Valdez Accident

After the *Exxon Valdez* spilled more than 240,000 barrels of oil into Alaska's Prince William Sound in March 1989, the federal government ordered Exxon Corporation to develop a clean-up plan, which it carried out until the weather prevented it from continuing in September. The *Valdez* captain, Joseph Hazelwood, was found guilty of negligence the following year. Exxon, the state of Alaska, and the U.S. Justice Department reached a settlement in October 1991 requiring Exxon to pay $1.025 billion in fines and restitution through 2001.

> **DID**YOU**KNOW?**
>
> The 2010 BP oil spill in the Gulf of Mexico released an estimated 172 million gallons of oil into the Gulf. That's nearly 16 times the 10.8 million gallons spilled in the *Exxon Valdez* accident (www.nwf.org).

Congressional Ethics Violations

After the House Ethics Committee released a report charging that Speaker Jim Wright had violated rules regulating acceptance of gifts and outside income, Wright resigned in May 1989. A short time later, the Democratic whip Tony Coelho resigned because of alleged improper use of campaign funds.

Pollution

The Clean Air Act, passed in October 1990 and updating the 1970 law, mandated that the level of emissions was to be reduced 50 percent by the year 2000. Cleaner gasolines were to be developed, cities were to reduce ozone (an ingredient in photo-chemical smog), and nitrogen oxide emissions were to be cut by one-third.

Civil Rights

The Americans with Disabilities Act, passed in July 1990, barred discrimination against people with physical or mental disabilities. In October 1990, Bush vetoed the Civil Rights Act on the grounds that it established quotas, but a year later he accepted a slightly revised version that, among other things, required that employers in discrimination suits prove that their hiring practices are not discriminatory.

Supreme Court Appointments

Bush continued to reshape the Supreme Court in a conservative direction when, upon the retirement of Justice William J. Brennan, he successfully nominated Judge David Souter of the U.S. Court of Appeals in 1989. Two years later, Bush nominated a conservative African American, Judge Clarence Thomas, also of the U.S. Court of Appeals, upon the retirement of Justice Thurgood Marshall. Thomas's nomination stirred up opposition from the NAACP and other liberal groups, which supported affirmative action and abortion rights. Dramatic charges of sexual harassment against Thomas from Anita Hill, a University of Oklahoma law professor, were revealed only days before the nomination was to go to the Senate. The charges provoked a reopening of Judiciary Committee hearings, which were nationally televised. Nonetheless, Thomas narrowly won confirmation in October 1991.

Bush's Activist Foreign Policy

Panama

Since coming to office, the Bush administration had been concerned with Panamanian dictator Manuel Noriega because he allegedly provided an important link in the drug traffic between South America and the United States. After economic sanctions, diplomatic efforts, and an October 1989 coup failed to oust Noriega, Bush ordered 12,000 troops into Panama on December 20. The Americans installed a new government headed by Guillermo Endara, who had earlier apparently won a presidential election which was then nullified by Noriega. On January 3, 1990, Noriega surrendered to the Americans and was taken to the United States to stand trial on drug-trafficking charges, a trial that began in September 1991. Found guilty in 1992, he was sentenced to 40 years' imprisonment. Twenty-three United States soldiers and three American civilians were killed in the Panamanian operation. The Panamanians lost nearly 300 soldiers and more than 500 civilians.

China

After the death in April 1989 of reformer Hu Yaobang, formerly general secretary and chairman of the Chinese Communist party, students began pro-democracy marches in Beijing. By the middle of May, more than one million people were gathering in Beijing's Tiananmen Square and elsewhere in China, calling for political reform. Martial law was imposed and in early June the army fired on the demonstrators. Estimates of the death toll in the wake of the nationwide crackdown on demonstrators ranged between 500 and 7,000. In July 1989 U.S. National Security Advisor Brent Scowcroft and Deputy Secretary of State Lawrence Eagleburger secretly met with Chinese leaders. When they again met the Chinese in December and revealed their earlier meeting, the Bush administration faced a storm of criticism for its policy of "constructive engagement" from opponents arguing that sanctions were needed. Although establishing sanctions on China in 1991 on high-technology satellite-part exports, Bush continued to support renewal of China's Most Favored Nation trading status.

Collapse of East European Communism

Bush-Gorbachev Summits

Amid the collapse of communism in Eastern Europe, Bush met with Mikhail Gorbachev in Malta from December 1 through 3, 1989; the two leaders appeared to agree that the Cold War was over. On May 30 and 31, 1990, Bush and Gorbachev met in Washington to discuss the possible reunification of Germany, and signed a trade treaty between the United States and the Soviet Union. The meeting of the two leaders in Helsinki on September 9 addressed strategies for the developing Persian Gulf crisis. At the meeting of the "Group of 7" nations (Canada, France, Germany, Italy, Japan, the United Kingdom, and the United States) in July 1991, Gorbachev requested economic aid from the West. A short time later, on July 30 and 31, Bush met Gorbachev in Moscow, where they signed the Strategic Arms Reduction Treaty (START), which cut United States and Soviet nuclear arsenals by 30 percent, and pushed for Middle Eastern talks.

Persian Gulf Crisis

July 1990: Saddam Hussein of Iraq charged that Kuwait had conspired with the United States to keep oil prices low and began massing troops at the Iraq Kuwait border.

August 1990: On August 2 Iraq invaded Kuwait, an act that Bush denounced as "naked aggression." One day later, 100,000 Iraqi soldiers were poised south of Kuwait City, near the Saudi Arabian border. The United States quickly banned most trade with

Iraq, froze Iraq's and Kuwait's assets in the United States, and sent aircraft carriers to the Persian Gulf. After the U.N. Security Council condemned the invasion, Bush on August 6 ordered the deployment of air, sea, and land forces to Saudi Arabia, dubbing the operation "Desert Shield." At the end of August there were 100,000 American soldiers in Saudi Arabia.

September 1990: Bush encouraged Egypt to support American policy by forgiving Egypt its debt to the United States. He also obtained pledges of financial support from Saudi Arabia, Kuwait, and Japan, among other nations, to help pay for the operation.

October 1990: On October 29 the Security Council warned Hussein that further actions might be taken if he did not withdraw from Kuwait.

November 1990: In November, Bush ordered that U.S. forces be increased to more than 400,000. On November 29 the United Nations set January 15, 1991, as the deadline for Iraqi withdrawal from Kuwait.

January 1991: On January 9 Iraq's foreign minister, Tariq Aziz, rejected a letter written by Bush to Hussein. Three days later, after an extensive debate, Congress authorized the use of force in the gulf. On January 17 an international force that included the U.S., Great Britain, France, Italy, Saudi Arabia, and Kuwait launched an air and missile attack on Iraq and occupied Kuwait. The United States called the effort "Operation Desert Storm." Under the overall command of the army's General H. Norman Schwarzkopf, the military effort emphasized high-technology weapons, including F-15E fighter bombers, F-117A stealth fighters, Tomahawk cruise missiles, and Patriot antimissile missiles. Beginning on January 17, Iraq sent SCUD missiles into Israel in an effort to draw that country into the war and hopefully break up the U.S.-Arabian coalition. On January 22 and 23, Hussein's forces set Kuwaiti oil fields on fire and spilled oil into the gulf.

February 1991: On February 23 the allied ground assault began. Four days later, Bush announced that Kuwait was liberated and ordered offensive operations to cease. The United Nations established the terms for the cease-fire: Iraqi annexation of Kuwait to be rescinded, Iraq to accept liability for damages and return Kuwaiti property, Iraq to end all military actions and identify mines and booby traps, and Iraq to release captives.

April 1991: On April 3 the Security Council approved a resolution to establish a permanent cease-fire; Iraq accepted U.N. terms on April 6. The next day the United States began airlifting food to Kurdish refugees on the Iraq-Turkey border who were fleeing the Kurdish rebellion against Hussein, a rebellion that was seemingly encouraged by Bush, who nonetheless refused to become militarily involved. The United States estimated that 100,000 Iraqis had been killed during the war, while the Americans had lost about 115 lives.

TEST **TIP**

If you are having a hard time understanding a question, try circling or underlining key words and ideas from the question stem. Then focus on defining or restating those parts in your own words to help you figure out the purpose of the question overall.

Toward a Middle East Conference

On February 6, 1991, the United States had set out its postwar goals for the Middle East. These included regional arms control and security arrangements, international aid for reconstruction of Iraq and Kuwait, and resolution of the Israeli-Palestinian conflict. Immediately after cessation of the conflict, Secretary of State James Baker toured the Middle East attempting to promote a conference to address the problems of the region. After several more negotiating sessions, Saudi Arabia, Syria, Jordan, and Lebanon had accepted the United States proposal for an Arab-Israeli peace conference by the middle of July; Israel conditionally accepted in early August. Despite continuing conflict with Iraq, including U.N. inspections of its nuclear capabilities, and new Israeli settlements in disputed territory which kept the conference agreement tenuous, the nations met in Madrid, Spain, at the end of October. Bilateral talks in early November between Israel and the Arabs concentrated on procedural issues.

Breakup of the Soviet Union

Collapse of Soviet Communism and the End of the Cold War

The Soviet Union began to break up in 1990, when Lithuania declared its independence. In the aftermath of an attemped coup by hard-line Communists later that year, other Soviet republics followed suit. For the United States, the collapse of the U.S.S.R. meant that the Cold War, which had begun in 1945, was finally over. The United States was now the world's only superpower. In September 1991 President Bush announced that the U.S. would carry out the unilateral removal and destruction of ground-based tactical nuclear weapons in Europe and Asia, removal of nuclear-armed Tomahawk cruise missiles from surface ships and submarines, immediate destruction of intercontinental ballistic missiles covered by the START treaty, and an end to the 24-hour alert for strategic bombers which the United States had maintained for decades. Gorbachev responded the next month by announcing the immediate deactivation of intercontinental ballistic missiles covered by START, removal of all short-range missiles from Soviet ships, submarines, and aircraft, and destruction of all ground-based tactical nuclear weapons. He also said that the Soviet Union would reduce its forces by 700,000 troops, and he placed all long-range nuclear missiles under a single command.

New foreign policy challenges emerged, however. Yugoslavia broke up into several different nations, and the region was plunged into a brutal war. Conflict threatened other parts of the world as well. The disintegration of the Soviet Union meant more nations had nuclear weapons, as several of the former Soviet republics had access to them.

The Election of 1992

William Jefferson Clinton, governor of Arkansas, overcame several rivals and won the Democratic presidential nomination, choosing Senator Al Gore of Tennessee as his candidate for vice-president. Clinton and Reform Party candidate H. Ross Perot, emphasized jobs and the economy, as well as the debt. Bush stressed traditional values and his foreign policy accomplishments. In the general election Clinton won 43 percent of the popular vote and 370 electoral votes, thereby defeating George Bush, who received 38 percent of the vote, and independent candidate Ross Perot, who took 19 percent of the vote but no electoral votes.

The Clinton Presidency

Rocky Start Upon taking office, Clinton created a storm of protest when he proposed lifting the ban on homosexuals in the military. In July 1993 a compromise "Don't ask, don't tell" policy was struck, requiring gays and lesbians to be discreet about their sexual orientation and not to engage in homosexual acts. On the legislative front, Clinton was strongly rebuffed in a first-term attempt, led by First Lady Hillary Rodham Clinton, to comprehensively reform the nation's healthcare system. In the 1994 mid-term elections, in what Clinton himself considered a repudiation of his administration, the Republicans took both houses of Congress from the Democrats and voted in Newt Gingrich of Georgia as Speaker of the House. Gingrich had helped craft the Republican congressional campaign strategy to dramatically shrink the federal government and give more power to the states.

Clinton, however, was not without his successes, both on the legislative and diplomatic fronts. He signed a bill establishing a five-day waiting period for handgun purchases, and he signed an anti-crime bill emphasizing community policing. He signed the Family and Medical Leave Act, which required large companies to provide up to 12 weeks' unpaid leave to workers for family and medical emergencies. He also championed welfare reform (a central theme of his campaign), but made it clear that the legislation he signed into law in August 1996 radically overhauling FDR's welfare system disturbed him on two counts—its exclusion of legal immigrants from getting most federal benefits and its deep cut in federal outlays for food stamps; Clinton said these flaws could be repaired with further legislation. In foreign affairs, Clinton signed the North American Free Trade Agreement (NAFTA), which, as of January 1994, lifted most trade barriers with Mexico and Canada. Clinton sought to ease tensions between Israelis and Palestinians, and he helped bring together Itzhak Rabin, prime minister of Israel, and Yasir Arafat, chairman of the Palestine Liberation Organization, for a White House summit. Ultimately, the two Middle East leaders signed a 1994 accord establishing Palestinian self-rule in the Gaza Strip and Jericho. In October 1994 Israel and Jordan signed a treaty to begin the process of establishing full diplomatic relations. Rabin was assassinated a year later by a radical, right-wing Israeli. The Clinton administration also played a key role in hammering out a peace agreement in 1995 in war-torn former Yugoslavia—where armed conflict had broken out in 1991 between Serbs, Croats, Bosnian Muslims, and other factions and groups.

President Clinton plays the saxophone he received as a gift from a beaming Russian President Yeltsin at a dinner party in 1994. White House photo by Bob McNeely.

Controversy Swirls Around the President The president came to be dogged by a number of controversies, including his and his wife's role in a complex Arkansas real estate deal called Whitewater, the removal of employees from the White House travel office, the suicide of Deputy White House Coun-

sel Vince Foster, and a sexual harassment suit (later settled out of court) brought against the president by Paula Jones, a former Arkansas state employee. Whitewater spawned the Justice Department's appointment of an independent counsel, Robert B. Fiske, to look into it. Fiske's successor, Kenneth W. Starr, would expand the scope of the investigation. (Congress ultimately soured on the independent counsel law—enacted as a kind of coda to Watergate—and allowed it to expire in mid-1999.)

The Election of 1996

Clinton recaptured the Democratic nomination without a serious challenge, while longtime GOP Senator Robert Dole of Kansas, the Senate majority leader, had to overcome several opponents but orchestrated a harmonious nominating convention with running mate Jack Kemp, a former New York congressman and Cabinet member during the Bush administration. In November 1996, with most voters citing a healthy economy and the lack of an enticing alternative in Dole or the Reform Party's Perot, Clinton received 49 percent of the vote (47 million popular votes and 379 electoral votes), becoming the first Democrat to be returned to the White House since FDR, in 1936. Dole won 41 percent (39 million popular votes, 159 electoral votes) and Perot polled eight percent of the total (8 million popular votes). The GOP retained control of both houses of Congress.

The Election of 1998 In the congressional elections of 1998, the Democrats gained seats in both the House and the Senate. Seldom does the president's party gain seats in a mid-term election, so it was widely believed that this—in part—might have been backlash to the continued Republican-led prosecution of Clinton for alleged perjury and obstruction of justice.

Domestic Policy Clinton sought a legacy as a preservationist by signing executive orders that set aside vast expanses of public lands, especially in the West.

Foreign Policy During his second term, Clinton faced continued political unrest and civil war in the Balkans. In 1999 the Serbian government attacked ethnic Albanians in Kosovo, a province of Serbia. In response, NATO forces, led by the United States, bombed Serbia. Several weeks of bombing forced Serbian forces to withdraw from Kosovo. Meanwhile, Clinton was instrumental in bringing about a historic peace agreement in Northern Ireland, while the land-for-peace accord he tried to broker between the Palestinians and Israel proved elusive. Clinton also continued to seek a policy of expanding international trade by relaxing or eliminating trade barriers.

Campaign Finance Reform Fails to Pass Though the issue of the influence of money on politics was not new, increasingly high levels of campaign spending and the contributions necessary to make such spending possible began to receive significant attention. Several bills were proposed in Congress, and Clinton pledged to support reform; by the end of his presidency in January 2001, however, no bill had passed.

Historic Economic Boom Falters As of February 1, 2000, the U.S. economy had enjoyed its longest stretch of uninterrupted growth in the nation's history. Much of this growth, which had begun in March 1991, was fueled by a new industry, electronic commerce on the Internet. Stock prices generally rose, but share prices for Internet companies rose especially fast, soaring to extraordinary heights. In 2000, investors came to see e-businesses' and high-tech stock prices as unreasonably high. A number of such stocks tumbled, with some losing as much as 90 percent of their value. Soon many formerly high-flying Internet companies were folding and by the close of 2000 the future of the surviving e-businesses, as well as the economy as whole, was uncertain.

Impeachment and Acquittal In December 1998 Clinton was impeached by the House and in January and February 1999 he was tried and acquitted by the Senate on charges that he had lied about an adulterous affair with a White House intern. The affair had been uncovered by Starr.

The Elections of 2000 and 2004

The Democrats nominated Vice-President Al Gore for president and Senator Joseph Lieberman for vice president. The Republican Party nominated Texas Governor George W. Bush (son of President George H. W. Bush). After some conflict, the Reform party nominated Patrick Buchanan. The Green Party ran Ralph Nader. After one of the tightest presidential elections ever, highlighted by a withdrawn initial concession by Gore, a recount in Florida, and several court challenges, Bush was declared the winner.

The 2004 election returned Bush to the White House, but only with a slender majority of both the electoral and popular vote over his Democratic rival, U.S. Senator John Kerry.

DIDYOUKNOW?

Press coverage of the Florida recount during the 2000 presidential election often focused on so-called hanging chads—small pieces of not-quite-fully-punched-out paper on a voter's ballot. The phrase was so ubiquitous that Lake Superior State University added the word *chad* to its light-hearted 2001 Banished Words list.

American Society at the Dawn of the Twenty-First Century

Terrorism Hits Home Major symbols of U.S. economic and military might—the World Trade Center in New York and the Pentagon just outside Washington, D.C.—were attacked on September 11, 2001, when hijackers deliberately crashed commercial jetliners into the buildings, toppling the trade center's 110-story twin towers. Thousands died in the worst act of terrorism in American history. The prime suspect, said President Bush, was Saudi exile Osama bin Laden, the alleged mastermind of previous attacks on U.S. interests overseas. Terrorist attacks had continued to be a grim reality overseas through the 1980s and early 1990s, with Americans frequently targeted. Yet such incidents had come to be viewed as something the United States wouldn't have to face on its own soil—until February 26, 1993, when a terrorist bomb ripped through the underground parking garage of the World Trade Center in New York City, killing six people and injuring more than 1,000. Convicted and sentenced to 240 years each were four Islamic militants. On April 19, 1995, the Oklahoma City federal building was bombed, killing 168 people and injuring 500. Timothy James McVeigh, a member of the American militia movement who had expressed hatred toward the U.S. government and was aggrieved over its assault two years earlier on a self-proclaimed prophet's compound in Waco, Texas, was put to death for the crime in May 2001. A second defendant, Terry Nichols, was convicted on federal charges of conspiracy and involuntary manslaughter and sentenced to life in prison.

A Modern Plague Descends on America In 1981 scientists announced the discovery of Acquired Immune Deficiency Syndrome, or AIDS, which was especially prevalent among—but not confined to—homosexual males and intravenous drug users. Widespread fear resulted, with an upsurge in homophobia. The revelation that a Florida dentist, who died in 1990, had transmitted human immunodeficiency virus, or HIV, to six patients led to calls for mandatory testing of healthcare workers. There were calls as well for fast-tracking drug approvals. In 1998 the federal Centers for Disease Control and Prevention estimated that between 400,000 and 650,000 Americans were HIV-positive, meaning that they had the virus that causes AIDS.

President George W. Bush and First Lady Laura Bush observe a moment of silence for the victims of the Sept. 11, 2001, terror attacks. White House photo by Eric Draper.

Urban America Rebounds America's cities showed renewed promise at the dawn of the new century—though much remained to be done to attack a host of social and economic ills. *The Economist* reported in January 1998 that unemployment in the 50 biggest cities had fallen by a third over the prior four years, to about 6 percent. Rates for serious crime fell to their lowest in a generation. Cities such as New York—which two decades before had nearly gone bankrupt—and Los Angeles, victim of race riots and an earthquake during the early and mid-'90s, were "growing in both population and confidence." There were also comebacks like that of New Brunswick, N.J. Moribund in the 1970s, it forged a public–private partnership that resulted in more than $1 billion in investments over 25 years. In 1999 this city of 42,000 boasted a vibrant downtown (with small-business loans awarded to city-based businesses topping $1.2 million), a

Patriot Act: Controversial Response to 9/11 Attacks

Following the terror attacks on the World Trade Center and the Pentagon on September 11, 2001, both houses of Congress passed and President Bush signed the USA Patriot Act, which strengthened the authority of U.S. law enforcement agencies to fight terrorist acts both in the United States and in foreign nations.

The Patriot Act has come under criticism by some individuals and groups who believe that portions of it are unnecessary and infringe upon American freedoms, including speech, press, and the right to privacy. The most controversial element is Section 215, which allows government agents to look into phone and Internet records on the basis of "an ongoing investigation concerning international terrorism or clandestine intelligence activities." In addition, this section allows FBI agents to obtain secret warrants from a federal court to review library or bookstore records of an individual connected with an international terrorism or spying investigation. Prior to the Patriot Act, such orders were granted only on the grounds of probable cause as detailed in the Fourth Amendment to the United States Constitution.

Public support for the Patriot Act, which was quite high in the period immediately after the September 11th attacks, began dropping in 2003. According to the Gallup Poll, in January 2002 47 percent of Americans wanted the U.S. government to stop terrorism even if it reduced civil liberties. By November 2003, this number had dropped to 31 percent. By 2005, the public was divided almost evenly for and against the Patriot Act.

One of the main arguments against the Patriot Act is that while significantly expanding federal investigative authority, it did not provide checks and balances protecting civil liberties that were normally included in legislation. The Act did, however, include "sunset," or temporary, provisions that were set to expire on December 31, 2005. After that date, the authority was to remain in effect only for investigations previously begun. The temporary provisions deal with wiretapping in terrorism and computer cases, sharing wiretap and foreign intelligence information, nationwide search warrants for electronic evidence, and several other areas. The Patriot Act was reauthorized, however, by two bills in 2005 and 2006.

The Patriot Act comprises a controversial aspect of post–9/11 American life, as it created a new crime category of "domestic terrorism." It amended immigration, banking and money laundering, and foreign intelligence laws in its attempt to enhance federal law enforcement capabilities. Hailed by many as an important and necessary reaction to terrorism, the Patriot Act also inspired serious concern among others who fear restrictions on civil liberties. The American Civil Liberties Union, for example, filed challenges to a number of Patriot Act provisions and ran an ad campaign beginning in August 2004, claiming, "So the government can search your house ... My house ... Our house ... Without notifying us. Treating us all like suspects. It's part of the Patriot Act."

jobless rate of 6.6 percent (down from as high as 11.8 percent in 1993), a 34 percent drop in crime since 1991 for which so-called community policing got much of the credit, and the U.S. Department of Education's coveted Blue Ribbon Award for one of its elementary schools.

The Election of 2008: History is Made

AP/Wide World Photos

Barack Obama

Barack Obama's presidential election victory in November 2008 marked a milestone in the progress of black political officeholders in the United States.

As race was no longer a barrier to voting with the 15th Amendment in 1865, some Reconstruction-era former slaves were elected to office in the South during the period immediately following the Civil War. But the enactment of black codes, grandfather clauses, and literacy tests effectively removed the franchise (or the right to vote) for blacks in Southern states and these black officials were turned out of office. The last black congressman elected in the 19th century was George Henry White of North Carolina, who took office in 1897. By the turn of the century, most Southern blacks had lost the right to vote.

All of the black Reconstruction-era elected officials ran as members of the Republican Party. Virtually all blacks who could vote were registered as Republicans from 1865 until the 1930s. The election of Democrat Franklin Roosevelt in 1932, however, caused a massive switch in allegiance from the Republican to the Democratic Party, as New Deal programs offering economic opportunities and labor protections benefited black voters. In addition, the migration of blacks from the deep South to the North and West which began during World War I accelerated during the 1930s, affecting local politics. By the election of John F. Kennedy in 1960, almost all black voters were Democrats and voting in regions outside of the former Confederacy.

The passage of the Voting Rights Act in 1965, following the voting registration drives by civil rights workers throughout Southern states in the early 1960s, finally provided blacks with unfettered access to the ballot box and, subsequently, black candidates were elected. However, with the Great Migration north and west since the 1940s, no states were comprised of black majority populations. This meant that candidates needed to broaden their appeal to other ethnic groups to become elected. Since 1965, 92 black House of Representative members have been elected to Congress. All but two were Democrats. In addition, three black senators have been elected in modern times: Edward Brooke of Massachusetts, and Carol Moseley Braun and Barack Obama, both of Illinois.

Obama's victory over fellow U.S. Senator John McCain in the 2008 presidential election was a milestone in a number of ways. It shattered the record of campaign contributions received by a candidate when his campaign raised over $640 million. The election also brought to the White House the first president born after the civil rights protests and reforms of the 1960s. However, the main message may be what the election says to blacks in America. In a *Time* magazine article written just before the election, *Atlantic Monthly* contributing editor Ta-Nehisi Coates wrote: "Consider this fact: the most famous black man in America isn't dribbling a ball or clutching a microphone. He has no prison record. ... Words like hope, change, and progress might seem like naïve campaign sloganeering in a dark age. But think of the way those words ring for a people whose forebears marched into billy clubs and dogs, whose ancestors fled north by starlight, feeling the moss on the backs of trees."

In the 232-year history of the United States, the presidential election of 2008 was truly a monumental event. A black man had been elected president.

Writers Explore the Kaleidoscope of U.S. Life The 1980s and 1990s saw the emergence of writers who threw light on various, sometimes hidden facets of national life—from the immigrant experience as told by Amy Tan in *The Joy-Luck Club* (1989) and Oscar Hijuelos in *The Mambo Kings Play Songs of Love* (1990) to Tom Wolfe's satirical take on greed and class and racial tensions in New York City in *The Bonfire of the Vanities* (1987) and, later, his look behind the patina of Deep South gentility in *A Man in Full* (1998). Toni Morrison's *Beloved* (1987) dramatized the African-American slave experience.

The U.S. Counts Its People The 2000 decennial census counted 281,421,906 Americans, a 13.2 percent increase since 1990. The most populous state was California (33,871,648), the least populous, Wyoming (493,782).

(Before taking the quiz noted below, please review the summary timeline for this chapter on the following pages.)

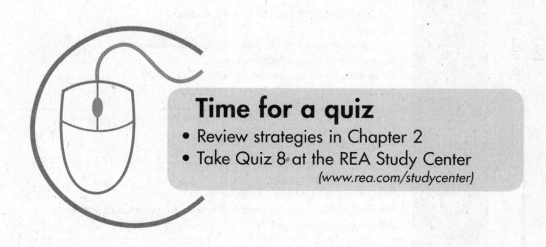

Time for a quiz
- Review strategies in Chapter 2
- Take Quiz 8 at the REA Study Center
  (www.rea.com/studycenter)

Watergate, Conservatism's Rise, and Post–Cold War Challenges (1972–2008)

Historical Timeline (1972–2008)

Year	Events
1972	Watergate break-in occurs at Democratic Headquarters Nixon defeats McGovern for presidency Haiphong Harbor in North Vietnam mined by U.S.
1973	U.S., North Vietnam sign Paris Peace Accords *Roe v. Wade* expands abortion rights Yom Kippur War in Israel Vice-President Agnew resigns in disgrace
1974	Impeachment proceedings begin against Pres. Nixon *U.S. v. Richard Nixon* rules that tapes must be turned over Nixon resigns; Vice-President Ford succeeds him Ford pardons Nixon
1975	U.S. abandons South Vietnam as it falls to North Vietnam
1978	Bakke vs. University of California Regents affirmative action case Camp David Accords between Israel and Egypt
1979	U.S. and China establish diplomatic relations Iran deposes shah Iran militants capture U.S. embassy and take hostages Soviet Union invades Afghanistan Three-Mile Island nuclear accident Sandinistas overthrow Somoza in Nicaragua
1980	U.S. boycotts Moscow Olympics Reagan elected president
1981	Iran releases hostages Reagan breaks air traffic controller strike Sandra Day O'Connor named first female Supreme Court justice AIDS epidemic reaches U.S.
1982	241 Marines killed in Lebanon U.S. invades Grenada
1985	Gorbachev takes power in Soviet Union
1986	Iran-Contra affair *Challenger* space shuttle explodes after takeoff

Watergate, Conservatism's Rise, and Post–Cold War Challenges (1972–2008)

(continued)

1989	*Exxon Valdez* oil tanker runs aground in Alaska Students begin pro-democracy demonstrations in China Berlin Wall falls
1990	Saddam Hussein of Iraq invades Kuwait
1991	Operation Desert Storm ends Iraq's occupation of Kuwait Soviet Union breaks up as Cold War ends
1992	Los Angeles riots follow Rodney King verdict Clinton elected president
1993	North American Free Trade Agreement approved
1995	U.S., NATO forces enforce peace in Bosnia
1999	Clinton acquitted following House impeachment
2000	George W. Bush defeats Gore in disputed election
2001	Hijackers crash planes into World Trade Center towers and Pentagon U.S. invades Afghanistan to overthrow Taliban government Patriot Act gives U.S. broad powers to investigate terrorism
2004	George W. Bush re-elected president
2006	Congress reauthorizes the USA Patriot Act
2008	Barack Obama becomes the first African-American to be elected President

Historical Timeline (1972–2008)

Take Mini-Test 2
on Chapters 11-17
Go to the REA Study Center
(www.rea.com/studycenter)

Practice Exam

Also available at the REA Study Center *(www.rea.com/studycenter)*

This practice exam is available at the REA Study Center. Although AP exams are administered in paper-and-pencil format, we recommend that you take the online version of the practice exam for the benefits of:

- Instant scoring
- Enforced time conditions
- Detailed score report of your strengths and weaknesses

Practice Exam
Section I

(Answer sheets appear in the back of the book.)

TIME: 55 minutes

80 questions

Directions: Each of the questions or incomplete statements below is followed by five suggested answers or completions. Select the one that is best in each case.

1. The Farmers' Alliances of the 1880s appealed primarily to

   (A) small farmers in the Northeast who found themselves unable to compete with large Western farms

   (B) Southern and Great Plains farmers frustrated with low crop prices and mired in the sharecrop and crop lien systems

   (C) established and well-to-do farmers who desired to limit production in order to sustain high prices

   (D) owners of the giant "bonanza" farms of the northern plains states who sought special advantages from the government

   (E) Chinese immigrants serving as agricultural workers with low pay and poor working conditions, primarily in the Eastern states

2. All of the following were among President Andrew Jackson's objections to the First Bank of the United States EXCEPT:

   (A) It allowed the economic power of the government to be controlled by private individuals

   (B) It threatened the integrity of the democratic system

   (C) It was preventing the government from achieving its policy of creating inflation

   (D) It could be used irresponsibly to create financial hardship for the nation

   (E) It benefited a small group of wealthy and privileged persons at the expense of the rest of the country

3. After 45 years of conflict, a series of developments in the 1990s showed improvement in relations between Israel and the Palestine Liberation Organization. Which of the following did not occur in the 1990s?

   (A) An agreement on Palestinian autonomy

   (B) Washington, D.C., ceremony signing an agreement to expand Palestinian West Bank self-rule

   (C) Israel and Jordan formally end the state of war between them

   (D) Egypt and Israel sign the Camp David Accords

   (E) In Cairo, leaders Yasir Arafat, Hosni Mubarek and Yitzhak Rabin condemn violence

4. During the Congressional campaigns in 1994, a year in which Republicans would take control of both houses of Congress, Newt Gingrich and 300 other Republican House candidates dramatically pledged to pass

   (A) health care reform

   (B) a Contract with America

   (C) social welfare legislation

   (D) increased funding for education

   (E) new civil rights measures

5. One mound-building culture, Cahokia, supported perhaps 40,000 people near what modern-day city?

   (A) New York City

   (B) Mexico City

   (C) St. Louis

   (D) Seattle

   (E) Miami

6. Which of the following factors came closest to giving the Confederacy what could have been a decisive foreign policy success during the Civil War?

   (A) The U.S. Navy's seizure of Confederate emissaries James M. Mason and John Slidell from the British mail steamer *Trent*

   (B) French objections to the Union blockade

   (C) The acute economic dislocation in Britain and France caused by the cut-off of cotton imports from the South

   (D) The concerns of French financial interests that had loaned large amounts of money to the Confederacy

   (E) The skillful negotiating of Confederate diplomats in Europe

7. The following map depicts the United States as it was immediately after which of the following events?

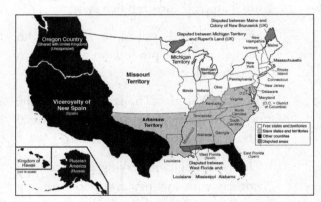

   (A) Passage of the Compromise of 1850

   (B) Passage of the Missouri Compromise

   (C) Passage of the Northwest Ordinance

   (D) Settlement of the Mexican War

   (E) Negotiation of the Webster-Ashburton Treaty

8. The 1932 demonstration known as the "Bonus March" involved

   (A) farmers disgruntled about low prices for meat, grain, and dairy products

   (B) homeless persons building shantytowns near Washington, D.C.

   (C) Japanese-Americans protesting forced relocation from the West Coast

   (D) World War I veterans demanding financial aid from the federal government

   (E) migrant farm workers seeking employment in California

9. Which of the following statements is true about the case of Julius and Ethel Rosenberg?

   (A) They were accused of giving atomic secrets to Germany during World War II.

   (B) They were exposed as spies by former Communist agent Whitaker Chambers.

   (C) They were convicted of espionage, condemned, and electrocuted.

   (D) They were convicted but were later pardoned by President Eisenhower because public opinion did not favor harsh treatment of accused Communist spies.

   (E) They confessed to having carried out espionage on behalf of the Soviet Union.

10. Which of the following best describes the methods advocated by Malcolm X?

    (A) Nonviolent defiance of segregation

    (B) Armed violence against police and troops

    (C) Patience while developing the skills that would make African Americans economically successful and gain them the respect of Whites

    (D) Gradual assimilation of the two races until they became indistinguishable

    (E) Meek acceptance of "Jim Crowism" until increasingly enlightened southern Whites were prepared to change it

11. In 1960 which of the following contributed most directly to Soviet leader Nikita Khrushchev's cancellation of a scheduled summit meeting with President Dwight Eisenhower?

    (A) The rise to power of Fidel Castro in Cuba

    (B) The failure, at the Bay of Pigs, of a U.S.-sponsored attempt to oust Castro

    (C) The sending of U.S. troops to Lebanon

    (D) The downing of an American U-2 spy plane over the Soviet Union

    (E) The success of the Soviet space program in launching the Sputnik satellite

Average Inland Freight Rates in the U.S.
1800–1830

CENTS PER TON-MILE

YEAR

12. Which of the the following was most responsible for the change shown between 1815 and 1830?

(A) The development of practical steam-powered railroad trains

(B) The development of a network of canals linking important cities and waterways

(C) The growth in the nation's mileage of improved roads and turnpikes

(D) Improvements in the design of keelboats and flatboats

(E) The development of steamboats

13. During the period of Reconstruction, most of the states of the former Confederacy, in order to regain admission to the Union, were required to

(A) grant Black people all the civil rights that Northern states had granted them before the war

(B) ratify the Fourteenth Amendment

(C) provide integrated public schools

(D) ratify the Sixteenth Amendment

(E) provide free land and farming utensils for the recently freed slaves

14. The primary function of the Food Administration during the First World War was to

(A) keep farm prices high by limiting the amount of food produced on American farms

(B) ensure an adequate supply of food for American needs by arranging for imports from America's British and French allies

(C) oversee the production and allocation of foodstuffs to ensure adequate supplies for the army and the Allies

(D) monitor the purity and wholesomeness of all food items shipped to France to feed the American Army there

(E) create and operate large-scale government-owned farms

15. The purpose of the Truman Doctrine was to

(A) aid the economic recovery of war-torn Europe

(B) prevent European meddling in the affairs of South American countries

(C) aid countries that were the targets of Communist expansionism

(D) reduce the dependence of the European economy on overseas empires

(E) expand the Monroe Doctrine to include Eastern Asia

16. The Molasses Act was intended to enforce England's mercantilist policies by

(A) forcing the colonists to export solely to Great Britain

(B) forcing the colonists to buy sugar from other British colonies rather than from foreign producers

(C) forbidding the colonists to engage in manufacturing activity in competition with British industries

(D) providing a favorable market for the products of the British East India Company

(E) creating an economic situation in which gold tended to flow from the colonies to the mother country

17. The British government imposed the Townshend Acts on the American colonies in the belief that

(A) the American position regarding British taxation had changed

(B) it was necessary to provoke a military confrontation in order to teach the colonists a lesson

(C) its provisions were designed solely to enforce mercantilism

(D) it had been approved by the colonial legislatures

(E) the Americans would accept it as external rather than internal taxation

18. In his famous "Freeport Doctrine" set forth in his debate with Abraham Lincoln at Freeport, Illinois, Stephen A. Douglas stated that

(A) any territory desiring to exclude slavery could do so simply by declining to pass laws protecting it

(B) any state wishing to secede from the Union could do so simply by the vote of a special state constitutional convention

(C) no state had the right to obstruct the operation of the Fugitive Slave Act by the passage of "personal liberty laws"

(D) the Dred Scott decision prohibited any territorial legislature from excluding slavery until a state constitution was drawn up for approval by Congress

(E) any slaveholder was free to take his slaves anywhere within the United States without hindrance by state, federal, or territorial governments

19. Government subsidies for the building of transcontinental railroads during the nineteenth century mainly took the form of

(A) large cash payments based on the mileage of track built

(B) a one-time blanket appropriation for the building of each separate transcontinental line

(C) generous land grants along the railroad's right-of-way

(D) the option of drawing supplies and materials from government depots

(E) the provision of large amounts of convict labor at no charge to the railroad company

20. During William H. Taft's administration, the federal government moved to strengthen its regulatory control over the railroad industry by

    (A) passage of the Mann-Elkins Act

    (B) creation of the Federal Trade Commission

    (C) passage of the "Granger Laws"

    (D) taking over and operating the railroads

    (E) removal of former legal obstacles to consolidation of the railroads into giant corporations

21. Which of the following regions was most heavily represented among immigrants to the United States during the years from 1865 to 1890?

    (A) Northern and Western Europe

    (B) Southern and Eastern Europe

    (C) Asia

    (D) Africa

    (E) Central and South America

22. The slogan "Fifty-four forty or fight" had to do with the

    (A) so-called "Aroostook War," involving a boundary dispute between Maine and New Brunswick

    (B) demand for the annexation of all of the Oregon country

    (C) demand for the readjustment of the boundary with Mexico

    (D) demand by free-soil Northerners that some limit be placed on the spread of slavery in the territories

    (E) demand by Southerners that the Missouri Compromise line be extended through the Mexican Cession

23. All of the following statements are true of William H. Taft EXCEPT:

    (A) He was an able and efficient administrator.

    (B) He was little inclined to making rousing speeches or engage in political conflict.

    (C) He reversed Theodore Roosevelt's conservationist policies.

    (D) He disliked publicity.

    (E) His administration was more active in prosecuting trusts than Roosevelt's had been.

24. The primary issue in dispute in Shays' Rebellion was

    (A) the jailing of individuals or seizure of their property for failure to pay taxes during a time of economic hardship

    (B) the underrepresentation of western Massachusetts in the state legislature leading to accusations of "taxation without representation"

    (C) the failure of Massachusetts to pay a promised postwar bonus to soldiers who had served in its forces during the Revolution

    (D) the failure of Massachusetts authorities to take adequate steps to protect the western part of the state from the depredations of raiding Indians

    (E) economic oppression practiced by the banking interests of eastern Massachusetts

25. All of the following were weaknesses of the Articles of Confederation government EXCEPT:

    (A) It lacked the power to levy taxes.

    (B) It lacked the power to regulate commerce.

    (C) It lacked the power to borrow money.

    (D) It could not compel the states to abide by the terms of international treaties it had made.

    (E) It lacked a strong executive.

26. Congress's most successful and effective method of financing the War of Independence was

    (A) printing large amounts of paper money

    (B) obtaining grants and loans from France and the Netherlands

    (C) levying heavy direct taxes

    (D) issuing paper securities backed by the promise of western land grants

    (E) appealing to the states for voluntary contributions

27. All of the following are true statements of the Compromise of 1850 EXCEPT:

    (A) It provided for the admission of California to the Union as a free state.

    (B) It included a tougher fugitive slave law.

    (C) It prohibited slavery in the lands acquired as a result of the Mexican War.

    (D) It stipulated that land in dispute between the state of Texas and the territory of New Mexico should be ceded to New Mexico.

    (E) It ended the slave trade in the District of Columbia.

28. A member of the Social Gospel movement would probably

    (A) consider such social sins as alcohol abuse and sexual permissiveness as society's most serious problems

    (B) assert that the poor were themselves at fault for their circumstances

    (C) maintain that abuses and social degradation resulted solely from a lack of willpower on the part of those who committed them

    (D) hold that religion is an entirely individualistic matter

    (E) argue that Christians should work to reorganize the industrial system and bring about international peace

29. In its decision in the case of *Plessy v. Ferguson*, the Supreme Court held that

    (A) separate facilities for different races were inherently unequal and therefore unconstitutional

    (B) no black slave could be a citizen of the United States

    (C) separate but equal facilities for different races were constitutional

    (D) affirmative action programs were acceptable only when it could be proven that specific previous cases of discrimination had occurred within the institution or business in question

    (E) imposition of a literacy test imposed an unconstitutional barrier to the right to vote

30. Henry Clay's "American System" advocated all of the following EXCEPT

    (A) federal funding for the building of roads

    (B) a national bank

    (C) high protective tariffs

    (D) an independent treasury

    (E) federal funding for the building of canals

31. Which of the following groups was the first target of congressional legislation restricting immigration expressly on the basis of national origin?

    (A) Northern and Western Europeans

    (B) Chinese

    (C) Italians

    (D) Africans

    (E) Latin Americans

32. The main issue of the 1850s Free-Soil party was that

    (A) the federal government should permit no further spread of slavery in the territories

    (B) a homestead act should be passed, granting 160 acres of government land in the West free to anyone who would settle on it and improve it for five years

    (C) the federal government should oversee immediate and uncompensated abolition of slavery

    (D) freed slaves should be provided with 40 acres and a mule to provide them the economic means of independent self-support

    (E) the United States should annex Cuba

33. The most controversial portion of Alexander Hamilton's economic program was

    (A) federal assumption of state debts

    (B) assessment of direct taxes on the states

    (C) creation of the Bank of the United States

    (D) imposition of high protective tariffs

    (E) establishment of a bimetallic system

34. In the Nullification Controversy, some Southerners took the position that

    (A) the federal government had the right to nullify state laws that interfered with the right to hold property in slaves

    (B) the federal courts had the right to nullify acts of Congress that restricted the spread of slavery in the territories

    (C) the states had the right to nullify acts of the federal government they deemed to be unconstitutional

    (D) Southern states had the right to nullify statutes of Northern states interfering with the recapture of escaped slaves

    (E) Congress should refuse to receive any petitions against slavery

35. The Mayflower Compact could best be described as

    (A) a detailed frame of government

    (B) a complete constitution

    (C) a business contract

    (D) a foundation for self-government

    (E) an enumeration of the causes for leaving England and coming to the New World

36. All of the following statements about the Taft-Hartley Act are true EXCEPT:

    (A) It had long been the goal of a number of large labor unions.

    (B) It allowed the president to call an eight-day cooling-off period to delay any strike that might endanger national safety or health.

    (C) It outlawed the closed shop.

    (D) It was backed by congressional Republicans.

    (E) It was vetoed by President Truman.

37. Which of the following statements is true of the Wade-Davis Bill?

    (A) It allowed restoration of a loyal government when as few as ten percent of a state's prewar registered voters swore future loyalty to the Union and acceptance of emancipation.

    (B) It explicitly required that the vote be accorded to the recently freed slaves.

    (C) It allowed high-ranking rebel officials to regain the right to vote and hold office by simply promising future good behavior.

    (D) It was pocket-vetoed by Lincoln.

    (E) It provided substantially more lenient terms of reconstruction than those favored by Lincoln.

38. Sinclair Lewis generally depicted small-town America as

    (A) an island of sincerity amid the cynicism of American life

    (B) the home of such traditional virtues as honesty, hard work, and wholesomeness

    (C) merely a smaller-scale version of big-city life

    (D) dreary, prejudiced, and vulgar

    (E) open and accepting but naive and easily taken in

39. As president, Calvin Coolidge generally

    (A) favored large government building projects

    (B) urged Congress to raise taxes

    (C) kept government spending low and encouraged private business

    (D) took an active role in pushing legislation through Congress

    (E) argued that the protective tariff should be lowered in order to provide a more healthy economic environment

40. A people who dominated a large kingdom in the Andes Mountains of Peru when the first Europeans arrived were the

    (A) Incas

    (B) Maya

    (C) Aztecs

    (D) Mohecans

    (E) Pueblos

41. The Spanish-American War spurred building of the Panama Canal by

    (A) demonstrating the need to shift naval forces quickly from the Atlantic to the Pacific

    (B) demonstrating the ease with which Latin American countries could be overcome by U.S. military force

    (C) discrediting congressional opponents of the project

    (D) removing the threat that any possible canal could be blockaded by Spanish forces based in Cuba and Puerto Rico

    (E) demonstrating that such tropical diseases as malaria and yellow fever could be controlled

42. "We have nothing to fear but fear itself" is a statement from

    (A) Woodrow Wilson's 1917 message to Congress asking for a declaration of war against Germany

    (B) a speech by President Herbert Hoover two weeks after the October 1929 stock market crash

    (C) Franklin D. Roosevelt's first inaugural address

    (D) Franklin D. Roosevelt's message to Congress asking for a declaration of war against Japan, December 8, 1941

    (E) Harry S. Truman's announcement of the dropping of the atomic bomb on Hiroshima

43. All of the following statements about the Civilian Conservation Corps are true EXCEPT:

    (A) Its members lived in camps, wore uniforms, and were under semi-military discipline.

    (B) It engaged in such projects as preventing soil erosion and impounding lakes.

    (C) It eventually came to employ over one-third of the American work force.

    (D) It provided that some of the workers' pay should be sent home to their families.

    (E) It was part of the New Deal.

44. In personally taking over the task of setting the dollar amount the government would pay for gold, Franklin D. Roosevelt's announced purpose was to

    (A) maintain the value of the dollar at a constant level

    (B) prevent inflation

    (C) prevent a run on the banks, which would be likely to deplete the nation's gold supply dangerously

    (D) manipulate the price of gold so as to raise prices

    (E) revise the value of the dollar so as to force prices down to affordable levels in America's depressed economy

45. The underlying issue that led to the outbreak of war between the United States and Japan in 1941 was

    (A) Japanese aid to the Germans in their war against Britain

    (B) U.S. desire to annex various Pacific islands held by Japan

    (C) Japanese desire to annex the Aleutian Islands

    (D) Japanese desire to annex large portions of China

    (E) American resentment of Japanese trading policies and trade surpluses

46. In the *Arabic* Pledge of 1916 Germany promised not to

    (A) aid Mexico in any war against the United States

    (B) attempt to buy war materials in the United States

    (C) use submarines for any purpose but reconnaissance

    (D) attempt to break the British blockade

    (E) sink passenger ships without warning

47. In the negotiations leading to the Treaty of Versailles, Woodrow Wilson was willing to sacrifice other portions of his Fourteen Points in order to gain Allied approval of

    (A) a ban on secret diplomacy

    (B) a strengthening of the Austrian Empire in order to restore the balance of power

    (C) a union of Germany and Austria in accordance with the right of self-determination of peoples

    (D) new rules of blockade that would provide more complete freedom of the seas

    (E) a League of Nations

48. Which of the following is true of W. E. B. Du Bois?

    (A) He founded the National Association for the Advancement of Colored People.

    (B) He was the chief author of the Atlanta Compromise.

    (C) He was an outspoken critic of the Niagara Movement.

    (D) He believed that Blacks should temporarily accommodate themselves to Whites.

    (E) He worked closely with Booker T. Washington.

49. In response to President Andrew Johnson's relatively mild reconstruction program, the Southern states did all of the following EXCEPT

    (A) refuse to repudiate the Confederate debt

    (B) elect many former high-ranking Confederates to Congress and other top positions

    (C) refuse to grant Blacks the right to vote

    (D) attempt to reinstitute slavery

    (E) pass special "Black codes" restricting the legal rights of Blacks

50. Andrew Johnson was impeached and nearly removed from office on the grounds of his

    (A) refusal to carry out the provisions of the Military Reconstruction Act

    (B) alleged involvement in a corrupt stock-manipulating scheme carried out by one of his associates

    (C) refusal to carry out the provisions of the Civil Rights Act of 1866

    (D) violation of the Tenure of Office Act in removing Secretary of War Edwin M. Stanton

    (E) general failure to cooperate with the Radical Republicans in their efforts to carry out Reconstruction

51. In speaking of "redemption" in a political sense, white Southerners of the Reconstruction era made reference to

    (A) ridding the South of the Reconstruction governments

    (B) atoning for their society's sin of slavery by granting full legal and social equality to Blacks

    (C) atoning for the Southern states' secession by displaying extreme patriotism to the restored United States

    (D) regaining personal rights of citizenship by taking an oath of allegiance to the Union

    (E) buying back from the federal government plantations confiscated during the war

52. The primary underlying reason that Reconstruction ended in 1877 was that

    (A) Southerners had succeeded in electing anti-Reconstruction governments in all the former Confederate states

    (B) all the goals set by the Radical Republicans at the end of the Civil War had been accomplished

    (C) leading Radicals in the North had become convinced that Reconstruction had been unconstitutional

    (D) Northern voters had grown weary of the effort to Reconstruct the South and generally lost interest

    (E) Republican political managers had come to see further agitation of North-South differences arising from the Civil War as a political liability

53. In the Second World War the Allied strategy, agreed upon by the U.S. and Great Britain, was to

    (A) concentrate on defeating Japan first before turning on Germany

    (B) divide all resources equally between the war against Japan and that against Germany

    (C) fight only against Japan, leaving the Russians to fight Germany alone

    (D) take a passive role and limit operations to reacting to Axis moves

    (E) concentrate on defeating Germany first before turning on Japan

54. The Marshall Plan was

    (A) a strategy for defeating Germany

    (B) a strategy for defeating Japan

    (C) an American economic aid program for Europe

    (D) an American commitment to give military and economic aid to any nation resisting Communist aggression

    (E) a civil-defense plan for surviving a Soviet nuclear strike

55. Which of the following was the most important factor in John F. Kennedy's 1960 presidential election victory over Richard Nixon?

(A) Americans' deep and growing dissatisfaction with the Eisenhower Administration

(B) Revelations of corrupt activities on the part of Nixon

(C) Kennedy's better showing in nationally televised debates

(D) Kennedy's long record of administrative experience as governor of Massachusetts

(E) Nixon's failure to serve in the armed forces during the Second World War

56. After concluding its investigation of the assassination of President John F. Kennedy, the Warren Commission announced its finding that

(A) Lee Harvey Oswald acted alone in assassinating the president

(B) Oswald was assisted by two other marksmen on the "grassy knoll" in front of the presidential motorcade

(C) Oswald had been the only gunman but was part of a widespread conspiracy

(D) Oswald in fact had nothing to do with the assassination

(E) the true facts of the assassination and any possible conspiracy involved with it will probably never be known

57. The chief significance of French explorer Samuel de Champlain's alienation of the Iroquois Indians was

(A) to prevent the French from establishing a profitable fur trade in Canada

(B) to prevent Champlain from founding any permanent settlement along the St. Lawrence River

(C) to prevent Champlain from making it back to France alive

(D) to prevent New France from expanding southward into what is now the United States

(E) the creation of an alliance of British and French colonists against the Iroquois

58. In founding the colony of Pennsylvania, William Penn's primary purpose was to

(A) provide a refuge for persecuted English Quakers

(B) provide a refuge for persecuted Christians of all sects from all parts of Europe

(C) demonstrate the possibility and practicality of establishing truly friendly relations with the Indians

(D) make a financial profit

(E) provide a refuge for English debtors

59. During the first two decades under the United States Constitution, the main factor that separated Federalists from Republicans was

    (A) whether they accepted the Constitution or opposed it

    (B) whether they favored the French Revolution or opposed it

    (C) whether they leaned more toward states' rights or national sovereignty

    (D) their personal like or dislike for the personalities of Thomas Jefferson and Alexander Hamilton

    (E) whether they had been patriots or loyalists during the American War of Independence

60. When colonial Massachusetts' Governor Thomas Hutchinson attempted to force the sale of taxed tea in Boston in 1773, Bostonians reacted with the

    (A) Boston Massacre

    (B) Boston Tea Party

    (C) Declaration of Independence

    (D) Articles of Confederation

    (E) Massachusetts Circular Letter

61. The international incident known as the XYZ Affair involved

    (A) a French foreign minister's demand for a bribe before he would meet with American envoys

    (B) the British refusal to evacuate their forts on American territory

    (C) General Andrew Jackson's incursion into Spanish-held Florida

    (D) the British seizure of American crewmen from a U.S. Navy warship in Chesapeake Bay

    (E) Aaron Burr's secret plot to detach the western United States in order to create a new nation of which he would be ruler

62. The most unusual feature of the charter of the Massachusetts Bay Colony was that it

    (A) provided that the colony should be run as a religious commonwealth

    (B) made the colony completely independent of all English authority

    (C) assured the colonists all the rights they would have had if they had been born and living in England

    (D) did not specify where the company's headquarters should be

    (E) specified that only Parliament, not the king, was to have authority over the colony

63. During the first two decades of the seventeenth century all of the following aided in the establishment and growth of the colony at Jamestown, Virginia, EXCEPT

    (A) the establishment of the Virginia House of Burgesses

    (B) the establishment of the ownership of private property

    (C) the beginning of tobacco cultivation

    (D) good relations with the local Indians

    (E) large influxes of supplies and colonists from England

64. The first religious development to have an impact throughout colonial America was the

    (A) establishment of religious toleration in Maryland

    (B) spread of Quaker ideas from Pennsylvania

    (C) Halfway Covenant

    (D) Parsons' Cause

    (E) Great Awakening

65. President Andrew Jackson's Maysville Road veto dealt with

    (A) federally financed internal improvements

    (B) foreign policy

    (C) the power of the Second Bank of the United States relative to that of other financial institutions

    (D) the efficiency and honesty of government employees

    (E) the purchase of government land with paper money

66. All of the following contributed to the coming of the War of 1812 EXCEPT

    (A) the *Chesapeake-Leopard* Incident

    (B) British impressment of American seamen from American ships on the high seas

    (C) the concerns of Western Americans that the Indian raids they suffered were being carried out with British encouragement

    (D) the Congressional "War Hawks'" desire to annex Canada

    (E) the armed confrontation between U.S. and British forces along the Maine-Canada border

67. The Monroe Doctrine stated that the United States

    (A) was not concerned with the type of government other countries might have

    (B) was concerned only with the type of government that the countries of the Western Hemisphere might have

    (C) would not tolerate any new European colonization in the New World

    (D) claimed the Western Hemisphere as its exclusive zone of influence

    (E) was prepared to drive out by force any European power that did not give up its colonies in the Western Hemisphere

68. The most divisive and controversial aspect of the slavery issue during the first half of the nineteenth century was the

    (A) status of slavery in the District of Columbia

    (B) right of abolitionists to send their literature through the U.S. mail

    (C) enforcement of the draconian Fugitive Slave Law

    (D) status of slavery in the territories

    (E) prohibition of the international slave trade

69. When President Andrew Jackson's enemies spoke of the "Kitchen Cabinet" they were referring to

    (A) a group of old friends and unofficial advisors of the president

    (B) a number of persons of low social standing, including a former cook, who were appointed by Jackson to high cabinet positions

    (C) a suggestion as to where Jackson might keep the federal government's money if he removed it from the Bank of the United States

    (D) a coterie of Jackson supporters in the U.S. Senate

    (E) several state governors who supported Jackson

70. The 1840s Pre-emption Act, signed by President John Tyler, provided that

    (A) the status of slavery in a territory was to be decided by the settlers there

    (B) slave law pre-empted free law in disputes involving escaped slaves

    (C) settlers who had squatted on government land would have first chance to buy it

    (D) the vice president automatically became president upon the death of the president

    (E) federal law pre-empted state law in matters pertaining to slavery

71. The Homestead Act provided

    (A) that Indians should henceforth own their lands as individuals rather than collectively as tribes

    (B) 160 acres of free land within the public domain to any head of household who would settle on it and improve it over a period of five years

    (C) large amounts of federal government land to Great Plains cattle ranchers who would contract to provide beef for the Union army

    (D) 40 acres of land to each former slave above the age of 21

    (E) that the land of former Confederates should not be confiscated

72. Henry George's most famous book was

    (A) *Looking Backward*

    (B) *Progress and Poverty*

    (C) *The Jungle*

    (D) *The Shame of the Cities*

    (E) *Sister Carrie*

73. All of the following statements are true of John Dewey EXCEPT:

    (A) He strove to alter radically both the content and purpose of schooling.

    (B) He strove to strengthen the child's respect for parental and other traditional authority.

    (C) He substituted the authority of the peer group for that of the teacher so that the child would be socialized and schooling would be made relevant to him.

    (D) He was much inflamed by William James.

    (E) He has been called the father of Progressive Education.

74. "Waving the bloody shirt" was the name given to the practice of

    (A) scaring potential black voters into staying away from the polls

    (B) voting large appropriations of federal funds for unnecessary projects in a powerful congressman's district

    (C) using animosities stirred up by the Civil War to gain election in the postwar North

    (D) inciting the country to go to war with Spain

    (E) machine politics as practiced in many major cities during the late nineteenth century

75. Which of the following expresses the first policy taken by the federal government toward the Indians of the Great Plains?

    (A) The Indians should be confined to two large reservations, one north of the Platte River and the other south of it.

    (B) Since the Great Plains are a desert anyway, the Indians may be allowed to keep the entire area.

    (C) Indians should be given individual parcels of land by the government rather than holding land communally as tribes.

    (D) Indians are subhuman and ought to be exterminated.

    (E) The Indians should be induced to accept permanent residence on a number of small reservations.

76. One of the goals of the Populist movement was to induce the government to introduce

    (A) free coinage of silver

    (B) prohibition of all immigration from China and Japan

    (C) the building of a transcontinental railroad at government expense

    (D) a "single tax" on land

    (E) more stringent regulations for the health and safety of factory workers

77. Georgia O'Keeffe, Thomas Hart Benton, and Edward Hopper were all

    (A) American painters of the 1920s

    (B) pioneers in the field of a distinctly American music

    (C) known for their abstract paintings of flowers and other objects

    (D) pioneers in the building of skyscrapers

    (E) American literary figures of the first decade of the twentieth century

78. The 1944 Dumbarton Oaks Conference involved primarily

    (A) the trial and punishment of Nazi war criminals

    (B) the decision on whether or not to use the atomic bomb

    (C) startling revelations of the Nazi atrocities against Jews

    (D) American plans for redrawing the map of Eastern Europe

    (E) the formation of the United Nations

79. Which of the following statements is true of the Bland-Allison Act?

    (A) It gave the president discretion to purchase up to 1 million ounces of silver per year.

    (B) It required the government to purchase from $2 million to $4 million worth of gold per month.

    (C) It was intended to raise the market price of gold and thus create a slight inflationary effect.

    (D) It provided for a floating rate of exchange between silver and gold.

    (E) It was vetoed by President Rutherford B. Hayes.

80. In the 1790s political conflict between Thomas Jefferson and Alexander Hamilton, Jefferson would have been more likely to

    (A) take a narrow view of the Constitution

    (B) favor Britain over France in the European wars

    (C) favor the establishment of a national bank

    (D) win the cooperation of presidents George Washington and John Adams

    (E) oppose the efforts of Citizen Genet in America

STOP
This is the end of Section I.
If time still remains, you may check your work only in this section.
Do not begin Section II until instructed to do so.

Section II
Part A - Document-Based Essay

TIME: Reading Period: 15 minutes
Writing Time: 45 Minutes
1 Essay Question

> **Directions:** Read over the Document-Based Essay question in Part A and the choices in Parts B and C during the Reading Period, and use the time to organize answers. All students must answer Part A (the Document-Based Essay question) and answer ONE question in both Parts B and C.

1. Using the following documents as well as your knowledge of the events surrounding the outbreak of the Civil War, assess the wisdom of Abraham Lincoln's decision to hold Fort Sumter and Jefferson Davis's decision to take it.

Document A

It is safe to assert that no government proper ever had a provision in its organic law for its own termination. . . . No state upon its own mere motion can lawfully get out of the Union. I shall take care, as the Constitution itself expressly enjoins upon me, that the laws of the Union be faithfully executed in all the states. Doing this I deem to be only a simple duty on my part; and I shall perform it, so far as practicable, unless my rightful masters, the American people, shall withhold the requisite means, or in some authoritative manner direct the contrary. . . . The power confided in me will be used to hold, occupy and possess the property and places belonging to the government, and to collect the duties and imposts. . . . In your hands, my dissatisfied fellow countrymen, and not in mine, is the momentous issue of civil war. The government will not assail you. You can have no conflict without being yourselves the aggressors. You have no oath registered in heaven to destroy the government, while I shall have the most solemn one to "preserve, protect and defend" it.

Source: Lincoln's first inaugural address (March 4, 1861)

Document B

.... The occupation or evacuation of Fort Sumter, although not in fact a slavery or a party question, is so regarded. Witness the temper manifested by the Republicans in the free States, and even by the Union men in the South.

I would therefore terminate it as a safe means for changing the issue. I deem it [un]fortunate that the last administration created the necessity.

Source: Memorandum from Secretary of State William H. Seward to Lincoln (April 1, 1861)

Document C

Border southern States will never join us until we have indicated our power to free ourselves — until we have proven that a garrison of seventy men cannot hold the portal of our commerce. Let us be ready for war. .... The fate of the Southern Confederacy hangs by the ensign halliards of Fort Sumter.

Source: Charleston Mercury (January 24, 1861)

Document D

The spirit and even the patriotism of the people is oozing out under the do-nothing policy. If something is not done pretty soon...the whole country will become so disgusted with the sham of southern independence that the first chance the people get at a popular election they will turn the whole movement topsy-turvy.

Source: A Mobile, Alabama, newspaper (January 1861)

Document E

The shedding of blood will serve to change many voters in the hesitating states, from the submission or procrastinating ranks, to the zealous for immediate secession.

Source: The diary of Edmund Ruffin (early 1861)

Document F

The firing on that fort will inaugurate a civil war greater than any the world has yet seen, and I do not feel competent to advise you. Mr. President, at this time it is suicide, murder, and you will lose us every friend at the North. You will wantonly strike a hornets' nest which extends from mountains to ocean. Legions now quiet will swarm out and sting us to death. It is unnecessary. It puts us in the wrong. It is fatal.

Source: Statement of Confederate Secretary of State Robert Toombs to Davis at cabinet meeting (April 9, 1861)

Document G

> I am directed by the President of the United States to notify you to expect an attempt will be made to supply Fort Sumter with provisions only, and that if such an attempt be not resisted, no effort to throw in men, arms, or ammunition will be made without further notice, or in case of an attack upon the fort.
>
> *Source: Note from U.S. State Department official R.S. Chew to South Carolina Governor F.W. Pickens (April 8, 1861)*

Document H

> If you have no doubt as to the authorized character of the agent who communicated to you the intention of the Washington government to supply Fort Sumter by force, you will at once demand its evacuation, and, if this is refused, proceed in such manner as you may determine to reduce it.
>
> *Source: Order from Davis to General Pierre G.T. Beauregard (April 10, 1861)*

Section II
Part B and C - Standard Essay Question

TIME: 70 minutes

Directions: Choose ONE question each from Part B and Part C. It is recommended that you spend 5 minutes planning and 30 minutes writing. Support your thesis with germane historical evidence and present your case logically and clearly.

Part B

2. The sectional compromises of the first half of the nineteenth century were not in fact compromises but rather "sectional sellouts" in which the North gave in to the insistent demands of the slaveholding South.

   Assess the validity of this statement.

3. Analyze the appeal of Dwight D. Eisenhower to voters in the 1950s.

Part C

4. The Spanish-American War was the result of shrewd maneuvering on the part of a number of Washington imperialists, such as Theodore Roosevelt, who pressured the weak and vacillating McKinley into war in order to gain a colonial empire in the Caribbean and the Western Pacific.

   Evaluate this statement.

5. The Civil War was doubly tragic because it was completely unnecessary. Slavery had been ended in other nations by the stroke of a pen, and so it could have been in the United States.

   Assess the validity of this statement.

Answer Key

Section I

1. (B)	21. (A)	41. (A)	61. (A)
2. (C)	22. (B)	42. (C)	62. (D)
3. (D)	23. (C)	43. (C)	63. (D)
4. (B)	24. (A)	44. (D)	64. (E)
5. (C)	25. (C)	45. (D)	65. (A)
6. (A)	26. (B)	46. (E)	66. (E)
7. (B)	27. (C)	47. (E)	67. (C)
8. (D)	28. (E)	48. (A)	68. (D)
9. (C)	29. (C)	49. (D)	69. (A)
10. (B)	30. (D)	50. (D)	70. (C)
11. (D)	31. (B)	51. (A)	71. (B)
12. (E)	32. (A)	52. (D)	72. (B)
13. (B)	33. (C)	53. (E)	73. (B)
14. (C)	34. (C)	54. (C)	74. (C)
15. (C)	35. (D)	55. (C)	75. (B)
16. (B)	36. (A)	56. (A)	76. (A)
17. (E)	37. (D)	57. (D)	77. (A)
18. (A)	38. (D)	58. (A)	78. (E)
19. (C)	39. (C)	59. (B)	79. (E)
20. (A)	40. (A)	60. (B)	80. (A)

Detailed Explanations of Answers

Section I

1. **(B)**

Farmers of the Great Plains and the South often saw the Alliance movement as the only way to get out of the seemingly endless cycle of debt (crop liens), sharecropping, and/or low commodity prices. Small farmers in the Northeast could not, in fact, compete with Western farms, but they had no need to since they could concentrate on production of perishable items for nearby metropolitan areas (A). This was also the age of the giant "bonanza" farms of the northern Plains, but neither the owners of such farms (D) nor established, well-to-do farmers (C) had any need for the kind of government help the Farmers' Alliances sought. There were also a number of Chinese immigrants in the Western states at this time, not, however, in the Farmers' Alliances.

2. **(C)**

Jackson did not object to the bank's preventing inflation, though some of his followers may have. Jackson, on the other hand, desired a gold standard. He believed the bank allowed the economic power of the government to be wielded by private individuals (A), the bank's directors. He believed it benefited this small and wealthy group, and their friends, at the expense of the rest of the country (E). He believed it could create economic hardship for the nation (D) and had in 1819; and he believed it threatened the integrity of the democratic system by using its influence in elections (B).

3. **(D)**

All events listed except the Camp David Accords (1979) occurred in the 1990s. The Camp David Accords saw the first comprehensive peace agreement between an Arab and an Israeli leader. In September of 1993 Israel and the Palestine Liberation Organization exchanged letters recognizing (A) each other. They also signed an agreement including Palestinian autonomy in Israeli-held territories. In 1994, Palestinian autonomy, to a limited extent, began in the Gaza Strip and the West Bank. Also in 1994, Israel and Jordan signed a peace treaty formally ending their 46 years of war (C). In February of 1995 leaders in the Middle East condemned violence (E). On September 28, 1995, during a White House ceremony (B), the Israelis and the Palestinians agreed to expand Palestinian West Bank self-rule.

4. **(B)**

On September 27, 1994, at the Capitol Building, Newt Gingrich and Republican House candidates pledged to pass a Contract with America, which called for legislation to lower taxes, increase defense spending and pass a balanced budget amendment to the Constitution. Concern regarding the return of Reaganomics and an increased budget deficit did not influence the majority of the voters. Health care reform (A) had failed to materialize in 1994 and had little chance in 1995, when the interest on Capitol Hill shifted to a balanced budget. The welfare legislation (C) taken up was welfare reform. The Republican House sought decreases in education funding (D). Opposition to unfunded mandates and affirmative action did not lead to new civil rights measures (E).

5. **(C)**

The largest of the mound-building centers, Cahokia, was located near the present city of St. Louis. This Mississippi Valley culture built massive earthen mounds of varying size and function. The Cahokia inhabitants built flat-top mounds for buildings and other types of mound structures for cemeteries. The largest Cahokian mound, Monks Mound, featured a massive base measuring over 700,000 square feet and two terraces and was 25 percent larger than the Great Pyramid of Giza. Cahokia's population was greater than any European city of its day, and the first European-American city that matched it in population was eighteenth-century Philadelphia. The other four cities (New York City, Mexico City, Seattle, and Miami) were settled by other Indian groups.

6. **(A)**

The U.S. Navy's seizure of Confederate emissaries James M. Mason and John Slidell from the British mail steamer *Trent* came closest to giving the Confederacy the foreign help it needed by nearly bringing on a war between Great Britain and the United States. Confederate diplomats were not, on the whole, very skillful negotiatiors (E). There was some objection in Europe to the Union blockade (B), but Britain, the only country that could have done anything about it, favored permissive rules for blockading. Large prewar stocks of cotton in Britain and France, along with the discovery of alternate sources of cotton, prevented the economic dislocation in those countries that Confederate leaders had hoped would bring their aid (C). Some French financiers did float a bond issue for the Confederacy, but they slyly made sure they got their money first, assuring that if anyone got bilked it would be the small, uninfluential investors.

7. **(B)**

This map depicts the United States as it was after the Missouri Compromise in 1820. Maine was admitted as a state on March 15, 1820, and Missouri would become a state on August 21, 1821. The territory remaining from the Louisiana Purchase has been divided between slave and free areas along the line of 36° 30'. Arkansas and Michigan have not yet become states as would have been the case before the Webster-Ashburton Treaty (E). The Mexican Cession has not yet been added as would have been the case after the settlement of the Mexican War (D) or the Compromise of 1850 (A). However, at the time of the Northwest Ordinance (C), the Louisiana Purchase area would not yet have been added.

8. **(D)**

The "Bonus March" involved World War I veterans demanding financial aid from the federal government during the Depression. A few of the Bonus Marchers did build shacks near Washington, D.C. (B). Many farmers — and others — were disgruntled in 1932 (A), but the means of expressing it was generally by voting for Franklin D. Roosevelt for president. There were also during this time a number of farm workers seeking employment in California (E). Later, during the Second World War, Japanese-Americans were relocated (C), but they could hardly have protested by marching on Washington.

9. **(C)**

Julius and Ethel Rosenberg were convicted of espionage, condemned, and electrocuted. They were accused of giving atomic secrets to the Soviet Union, not Germany (A), but they refused to confess (E). Public opinion was very much in favor of harsh treatment of Communists, and Eisenhower did not pardon the Rosenbergs (D). It was not the Rosenbergs but Alger Hiss who was exposed as a spy by Whitaker Chambers (B).

10. **(B)**

Malcolm X advocated armed violence against police and troops. Nonviolent defiance of segregation (A) was the policy of Martin Luther King Jr. Patience while developing the skills that would make Blacks economically successful and gain them the respect of Whites (C) and (E) was the policy of Booker T. Washington. Gradual assimilation of the two races (D) was exactly the opposite of what Malcolm X taught.

11. **(D)**

Khrushchev used the Soviet downing of the U-2 spy plane as a pretense to cancel the summit, thereby embarrassing Eisenhower. Castro had recently risen to power in Cuba (A), but the Bay of Pigs fiasco (B) was yet to come. Several years earlier, in unrelated incidents, the U.S. had sent troops into Lebanon (C) and the Soviet Union had launched *Sputnik* (E).

12. **(E)**

The largest impact on the reduction of inland freight rates during this period was created by the introduction of steamboats. Railroads (A) came somewhat later. Keelboats, flatboats (D), turnpikes (C), and canals (B) were of less importance.

13. **(B)**

Southern states were required to ratify the Fourteenth Amendment. Actually, Blacks had not always been granted full civil rights even in Northern states before the Civil War and after (A). Integrated public schools were more than a century off (C). The Sixteenth Amendment (D), allowing a federal income tax, was ratified in 1913. Some radicals talked of providing land to the freed slaves (E) but nothing ever came of it.

14. **(C)**

The primary function of the World War I Food Administration was to oversee the production and allocation of foodstuffs to ensure adequate supplies for the army and the Allies. It did not become involved in operating farms (E) nor did it, as a general rule, specially monitor the food produced (D). Farm prices were considered to be high enough already (A), and the U.S. would hardly have imported food from its somewhat undernourished Allies (B).

15. **(C)**

The purpose of the Truman Doctrine was to aid countries that were the targets of Communist expansionism. Preventing European meddling in the affairs of South American countries (B) was the essence of the Monroe Doctrine, which was not directly related to the Truman Doctrine (E). It was the Marshall Plan, also instituted during Truman's presidency, that aided the economic recovery of Europe from the Second World War (A).

16. **(B)**

The Molasses Act was intended to force the colonists to buy sugar from more expensive British colonial sources rather than from foreign producers. Forcing the colonists to export solely to Great Britain (A), forbidding them to engage in manufacturing activity in competition with British industries (C), and creating an economic situation in which gold tended to flow from the colonies to the mother country (E) were also goals of mercantilism. Providing a favorable market for the products of the British East India Company (D) was the purpose of the Tea Act.

17. **(E)**

The British government mistakenly thought the colonists would accept the Townshend Act as an external tax after having rejected the previous Stamp Act, an internal tax. They were under no illusions about the American position on taxation having changed (A), and they had not yet decided to provoke a military confrontation to teach the colonists a lesson (B). The act was designed to collect revenue, not merely enforce mercantilism (C), and it had not been approved by the colonial legislatures (D), though in either case the Americans would probably have accepted it.

18. **(A)**

Douglas's Freeport Doctrine was that any territory desiring to exclude slavery could do so simply by declining to pass laws protecting it, notwithstanding the Dred Scott decision (D). That decision had also asserted that any slaveholder was free to take his slaves anywhere within the United States without hindrance by state, federal, or territorial governments (E). Many Northern states were, by this time, attempting to block the operation of the Fugitive Slave Law through their own "personal liberty laws" (C). Douglas did not believe that a state had the right to secede (B).

19. **(C)**

Subsidies to transcontinental railroads generally took the form of land grants along the railroad's right-of-way. Occasionally, loans, rather than cash payments (A), were granted on a per-mile basis. Blanket appropriations (B) and provision of supplies and materials (D) were generally not used. In the Southeastern U.S., convict labor was sometimes rented to railroads (E), but not for the trans-continental railroads, much of whose track lay, of necessity, far from centers of population.

20. **(A)**

The Mann-Elkins Act strengthened government regulation of the railroads during Taft's administration. The Federal Trade Commission (B) did not apply primarily to the railroads. The Granger Laws (C) did, but came long before Taft's administration. The government was still opposed to large business combinations (E), as Taft broke up more trusts than famed "trust-buster" Theodore Roosevelt. The government did not, however, take over and run the railroads (D) until during the First World War, under Wilson.

21. **(A)**

Surprisingly, the Old Immigration, made up of those from Northern and Western Europe, still predominated after the Civil War until about 1890. Thereafter, the New Immigration, composed primarily of those from Southern and Eastern Europe (B), was most prevalent.

22. **(B)**

The 1844 campaign slogan of the supporters of James K. Polk called for annexation of all of the Oregon country. After being elected Polk settled for a compromise deal. During Polk's presidency the readjustment of the nation's border with Mexico (C) and the demand by Northern free-soilers that limits be placed on the spread of slavery (D) were both significant issues. In response to the latter, Southerners suggested that the Missouri Compromise line be extended through the Mexican Cession (E). The "Aroostook War" (A) was settled by the Webster-Ashburton Treaty during the presidency of Polk's predecessor, John Tyler.

23. **(C)**

Taft did not reverse Theodore Roosevelt's conservationist policies but in fact advanced them more than Roosevelt had. He did this, however, in a quiet way, since he disliked publicity (D) and was little inclined to make rousing speeches or engage in political conflict (B). In much the same way, he went about prosecuting trusts to a greater degree than Roosevelt had done (E). He was also an able administrator (A).

24. **(A)**

The primary issue in Shays' Rebellion was the jailing of individuals or seizure of their property for failure to pay taxes during a time of economic hardship. Economic oppression by eastern Massachusetts bankers (E) and underrepresentation of the western part of the state (B) may have been contributing factors. Indians were by this time not a serious problem in Massachusetts (D), and there was no unpaid bonus (C).

25. **(C)**

The Articles of Confederation government did have the power to borrow money and that is how it financed most of what it did. It did not, however, have the power to levy taxes (A), regulate commerce (B), or compel the states to abide by treaties (D), and it lacked a strong executive (E).

26. **(B)**

The most successful method of financing the War of Independence was by obtaining grants from foreign countries. Printing large amounts of paper money (A), issuing paper securities backed by the promise of Western land grants (D), and appealing to the states for voluntary contributions (E) were tried with very little success. Congress did not have the power to levy direct taxes (C).

27. **(C)**

It did not prohibit slavery in the lands acquired as a result of the Mexican War. Although California was admitted as a free state (A), the Utah and New Mexico Territories were left open on the subject of slavery. The Compromise also included a tougher fugitive slave law (B), stipulated that land in dispute between Texas and New Mexico should go to New Mexico (D), and ended the slave trade — but not slavery — in the District of Columbia (E).

28. **(E)**

A member of the Social Gospel movement would probably argue that Christians should work to reorganize the industrial system and bring about international peace. He would probably not be very concerned about such "ordinary" sins as alcohol abuse and sexual permissiveness (A), nor would he hold the poor at fault for their plight (B) or suggest that those who committed abuses simply lacked will-power (C) — all this was society's fault. He did not see religion as individualistic (D) but rather as a social matter.

29. **(C)**

In *Plessy v. Ferguson* (1896), the Supreme Court upheld separate but equal facilities. It overturned this ruling with *Brown v. Topeka Board of Education* in 1954 (A). The ruling that no black slave could be a citizen of the United States was in the 1857 case *Dred Scott v. Sanford*. Various Supreme Court decisions in the 1950s, '60s, and '70s dealt with affirmative action (D) and literacy tests (E).

30. **(D)**

Henry Clay's "American System" did not call for an independent treasury, which actually became a goal of Clay's opponents, the Democrats. Instead, Clay favored a national bank (B). His system also called for federal funding for the building of roads (A), high protective tariffs (C), and federal funding for the construction of canals (E).

31. **(B)**

The first national group upon whom Congress placed immigration restrictions was the Chinese. The Chinese Exclusion Act of 1882 was the vehicle for doing so. The first quantitative U.S. immigration law was adopted in 1921. It set temporary annual quotas according to nationality; quotas were made permanent in 1924. In 1952, the United States' many immigration and naturalization laws then on the books were brought under one comprehensive statute that limited immigration from the Eastern Hemisphere while leaving immigration from within the Western Hemisphere unrestricted. It wasn't until 1978 that the separate caps for Eastern and Western hemispheric immigration were combined into one global limit of 290,000.

32. **(A)**

The Free-Soil party's main issue was a federal ban on the spread of slavery in the territories. Later in the decade the Free-Soil party was swallowed up by the Republican party, which also espoused its chief issue as well as calling for a homestead act (B). Only the radical abolitionists during the 1850s called for the immediate and uncompensated abolition of slavery (C), just as after the Civil War it was only the most radical of the Republicans who called for providing the freed slaves with "forty acres and a mule" (D). During the 1850s it was Southerners who desired to annex Cuba (E), hoping it would become a slave state.

33. **(C)**

Creation of the Bank of the United States was more controversial than federal assumption of state debts (A) or the imposition of protective tariffs (D), though these, too, were controversial to a degree. Neither direct taxes (B) nor establishment of a bimetallic system (E) were part of Hamilton's program, though a century later the bimetallic issue did become very controversial.

34. **(C)**

The position of the Nullifiers was that the states could nullify acts of the federal government they held to be unconstitutional. That the federal courts had the right to nullify acts of Congress that restricted the spread of slavery in the territories (B) was expressed in the Supreme Court's 1857 Dred Scott decision. The idea that Southern states had the right to nullify statutes of Northern states interfering with the recapture of escaped slaves (D) is similar to the idea behind the Fugitive Slave Act except in that case it was the federal government that was overriding free-state law. That Congress should refuse to receive any petitions against slavery (E) was the "gag rule." Free states, of course, still had the right to prohibit the ownership of property in slaves, but only for their own citizens, not for Southerners passing through.

35. **(D)**

The Mayflower Compact could best be described as a foundation for self-government. It was not a detailed frame of government (A) or a complete constitution (B), and it was certainly not a business contract (C). It did not deal with the causes for leaving England and coming to the New World (E).

36. **(A)**

    The Taft-Hartley Act was definitely not sought but rather vehemently opposed by the labor unions. It did allow the president to call a cooling-off period (B), and it outlawed the closed shop (C). It was backed by Congressional Republicans (D), vetoed by President Truman (E), and passed over his veto.

37. **(D)**

    The Wade-Davis Bill was pocket-vetoed by Lincoln. Allowing restoration of a loyal government when as few as ten percent of the state's total prewar registered voters would take the oath of allegiance (A) was part of Lincoln's Ten Percent Plan, which the Wade-Davis Bill was meant to supersede with far harsher terms (E). It did not explicitly demand the vote for Blacks (B), but under its terms no Southern state could have established a government without doing so unless it waited for a whole new generation to rise to voting age. Its terms toward former high-ranking rebels were not at all lenient (C).

38. **(D)**

    Sinclair Lewis depicted small-town America as dreary, prejudiced, and vulgar, rather than in any of the more traditional and positive ways reflected in the other answer choices.

39. **(C)**

    Coolidge kept government spending low and encouraged private business. He kept taxes low (B), except for the tariff (E), and opposed government involvement in major projects (A). As was still traditional for presidents at that time, he did not take an active role in pushing legislation through Congress (D).

40. **(A)**

    The Incas built the most advanced culture in South America in the Andes Mountains region of Peru. At their zenith, in the sixteenth century, they may have controlled a population of about 12 million people. Inca society was strictly stratified and the emperor ruled with the assistance of an aristocratic bureaucracy. The Incas developed an elaborate irrigation system to support their agricultural economy, which grew maize, potatoes, squash, tomatoes, cassava, and cotton. They built an extensive network of roads, one of which was about 2,250 miles long. They also constructed suspension bridges made of vines and dug rock tunnels through the mountains. A message system based on relay runners was able to deliver news as fast as 150 miles per day. The other tribes did not live in South America.

41. **(A)**

   The Spanish-American War showed the need of shifting naval forces rapidly between the Atlantic and the Pacific. There had never been much doubt about overcoming Latin American countries if that were necessary, or of dealing with any (highly unlikely) threat from Spain (D). The war did nothing to discredit opponents of the project (C), and such tropical diseases as malaria and yellow fever were not dealt with successfully (E) until during the actual building of the canal.

42. **(C)**

   Though one can easily imagine it being said by any of the other persons on any of the other occasions, this statement was part of Franklin Roosevelt's first inaugural address.

43. **(C)**

   The Civilian Conservation Corps never employed anywhere near one-third of the U.S. work force, but it was part of FDR's New Deal (E). Its workers did live in camps under semi-military discipline (A) and work on such projects as preventing soil erosion (B), and it did provide that some of the workers' pay be sent home to help their families.

44. **(D)**

   Roosevelt wanted to manipulate the dollar amount the government would pay for gold in order to raise prices, since it was believed this would relieve the Depression. Since Roosevelt had already made it impossible for Americans to own gold, there could be no run on the banks by people wanting to get it (C). Maintaining the dollar's value at a constant level (A), preventing inflation (B), or lowering prices (E) were all just the opposite of what Roosevelt hoped to accomplish.

45. **(D)**

   The basic issue in the coming of war between the U.S. and Japan in 1941 was Japan's desire to annex large portions of China. The Japanese were not yet aiding the Germans in their war against Britain (A) and did not desire to annex the Aleutians (C) — although during the course of the war they did attack and occupy a couple of them. The U.S. did not desire the Japanese-held islands in the Pacific (B) — though during the war it wound up taking a great many of them. American resentment of Japanese trading policies (E) characterizes more the last quarter of the twentieth century.

46. **(E)**

The Arabic Pledge, named after a torpedoed British liner, was a German promise not to sink passenger ships without warning. German submarines could still be used to attack warships without warning or passenger ships after giving warning (C). The Germans, of course, made no promise not to try to break the British blockade (D) but had little hope of doing so, and unless they did could not hope to buy war supplies in the U.S. (B). The following year, 1917, the Germans did offer to aid Mexico in a war against the United States (A), an offer contained in the famous Zimmermann Telegram.

47. **(E)**

Woodrow Wilson's most prized part of his Fourteen Points was the League of Nations. The Fourteen Points also included freedom of the seas (D), open diplomacy (A), and the right of self-determination — though not of a union of Germany and Austria in accord with such a right (C). Wilson would definitely have opposed either strengthening the Austrian Empire or restoring the balance of power (B).

48. **(A)**

W. E. B. Du Bois founded the National Association for the Advancement of Colored People. He was a leader of the Niagara Movement (C) and an outspoken critic of the Atlanta Compromise (B), which was the work of Booker T. Washington (E) whose teaching was that Blacks should temporarily accommodate themselves to Whites (D).

49. **(D)**

The Southern states did not attempt to reinstitute slavery, but some or all of them did refuse to repudiate the Confederate debt (A), elect former Confederates to high positions (B), refuse to grant Blacks the right to vote (C), and pass special "black codes" restricting the legal rights of Blacks (E), resulting in the imposition of harsh congressional Reconstruction despite Johnson's efforts to prevent it.

50. **(D)**

It was for violation of the Tenure of Office Act in removing Secretary of War Stanton that Johnson was impeached and almost removed from office. His refusal to cooperate with the Radical Republicans (E) or to carry out the spirit, if not the letter, of the Military Reconstruction Act (A) and the Civil Rights Act (C) were the reasons the heavily radical Congress was anxious to be rid of him, but even they could not bring themselves to impeach him without some actual breach of a law — thus, the Tenure of Office Act. It was Grant, rather than Johnson, whose associates were involved in not one but a number of highly questionable schemes (B).

51. **(A)**

When white Southerners during the era of Reconstruction spoke of "redemption" in political terms they meant ridding their states of the Reconstruction governments. They would hardly have thought it necessary to atone for slavery or secession (B) and (C), and regaining personal rights (D) was relatively easy for the great majority of Southerners who had not held high positions in the Confederacy or in the U.S. government before joining the Confederacy. Very few, if any, plantations were confiscated as a result of the war (E).

52. **(D)**

Northern voters simply lost interest and grew tired of Reconstruction. Leading Radicals in the North had never cared much whether Reconstruction was constitutional or not (C), but many of them were dead by 1877. Agitating wartime animosities was still a useful electoral tactic (E), but it did not necessarily need to be linked to reconstructing the South. The goals of the Radical Republicans had not been accomplished (B), but neither had the Southerners regained all the state governments (A).

53. **(E)**

Allied strategy was to beat Germany first rather than the other way around (A) or an even division of resources (B).

54. **(C)**

The Marshall Plan was an American economic aid program for Europe. The Truman Doctrine was the American commitment to help countries threatened by Communism (D).

55. **(C)**

Kennedy came off looking better in the televised debates. Americans were perhaps somewhat bored with Eisenhower, though not deeply dissatisfied (A). There were no revelations of corruption on Nixon's part during this election (B), though there were during his 1952 run for vice president and his 1972 run for re-election as president. Kennedy had never been governor of Massachusetts and was short of administrative experience (D). Nixon, like Kennedy, had served in the Navy during World War II (E), though without achieving the fame Kennedy had gained on the PT-109.

56. **(A)**

The Warren Commission held that Oswald acted alone. Many since then, however, have suggested that Oswald was part of a large conspiracy (C) and that he was aided by marksmen on a "grassy knoll" (B). Some have indeed gone so far as to suggest that Oswald had nothing to do with the assassination (D). In fact, there are very few allegations, however bizarre, that have not been made about the Kennedy assassination, and, not surprisingly, many Americans seem to believe that the true facts of the matter will probably never be known (E).

57. **(D)**

The hostility of the fierce Iroquois helped keep the French out of what is now the United States. The French did establish a profitable fur trade in Canada (A), and Champlain did found a permanent settlement, Quebec, along the St. Lawrence (B) and did make it back to France alive (C). Instead of a British-French alliance against the Iroquois (E), what developed was an alliance system that pitted the British and Iroquois against the French and Algonquins.

58. **(A)**

Penn's purpose was to create a refuge for Quakers, but other persecuted sects also found a haven there (B). Penn was also able to establish friendly relations with the Indians (C), and while he had hoped to make a financial profit out of the colony while he was at it (D), in this he was disappointed. The colony founded as a refuge for debtors was Georgia.

59. **(B)**

Though many factors might contribute to an individual's choice of party, including, perhaps, the character of the party's leader (D), and the party's stand on such issues as states' rights (C), the chief factor during this period was acceptance or rejection of the French Revolution — Jefferson and his supporters saw it as good, Hamilton and the Federalists did not. By this time the Constitution had virtually universal acceptance in the U.S. (A). Though during the days of the fight over ratification, those favoring the Constitution were known as Federalists; they are not to be confused with the political party bearing the same name that gradually took form *after* the Constitution was in effect. Patriot and Loyalist divisions came to mean increasingly less (E).

60. **(B)**

The Bostonians reacted by throwing the tea into the harbor rather than allow the tax to be paid on it. The Boston Massacre (A) was a bloody clash between British troops and American colonists during the unrest growing out of the Townshend Acts. The Massachusetts Circular Letter (E) was also part of the colonial reaction to the Townshend Acts. The Declaration of Independence (C) did not come for another three years after the Boston Tea Party, and the Articles of Confederation (D), the nation's first frame of national government, came after that.

61. **(A)**

The XYZ Affair involved the demand of French Foreign Minister Talleyrand that he receive a bribe before he would meet with American envoys. Immediately following the War of Independence, the British did refuse to evacuate their forts on American territory, particularly on the northwestern frontier (B). In 1818 Andrew Jackson did lead an incursion into Spanish-held Florida (C) in pursuit of raiding Indians. The 1807 British seizure of American crewmen from a U.S. Navy warship in Chesapeake Bay (D) was the Chesapeake-Leopard Incident. Finally, Aaron Burr did indeed seem to have some sort of bizarre plot in mind during the first decade of the 1800s though nothing came of it (E).

62. **(D)**

The most unusual feature of the charter of the Massachusetts Bay Colony was that it did not specify where the company's headquarters should be. It did not specify that the colony should be run as a religious commonwealth (A) or make the colony completely independent of all English authority (B), but by allowing the headquarters to be moved to America, it allowed the former and virtually insured the latter for the time being. It did not specify that Parliament rather than the king should have authority of the colony (E), and it did assure that the colonists were to enjoy all the rights they would have had if they had been born and living in England (C), but so did the rest of the colonial charters.

63. **(D)**

Relations with the Indians in colonial Virginia were not especially good. The colonists lived in constant fear of them and for good reason. The colony was kept alive by large influxes of supplies and recruits (E), drawn by promises of political rights represented by the House of Burgesses (A), and the hope of becoming rich through the cultivation of tobacco (C) on their own private property (B).

64. (E)

The Great Awakening was the first religious development to have an impact throughout colonial America. Toleration in Maryland (A) and Quakerism in Pennsylvania (B) showed little tendency to spread to the other colonies. The Half-Way Covenant (C) was a late-seventeenth-century religious compromise involving only colonial New England. The Parsons' Cause (D) involved Anglican Church establishment in eighteenth-century Virginia.

65. (A)

Jackson's veto of the Maysville Road dealt with the matter of federally financed internal improvements. The power of the Second Bank of the United States (C) was the issue in Jackson's "Bank War," and the efficiency and honesty of government employees (D) was the issue in Jackson's so-called "Spoils System." Jackson's *Specie Circular* forbade the purchase of government land with paper money (E).

66. (E)

The armed confrontation — brief and bloodless — along the Maine-Canada border was the "Aroostook War" and took place in 1842, 30 years after the outbreak of the War of 1812. The other items, the Chesapeake-Leopard Incident (A), the British impressment of American seamen from American ships on the high seas (B), the concerns of Western Americans that the British were inciting the Indians (C), and the "War Hawks'" desire to annex Canada (D) were all real and all contributed to the coming of the war.

67. (C)

The Monroe Doctrine stated that the United States would not tolerate any new European colonization in the New World. The U.S. did desire to see republican governments instituted in countries all over the world (A) and (B), it stated, but would intervene only to prevent new, not to remove existing (D) and (E) European colonization in the New World.

68. (D)

The status of slavery in the territories proved the most divisive aspect of the slavery issue. Relatively little controversy surrounded the international slave trade (E), and Congress prohibited it in 1808, as soon as it was constitutionally empowered to do so. The status of slavery in the District of Columbia (A), the right to send antislavery literature through the mail (B), and the enforcement of the Fugitive Slave Law (C) were all highly controversial and divisive issues though ultimately not to the degree of the territorial issue that eventually led to civil war.

69. **(A)**

The "Kitchen Cabinet" was a group of old friends and unofficial advisors to Andrew Jackson, so called by his political enemies from the derisive suggestion that they entered the White House through the kitchen, or servants' entrance. Jackson's cabinet may not have been socially acceptable among some of Jackson's aristocratic critics, but it certainly included no former cooks (B). It was not suggested that government funds be kept on the premises of the White House (C).

70. **(C)**

The Pre-emption Act provided that those who settled on government land would have first chance to buy it. Tyler did set a precedent for the vice president's becoming a full-fledged (rather than merely acting) president when the incumbent dies (D). The idea that the status of slavery in a territory should be decided by the settlers there (A) was popular sovereignty. Slave law pre-empted free law in disputes involving escaped slaves (B) by means of the Fugitive Slave Law, and that was the only case in which federal law pre-empted state law in matters pertaining to slavery (E).

71. **(B)**

The Homestead Act granted 160 acres to anyone who would settle on it and improve it. It was the Dawes Severalty Act of 1887 that provided for Indians to own their land individually (A). The Homestead Act was sometimes abused by Great Plains ranchers to obtain control of large amounts of land (C), though not in exchange for supplying beef to the Army. Talk of giving land to former slaves during the Reconstruction (D) era came to nothing, and, once again, there were virtually no confiscations as a result of the Civil War (E).

72. **(B)**

Progress and Poverty was Henry George's most famous book. The other books listed were all written by George's contemporaries and, like George, all intended to make social statements: *Looking Backward* (A) by Edward Bellamy, *The Jungle* (C) by Upton Sinclair, *The Shame of the Cities* (D) by Lincoln Steffens, and *Sister Carrie* (E) by Theodore Dreiser.

73. **(B)**

Dewey was not concerned with strengthening a child's respect for parental or other traditional authority. He has been called the father of Progressive Education (E); he was influenced by the ideas of "Pragmatist" philosopher William James (D); he strove to alter the content and purpose of schooling (A) and to socialize the child through his peer group (C).

74. **(C)**

"Waving the bloody shirt" was the practice of using wartime animosities to gain election in the North. Machine politics were practiced in many cities during the late nineteenth century (E), though there is no special name for this other than "corruption." The voting of large appropriations of federal funds for unnecessary projects in a powerful congressman's district (B) might also be called corruption but is more often referred to as a "pork barrel scheme," a general term for a politician's buying of votes with government appropriations. Inciting the country to go to war with Spain (D) was one of the things accomplished just before the turn of the century by "Yellow Journalism."

75. **(B)**

The first policy toward the Plains Indians was simply to let them have the entire area, which was actually believed to be a desert. Later the policy changed to dividing the Indians between two large reservations (A), then to confining them to a number of small reservations (E), then to giving them their land in individual parcels (C), and then back to reservations again. The idea that Indians should be exterminated (D) was never a policy of the government but, unfortunately, was held by some individuals.

76. **(A)**

The main goal of the Populist movement was free coinage of silver. Prohibition of immigration from China and Japan (B) was a popular idea on the West Coast during that era. The transcontinental railroad (C) had been completed 20 years before the Populist movement got under way. A "single tax" on land (D) was Henry George's idea. And stringent regulations for the workplace (E) was one of the reforms sought by the Progressive movement.

77. **(A)**

Georgia O'Keeffe, Thomas Hart Benton, and Edward Hopper were all American painters of the 1920s (E). This was the age of jazz (B) and of skyscrapers (D). Georgia O'Keeffe was known for her abstract paintings of flowers and animal skulls against the background of the New Mexico desert (C).

78. (E)

The Dumbarton Oaks Conference was one of the important meetings that led to the formation of the United Nations. Punishment of Nazi war criminals (A) was dealt with at the Nuremberg Trials. The map of Eastern Europe (D) was discussed at the Yalta Conference. The decision to drop the atomic bomb (B) was made by President Truman.

79. (E)

The Bland-Allison Act, requiring the government to purchase silver, not gold (B) and (C), was vetoed by President Hayes but subsequently passed over his veto. It did not give the president discretion as to whether or not silver should be bought (A), and it did not provide for a floating rate of exchange between gold and silver (D), probably one of its greatest weaknesses.

80. (A)

Jefferson would have been more likely to take a narrow view of the Constitution, Hamilton a broad and permissive one. Hamilton, rather than Jefferson, also favored Britain over France in the European war (B), favored the establishment of a national bank (C), won the cooperation of presidents George Washington and John Adams most of the time (D), and opposed the efforts of Citizen Genet in America (E).

Detailed Explanations of Answers

Section II

Sample Answer to Document-based Question

1. Few leaders have faced decisions as difficult as those confronting Abraham Lincoln and Jefferson Davis in April 1861. At stake was the allegiance of the northern tier of slaves states, wavering between the Union and their sister slave states. Beyond that, Lincoln had to find some way to get all the states back into the Union, and Davis to prevent it. All this now focused on Fort Sumter.

Located on an island inside the harbor of Charleston, South Carolina, and garrisoned by less then 100 U.S. soldiers, Fort Sumter was to both North and South a symbol of national authority in the states claiming to have seceded. At his inaugural Lincoln promised not to initiate hostilities against the South but nevertheless to "hold, occupy and possess the property and places belonging to the government." This wise policy avoided alienating the border states, for the time being, but also maintained the federal government's claim to sovereignty in South Carolina. Some disagreed. Secretary of State William H. Seward was foremost in urging that the fort be abandoned in order to mollify the South and keep the issue from being seen as one of slavery versus abolitionism or Democratic versus Republican party. Against all such urgings, Lincoln remained firm.

Davis was faced with the problem of whether to await the hoped-for Northern evacuation of the fort or to order a Southern attack. It was an unpleasant dilemma. To allow a garrison of "foreign" troops to remain in a fort in the harbor of one of its chief cities would appear to indicate the Confederacy was neither independent nor in earnest about becoming so. On the other hand, to attack the fort would be to take upon the South the onus of firing the first shot and initiating a civil war, making the South appear the aggressor, rather than the victim of aggression, as Davis and most other Southerners believed it to be. Meanwhile, the South clamored for Davis to take some sort of action. "The border states will never join us," complained the *Charleston Mercury*, "until we have indicated our power to free ourselves" by taking Fort Sumter. An Alabama newspaper even suggested that at the present rate the people would soon consider Southern independence mere hollow words and give up and go back to the Union. From elsewhere came assertions that all that was needed to rally every slave state around the cause of the Confederacy was "the shedding of blood."

Davis's hope in all of this was Lincoln's dilemma: the fort was running out of food. Unless supplies could be gotten to it soon, its commander, Major Robert Anderson, would have to evacuate. Davis waited to see if this would spare him the necessity of choosing one unpleasant alternative or the other. Lincoln was determined to do something about it. An expedition was sent to re-supply the fort, and notice duly given the South Carolina governor. No effort was to be made "to throw in men, arms, or ammunition. . . . without further notice" unless Sumter was attacked. With that Lincoln had checkmated his Confederate counterpart, who would now have to acquiesce in the permanent presence of a federal garrison in Charleston harbor or else take the responsibility of firing the first shot and firing it to keep food from hungry men. Lincoln probably hoped Davis would not choose war, but he was willing to risk the result if he did.

The Confederacy's own secretary of state, Robert Toombs, pleaded with Davis not to attack. "You will want only strike a hornets' nest...," he warned. "Legions now quiet will swarm out and sting us to death. It is unnecessary. It puts us in the wrong. It is fatal." Davis did not take Toombs' advice, but it was eventually proved at least partially correct. The Confederate firing on Fort Sumter and Lincoln's response in calling for 75,000 volunteers to put down the rebellion did have the effect of galvanizing the South. Arkansas, Tennessee, North Carolina, and crucial Virginia seceded and joined the Confederacy. Yet it also rallied the loyal states in a way that probably nothing else could have. The flag had been fired on; war had been initiated by Southern aggression. A wave of martial enthusiasm swept over the North.

Ultimately, Lincoln's course must appear the wiser. Davis, by initiating the conflict had given the North a strength and unity without which it probably could not have won the war that followed. Yet in fairness it must be said that for the Confederate president there were no easy alternatives.

Sample Answers to Essay Questions

2. Two major compromises marked the sectional relations of the first half of the nineteenth century, the 1820 Missouri Compromise and the Compromise of 1850. The Missouri Compromise settled a controversy arising from the petition of Missouri, a part of the Louisiana Purchase, to be admitted to the Union as a slave state. The slave state of Louisiana had already been formed out of the Louisiana Purchase, but slavery had existed there before U.S. ownership. Missouri represented an area settled largely by Americans, and Northerners were loath to see slavery following the flag to areas where it was previously unknown. Anxious to see some limit placed on the spread of slavery, they moved to admit Missouri on the condition that it emancipate its slaves within a generation.

Southerners were outraged at this not only because it would have assured their section the minority status in the Senate that it already had in the House, but also because they considered it an insult. The compromise that resolved this crisis stipulated that Missouri be admitted as a slave state but that the remaining Louisiana Territory be divided along latitude 36° 30', the area south of the line reserved for slavery, north of it, forever free.

Here the charge of "sectional sellout" is partially true. Southerners obtained Missouri as a slave state, and though the division of the remaining territory seemed favorable to the North, it actually gave the South at least half and probably two-thirds of the area suitable for the establishment of slavery in the first place. Yet the North did at least win the principle that slavery could be excluded in some of the territories, and a small area of land that might have been suitable for slavery was reserved for freedom.

The Compromise of 1850 quieted the uproar over the status of slavery in the lands acquired through the Mexican War. Sectional tempers had heated over the past quarter century, and many Northerners were prepared to see the war as a plot to add new slave states to the Union. Their feeling that the war should be fought, if at all, for national, rather than slave, expansion, was expressed in the Wilmot Proviso, stipulating that slavery be prohibited throughout the Mexican Cession. Introduced several times in Congress during the late 1840s, it was never passed.

Southerners were again outraged. Since the majority of the nation's unorganized land holdings had previously lain in the North and been closed to slavery, they felt the new lands added in the South should naturally be open to slavery. The matter was brought to a head when California petitioned for admission to the Union as a free state. The resulting compromise must again be considered at least in part a sectional sellout. Though the North got California and at least a chance at the rest of the Mexican Cession, it is doubtful if slavery could have prospered in that arid region anyway. The South got Congress to profess its lack of power to do two things the Constitution and laws clearly gave it power to do: abolish slavery in the District of Columbia and ban the interstate slave trade. In the odious Fugitive Slave Law, another part of the compromise, the federal government was made the instrument of some of the ugliest abuses of the system of slavery.

In short, it can be concluded that though "sectional sellout" may be too strong a word for agreements from which the North clearly received some gains, it is also clear that the compromises did to a large extent sacrifice justice and the national interest to the aggressive demands of the militant slaveholding South.

3. Dwight D. Eisenhower had enormous appeal with voters in the 1950s because he was a war hero, because he had the common touch, because he was reassuring, and because he was seen as moderate and non-partisan.

During the Second World War Eisenhower had been a supreme allied commander in Europe, where he had gained a reputation as a skillful manager and conciliator. One of the most distinguished generals of the war, he was seen by the public as the man who beat Hitler, and this was a major source of his popularity.

Yet at the same time he had the appeal of the common man, having been born in a small town in Texas and grown up in a poor but hard-working family in Abilene, Kansas. He expressed issues in simple terms and had the air of an ordinary, honest man.

Eisenhower was also reassuring. The country had just come through more than two decades of constant upheaval: stock market crash, Depression, government reforms on a magnitude previously unheard of, a World War, the Korean War, and the threat of Soviet Communism. Eisenhower, without doing very much — or perhaps because he did not do very much — was a reassuring influence to the American people. He was a president who would not "rock the boat" with drastic reforms or overseas emergencies.

He was also seen as moderate and non-partisan. Not having been a professional politician before coming to the presidency, he could project the image of being above partisan bickering. His moderation consisted of steering a middle course between the bureaucratic welfare state and the traditional laissez-faire republic of pre-New Deal days. Americans, still somewhat enamored of some of the New Deal programs but uncomfortable with this radical departure from their traditions of government, appreciated Eisenhower's moderate mixing of the two.

Taken together, these factors made Eisenhower one of the most popular presidents of the post-World War II era.

4. While the influence of Theodore Roosevelt and other influential and empire-minded persons may have helped to persuade McKinley to enter the Spanish-American War, the weight of public opinion must be considered as a major factor in the president's decision.

The 1890s were the heyday of "Yellow Journalism." Named for "the Yellow Kid," a cartoon character regularly appearing in the mass circulation papers of the time, Yellow Journalism grew out of the competition for circulation between the mass-market papers of William Randolph Hearst and Joseph Pulitzer. In order to boost their circulation, the papers were not above sensationalizing, distorting, falsifying, or even creating news.

This had its most striking effect in helping to bring on the Spanish American War. Newspapers gave sensationalized reports of Spanish attempts to suppress a rebellion in Cuba, making it appear that the Spaniards were guilty of extreme human rights violations. As public outrage grew, so too did pressure on the McKinley administration to take a hard line with Spain. Spain was conciliatory, but McKinley felt compelled to send the battleship U.S.S. *Maine* to the harbor of Havanna, Cuba, to show the flag and generally uphold American interests. While there the *Maine* was torn by an explosion and sank with heavy loss of life. The yellow press immediately roared its opinion that this was the doing of Spain, though the cause of the explosion was and remains unknown.

The public outcry raised by such reporting, coupled with the public's sincere but in part mislead humanitarian desire to free the Cubans from Spanish tyranny and bestow on it the benefits of a free government, finally drove McKinley to decide for war with Spain. Though imperialists in high places in Washington may have helped him toward such a decision for reasons of their own, the primary reason must be viewed as the pressure of public opinion, artificially created by an irresponsible press, on an astute politician like William McKinley.

5. While it is true that other countries did away with slavery without the resort to civil war, this could have happened in the United States only had the South been willing to part with slavery under some other circumstances. Unfortunately, that was not the case.

Attempts to deal with the issue of slavery in the United States go back to the period of the Articles of Confederation. The Northwest Ordinance, drafted in 1787 by Virginia slaveholder Thomas Jefferson, prohibited slavery in what was to become the states of Ohio, Indiana, Illinois, Michigan, and Wisconsin. Jefferson believed slavery was evil and inconsistent with American ideals but that it could not be abolished suddenly in the areas where it already existed. He did not, however, desire its spread — an attitude reflected in the Northwest Ordinance and shared by most Southerners throughout the United States' first half-century of independence. The slave trade was abolished in 1808 without controversy, and various schemes were discussed for the gradual and compensated emancipation of the slaves, usually coupled with plans to repatriate them to Africa. In these, Northerners and Northern state legislatures offered their financial help, but little came of them as most slaveholders seemed more willing to confess the evil of slavery in principle than to part with their own valuable investments in human chattels.

As the 1830s began both anti-slavery rhetoric on the part of Northern opponents of the institution as well as the attitudes of the slaveholders themselves began to become more extreme. It is hard to say which phenomenon was caused by the other. They were mutually aggravating. Abolitionists denounced slavery as a national sin, and slaveholders began to defend it not as an unavoidable evil but now as a positive good for both white man and black.

The issue that finally led to civil war was that of slavery in the territories. Northerners, or at least the vast majority of them, freely conceded that the federal government had no right to prohibit slavery in the states were it existed, and repeatedly assured the South that they had no intention of doing so. They did, however, believe the federal government had the right to keep slavery from spreading into new territories and felt it their duty to achieve this. As expressed by Abraham Lincoln, their goal in this was to "place slavery where the public may rest assured that it is in the course of ultimate extinction." This was much the same attitude Thomas Jefferson had held with regard to the Northwest Ordinance, but by the mid-nineteenth century Southern attitudes had changed. Southerners too saw the limitation of slavery expansion as an indication that slavery would some day in the distant future cease to exist in their states as well, and as such they rejected it, determined to have slavery not only for the present but for the indefinite future as well.

Several attempts were made to limit the spread of slavery — the Missouri dispute of 1819–20 and the struggle over the Wilmott Proviso (1846–50) — but each ended in a compromise that gave more land to slavery. When in 1861 the Republican party came to power on a platform calling for no further spread of slavery and then refused to compromise away the results of the election, Southerners responded by seceding and setting up their own republic where slavery might never be threatened.

Thus, while it is possible to say that slavery could have been ended in the United States without a civil war — if the South would have agreed to give up its slaves on any other terms — Southern determination to preserve the institution at all costs made such a course impossible and war was the only means to rid the country of slavery.

Answer Sheet

Section I

1. Ⓐ Ⓑ Ⓒ Ⓓ Ⓔ
2. Ⓐ Ⓑ Ⓒ Ⓓ Ⓔ
3. Ⓐ Ⓑ Ⓒ Ⓓ Ⓔ
4. Ⓐ Ⓑ Ⓒ Ⓓ Ⓔ
5. Ⓐ Ⓑ Ⓒ Ⓓ Ⓔ
6. Ⓐ Ⓑ Ⓒ Ⓓ Ⓔ
7. Ⓐ Ⓑ Ⓒ Ⓓ Ⓔ
8. Ⓐ Ⓑ Ⓒ Ⓓ Ⓔ
9. Ⓐ Ⓑ Ⓒ Ⓓ Ⓔ
10. Ⓐ Ⓑ Ⓒ Ⓓ Ⓔ
11. Ⓐ Ⓑ Ⓒ Ⓓ Ⓔ
12. Ⓐ Ⓑ Ⓒ Ⓓ Ⓔ
13. Ⓐ Ⓑ Ⓒ Ⓓ Ⓔ
14. Ⓐ Ⓑ Ⓒ Ⓓ Ⓔ
15. Ⓐ Ⓑ Ⓒ Ⓓ Ⓔ
16. Ⓐ Ⓑ Ⓒ Ⓓ Ⓔ
17. Ⓐ Ⓑ Ⓒ Ⓓ Ⓔ
18. Ⓐ Ⓑ Ⓒ Ⓓ Ⓔ
19. Ⓐ Ⓑ Ⓒ Ⓓ Ⓔ
20. Ⓐ Ⓑ Ⓒ Ⓓ Ⓔ
21. Ⓐ Ⓑ Ⓒ Ⓓ Ⓔ
22. Ⓐ Ⓑ Ⓒ Ⓓ Ⓔ
23. Ⓐ Ⓑ Ⓒ Ⓓ Ⓔ
24. Ⓐ Ⓑ Ⓒ Ⓓ Ⓔ
25. Ⓐ Ⓑ Ⓒ Ⓓ Ⓔ
26. Ⓐ Ⓑ Ⓒ Ⓓ Ⓔ
27. Ⓐ Ⓑ Ⓒ Ⓓ Ⓔ

28. Ⓐ Ⓑ Ⓒ Ⓓ Ⓔ
29. Ⓐ Ⓑ Ⓒ Ⓓ Ⓔ
30. Ⓐ Ⓑ Ⓒ Ⓓ Ⓔ
31. Ⓐ Ⓑ Ⓒ Ⓓ Ⓔ
32. Ⓐ Ⓑ Ⓒ Ⓓ Ⓔ
33. Ⓐ Ⓑ Ⓒ Ⓓ Ⓔ
34. Ⓐ Ⓑ Ⓒ Ⓓ Ⓔ
35. Ⓐ Ⓑ Ⓒ Ⓓ Ⓔ
36. Ⓐ Ⓑ Ⓒ Ⓓ Ⓔ
37. Ⓐ Ⓑ Ⓒ Ⓓ Ⓔ
38. Ⓐ Ⓑ Ⓒ Ⓓ Ⓔ
39. Ⓐ Ⓑ Ⓒ Ⓓ Ⓔ
40. Ⓐ Ⓑ Ⓒ Ⓓ Ⓔ
41. Ⓐ Ⓑ Ⓒ Ⓓ Ⓔ
42. Ⓐ Ⓑ Ⓒ Ⓓ Ⓔ
43. Ⓐ Ⓑ Ⓒ Ⓓ Ⓔ
44. Ⓐ Ⓑ Ⓒ Ⓓ Ⓔ
45. Ⓐ Ⓑ Ⓒ Ⓓ Ⓔ
46. Ⓐ Ⓑ Ⓒ Ⓓ Ⓔ
47. Ⓐ Ⓑ Ⓒ Ⓓ Ⓔ
48. Ⓐ Ⓑ Ⓒ Ⓓ Ⓔ
49. Ⓐ Ⓑ Ⓒ Ⓓ Ⓔ
50. Ⓐ Ⓑ Ⓒ Ⓓ Ⓔ
51. Ⓐ Ⓑ Ⓒ Ⓓ Ⓔ
52. Ⓐ Ⓑ Ⓒ Ⓓ Ⓔ
53. Ⓐ Ⓑ Ⓒ Ⓓ Ⓔ
54. Ⓐ Ⓑ Ⓒ Ⓓ Ⓔ

55. Ⓐ Ⓑ Ⓒ Ⓓ Ⓔ
56. Ⓐ Ⓑ Ⓒ Ⓓ Ⓔ
57. Ⓐ Ⓑ Ⓒ Ⓓ Ⓔ
58. Ⓐ Ⓑ Ⓒ Ⓓ Ⓔ
59. Ⓐ Ⓑ Ⓒ Ⓓ Ⓔ
60. Ⓐ Ⓑ Ⓒ Ⓓ Ⓔ
61. Ⓐ Ⓑ Ⓒ Ⓓ Ⓔ
62. Ⓐ Ⓑ Ⓒ Ⓓ Ⓔ
63. Ⓐ Ⓑ Ⓒ Ⓓ Ⓔ
64. Ⓐ Ⓑ Ⓒ Ⓓ Ⓔ
65. Ⓐ Ⓑ Ⓒ Ⓓ Ⓔ
66. Ⓐ Ⓑ Ⓒ Ⓓ Ⓔ
67. Ⓐ Ⓑ Ⓒ Ⓓ Ⓔ
68. Ⓐ Ⓑ Ⓒ Ⓓ Ⓔ
69. Ⓐ Ⓑ Ⓒ Ⓓ Ⓔ
70. Ⓐ Ⓑ Ⓒ Ⓓ Ⓔ
71. Ⓐ Ⓑ Ⓒ Ⓓ Ⓔ
72. Ⓐ Ⓑ Ⓒ Ⓓ Ⓔ
73. Ⓐ Ⓑ Ⓒ Ⓓ Ⓔ
74. Ⓐ Ⓑ Ⓒ Ⓓ Ⓔ
75. Ⓐ Ⓑ Ⓒ Ⓓ Ⓔ
76. Ⓐ Ⓑ Ⓒ Ⓓ Ⓔ
77. Ⓐ Ⓑ Ⓒ Ⓓ Ⓔ
78. Ⓐ Ⓑ Ⓒ Ⓓ Ⓔ
79. Ⓐ Ⓑ Ⓒ Ⓓ Ⓔ
80. Ⓐ Ⓑ Ⓒ Ⓓ Ⓔ

Section II

Use the following pages on which to write your essays. If you need more space than is provided here, use your own standard ruled paper on which to complete additional pages.

Section II (Continued)

Glossary

9/11 Attacks Series of attacks by radical Islamic group al-Qaeda that took place on September 11, 2001; resulted in the destruction of New York City's World Trade Center, significant damage to the Pentagon, and thousands of civilian casualties.

Abolitionist movement Anti-slavery movement that grew greatly from 1830 until the Civil War; some abolitionists supported the immediate and complete emancipation, while others promoted working through Congress; major movement leaders included William Lloyd Garrison and Frederick Douglass.

Act of Religious Toleration Law guaranteeing political rights to all Christians, both Catholic and Protestant, in the proprietary colony of Maryland; signed by proprietor George Calvert in 1649.

Adams-Onis Treaty Treaty between the United States and Spain ratified in 1819; granted the United States control of Florida and extended the Mexican border to the Pacific in exchange for U.S. assumption of $5 million in Spanish debts to U.S. merchants.

Agricultural Adjustment Act Legislation passed in 1933 to support farm-product prices; gave farmers a subsidy to reduce production; found unconstitutional in 1936 over a tax issue.

Agricultural Marketing Act Legislation passed in 1929 that created a Federal Farm Board to support agricultural commodity prices.

AIDS Sexually transmitted disease that damages the function of the immune system; first arose as a major killer of homosexual men and drug users in the early 1980s before spreading to the general population.

Alien and Sedition Acts Controversial legislation passed by the Federalists in 1798; Alien Act made it more difficult for immigrants to obtain U.S. citizenship; Sedition Act granted Adams administration more power to censor newspapers that criticized the government.

Alliance for Progress Kennedy initiative that worked to provide aid to Latin America.

American Federation of Labor (AFL) Major national labor union combining the strength of several smaller craft unions; used strikes and collective bargaining to achieve labor goals, but remained unaffiliated with radical movements.

American Indian Movement (AIM) Civil rights group that strove to achieve greater rights for Native Americans; founded in 1968.

American System Political program promoted by Henry Clay that proposed high tariffs on imports to generate revenue to pay for internal improvements; foundation of Clay's unsuccessful 1824 bid for the presidency.

Anaconda Plan Union plan engineered by General Winfield Scott in the early portion of the Civil War; relied on a combination of a naval blockade and Union control of the Mississippi River to split the South and squeeze out its incoming resources.

anarchist Radical who supports the end of all government.

Anasazi Pre-Columbian civilization in the Southwest; built cliff dwellings called pueblos and extensive systems of roads and irrigation canals; declined in the fourteenth century.

Annapolis Convention Convention held in September 1786 intended to discuss problems relating to interstate commerce; attended by delegates from only five states; major effect was decision to hold Philadelphia convention in 1787 to revise the Articles of Confederation.

mechanization Process of employing standardized mechanical processes to do work previously done by humans; mechanical inventions such as the sewing machine and reaper helped speed industrialization in the North before the Civil War.

mercantilism Economic theory that underlaid British policy during the colonial era; believed in government control of the economy in order to support political authority; encouraged the establishment of colonies that could provide raw materials to the mother country and serve as markets for that country's exports; focused on achieving a favorable trade balance for colonizing power.

Mexican War War between the United States and Mexico that began in 1846 after years of growing tensions over the admission of Texas as a state and other territorial disputes; ended by the Treaty of Guadalupe-Hidalgo in 1848, which granted the United States a great deal of land in the West known as the Mexican Cession for $15 million, and U.S. assumption of $3.25 million in Mexican debts to U.S. citizens.

Military Reconstruction Act Legislation dividing the South, except Tennessee, into five military districts overseen by strong military governors.

missionaries Priests and other religious persons who travel to a place to convert that place's inhabitants to their own religion.

Missouri Compromise Congressional compromise reached in 1820 that admitted Missouri as a slave state and Maine as a free state, to maintain the balance of free and slave representation in the Senate; barred the expansion of slavery in the rest of Louisiana Territory north of the southern border of Missouri; engineered by House Speaker Henry Clay.

Monroe Doctrine Policy instituted by President James Monroe in 1823; stated the United States considered the Western Hemisphere no longer available for European colonization.

Moral Diplomacy Foreign policy, promulgated mostly under President Woodrow Wilson, that aimed to encourage the growth of democratic capitalist governments around the world by offering U.S. support only to democratic capitalist governments.

Moral Majority Conservative Christian group under leader Jerry Falwell that began to exercise greater political influence during the 1980s; promoted conservative social values and a strong national defense.

Mormons Religious group founded by Joseph Smith in 1830; forced to leave New York, first for the Midwest and later for the area around the Great Salt Lake that is now Utah, because of popular objections to their practice of polygamous marriage.

Morrill Land Grant Act Legislation passed in 1862 that granted large tracts of federal lands to states for the construction of agricultural and technical colleges; encouraged the creation of several major state universities.

muckrakers Investigative journalists and authors who worked to encourage Progressive reforms through their stories; included Lincoln Steffens, Ida Tarbell, and Upton Sinclair.

NAFTA (North American Free Trade Agreement) Treaty among the United States, Canada, and Mexico, signed in 1994, that eliminated most trade barriers; critics argue that the treaty has damaged U.S. industry and factory workers.

Natchez Warlike pre-Columbian people of the Mississippi Valley who endured for a time past contact with Europeans; class-based society ruled by leader called the Great Sun; organized into confederacies of farming villages.

National Association for the Advancement of Colored People (NAACP) Civil rights organization founded in 1909 to work for improved civil rights for ethnic minorities; early efforts included the promotion of anti-lynching legislation.

National Industrial Recovery Act New Deal legislation that worked to stabilize the economy by providing federal guidelines for wages, prices, production levels, and quotas; granted workers the right to unionize; enforced by National Recovery Administration; eventually found unconstitutional.

National Origins Act Legislation passed in 1924 that set strict immigration quotas favoring Northern and Western Europeans and greatly limiting or eliminating immigration for other groups, particularly Southern and Eastern Europeans and Asians; remained in effect until the mid-1960s.

nationalism Feeling of great pride in the characteristics and achievements of one's own nation; may be expressed through cultural, social, or political means.

nativism Belief that American-born U.S. citizens were superior to immigrants; generally anti-immigrant and anti-Catholic.

natural rights Enlightenment-era series of human and political rights considered vital and unbreakable; also known as inalienable rights.

naval blockade Act of using ships to prevent supplies and trade vessels from reaching their intended ports.

Navigation Acts Series of four laws passed between 1651 and 1673 that required colonial goods to be shipped only on English or American ships; required certain "enumerated" goods to be shipped to only England or English-controlled colonies; required practically all colonial imports to first enter an English port.

Neutrality Acts Series of legislation in the mid- to late 1930s, asserting U.S. neutrality in the growing conflict in Europe; permitted Britain to buy war goods on a "cash and carry" basis.

New Deal coalition New coalition of Democratic voters including Southerners, farmers, union workers, and African Americans that emerged during the FDR administration.

New Federalism Political agenda under the Nixon administration that aimed to increase state-level

authority; a contrast to the escalation of federal authority under Kennedy and Johnson.

New France Territory controlled by France in parts of what is now Canada and the United States between the early sixteenth century and the end of the French and Indian War; sparsely populated; mostly centered on the fur trade.

New Freedom Program of legislation pursued under the Wilson administration; included major efforts in banking reform, tariff reduction, and anti-trust legislation.

New Jersey Plan Plan for government proposed by William Paterson; called for a Congress with one house; equal representation among all states.

New Spain Territory controlled by Spain in the Americas from the early sixteenth century into the early nineteenth century; economy characterized first by large-scale agriculture on *encomiendas* and later *haciendas,* both known for their harsh working conditions; highly segmented social system populated by a mix of Spaniards, African slaves, and Native Americans.

nonviolent protest Form of protest involving the use of peaceful methods such as boycotts and sit-ins to effect social change; primary method employed by civil rights protestors of the 1950s and early 1960s.

North African Theatre Area of North African operations by the U.S. military during World War II; included a notable effort to defeat German General Erwin Rommel's Afrika Korps at the Battle of Kassarine Pass.

North Atlantic Treaty Organization (NATO) Treaty signed by numerous Western European and North American powers providing for mutual self-defense in the event of foreign aggression.

Northwest Ordinance of 1787 Law granting western settlers a bill of rights and barring slavery north of the Ohio River.

Northwest Passage Water route through or around North America to Asia; explorers unsuccessfully searched for this route from the fifteenth century into the nineteenth century.

Nullification Crises Set of two political crises, first in 1828 and later in 1832, over federal tariffs; during each crisis, Southern interests threatened to refuse to collect federal tariffs within their states, claiming states had the right to nullify certain federal laws; Jackson used force to collect taxes during the Second Nullification Crisis, but agreed to a gradual reduction of tariffs.

Oklahoma City bombing Bombing of an Oklahoma City federal building in 1995 that resulted in 168 deaths; deadliest act of domestic terrorism in U.S. history.

oligopoly Business structure under which a few large corporations dominate a particular industry.

open shop Unionized workplace allowing nonunion workers.

Oregon Treaty Treaty between the United States and Great Britain ratified in 1846 that set the U.S.-Canada border at the 49th parallel.

Pacific Theatre Area of Asian and Pacific island operations by the U.S. military during World War II; included the Battle of Midway.

Palmer Raids Series of raids in late 1919 and early 1920 that resulted in the arrests of thousands of purported communists and illegal aliens; discredited when only a small number of the arrests were found to be justified, contributing to the end of the first Red Scare.

Panama Canal Canal built across the Isthmus of Panama to link the Atlantic and Pacific Oceans; first initiated by the French, the project later came under the control of the United States, which then administered the canal until the late twentieth century.

pan-Americanism U.S. foreign relations stance begun in the Gilded Age that worked to achieve peaceful conflict resolution and support a shared customs union among nations in the Americas.

Panic of 1857 Brief but intense economic depression that resulted from problems with overspeculation, banking, and capital availability.

Peace Corps Kennedy initiative that sent young volunteer workers to engage in various service projects in the developing world.

Pearl Harbor Site of a U.S naval base in Hawaii; surprise Japanese attack on Pearl Harbor on December 7, 1941, brought the United States into World War II.

Pendleton Act Legislation passed in 1883 aimed at reforming the federal civil service system by instituting a series of open, competitive examinations to fill civil service jobs.

Peninsula Campaign Union plan engineered by General George B. McClellan in 1862 that saw slow Union advancement through Virginia toward Richmond; ultimately resulted in a Union retreat to Washington, D.C.

Pentagon Papers Classified Defense Department documents leaked to the press and published in 1971 that revealed government efforts to misinform the U.S. public about the Vietnam War.

Persian Gulf Conflict War between the United States and Iraq in 1991 over the Iraqi invasion of Kuwait; ended in U.S. victory after less than two months, but left a great deal of instability in the region.

Pilgrims Group of English religious dissidents who immigrated to America aboard the *Mayflower;* wrote the *Mayflower Compact;* founded Plymouth Colony in 1620.

Pinckney Treaty Treaty between the United States and Spain, signed in 1796, that granted the United States commercial access to the Mississippi River, allowed U.S. right of deposit at the port of New Orleans, and set the northern boundary of Florida at the 31st parallel; named for U.S. negotiator Thomas Pinckney.

plantation Large farms dedicated to growing cash crops in the American South; relied heavily on enslaved labor; dominated Southern economy from colonial times until the Civil War era, but made up only a small minority of Southern farms.

Platt Amendment Legislative amendment passed in 1901 that granted the United States considerable control over Cuba; required Cuba to allow U.S. forces to maintain a military base at Guantanamo Bay.

pocket veto Form of indirect presidential veto by which the president simply fails to sign a bill into law in a 10-day period after its period during which Congress has adjourned.

political machine Informal political organization dominated by a specific political party that controlled a certain city or region and rewarded party loyalists with government jobs or contracts.

popular sovereignty Political process by which government reflects the will of the people; often used to describe the process by which voters decided whether a state would allow or bar slavery in the years just preceding the Civil War.

Populist Party Political party that gained strength in the early 1890s; founded as a coalition of farmers, urban workers, and the middle class; supported reforms including the coinage of silver, labor reform, and the direct election of senators; declined after the 1896 presidential election.

Potsdam Conference Meeting of Truman, Stalin, and British prime minister Clement Atlee that resulted in agreements on war crimes tribunals and plans to demilitarize and reorganize Nazi Germany.

price discrimination Practice of charging less in some areas than in others in order to undercut competition; barred under the Clayton Antitrust Act of 1914.

Proclamation of 1763 British declaration formally barring American settlement west of the Appalachians; issued in the wake of the French and Indian War to help ease tensions with Native Americans; angered colonists, who wished to build settlements and establish trade in the West.

Proclamation of Neutrality Statement issued by Washington in 1792 formally asserting U.S neutrality in the war between France and other European powers; broken by Citizen Genet, who tried to generate popular support for the French cause.

progressive reforms Wide-reaching series of reforms calling for changes in such fields as politics, labor, monopolies, and racial and gender equality; resulted in the direct election of senators, the creation of new forms of city government, child labor laws, conservation policies, anti-trust actions, and other reforms.

Progressives Loose coalition of reform-minded individuals who worked to effect change during the early twentieth century; included members of all social classes and both major political parties.

Prohibition Ban on the manufacture and sale of alcohol in the United States instituted by the Eighteenth Amendment in 1918; enforced only weakly; led to the rise of organized crime in major cities such as New York and Chicago; repealed by the Twenty-third Amendment in 1933.

Prohibitory Act British declaration in 1775 that the colonies were in rebellion and no longer enjoyed the protection of the king.

proprietary colony English colony under the direct control of a proprietor or group of proprietors.

Pueblo Pre-Columbian peoples in the Southwest named for their distinctive cliff dwelling; influenced by the building styles and religious practices of the Anasazi; developed drought-resistant crops.

Pullman Strike Major labor strike in 1894 by the American Railway Union under the leadership of activist Eugene V. Debs; ended after federal troops violently broke up the strike.

Puritans Group of English religious dissidents who had experienced great conflict with the English king; formed a joint-stock company called the Massachusetts Bay Company in 1629; established

Massachusetts Bay Colony under the authority of John Winthrop in 1630.

Quakers Religious sect with beliefs in direct connections with God, pacifism, and the unimportance of human institutions; became the core settlers of the Pennsylvania colony, founded on principles of religious freedom, in the late seventeenth century.

Quartering Act British law passed in 1765 that required American colonists to pay for a standing British army of up to 10,000 troops.

Quasi-War Undeclared naval war between the United States and France that took place during 1798 and 1799; erupted as a result of the XYZ Affair; all trade ended between the United States and France, and U.S. captains were permitted to attack and take French ships; ended after the ascension of Napoleon.

Quebec Act British law passed in 1774 that expanded the colony of Quebec to the Ohio River, established Roman Catholicism as that colony's official religion, and set up a representative government in Quebec; angered colonists because it hampered colonial hopes of expansion west; grouped with the Coercive Acts as the Intolerance Acts.

Radical Republicans Political faction composed of fervently anti-slavery Republicans; significant force in Congress during the Civil War and Reconstruction.

radio Primary form of mass communication and entertainment in the United States from the 1920s to the birth of television in the 1950s; helped create a U.S. mass culture.

Realism Literary movement of the Gilded Age that explored social problems, urban landscapes, and other real-life problems; major writers included Mark Twain, Henry James, and William Dean Howell.

Reconstruction Finance Corporation Congressional corporation authorized to provide up to $2 billion in loans to support railroads and financial institutions; helped prevent the failure of firms but did not provide immediate relief to average citizens.

Red Scare (1919) Period of intense fear and concern that swept the United States in 1919 about the influence of communists, radicals, and those perceived to support those causes, such as immigrants and labor union members.

Red Scare (late 1940s–early 1950s) Period of intense fear and concern that swept the United States in the late 1940a and early 1950s about the influence of communists; saw numerous people investigated as potential communists by the House Committee on Un-American Activities and rabid anti-communist Senator Joseph McCarthy.

reparations Payments made by one power to recompense another power for costs incurred because of a war; typically made from a losing aggressive force to a winning defensive forces.

Republican Party (1850s–present) Political party that emerged to replace the Whigs in the 1850s; opposed the expansion of slavery; forerunner of the modern Republican Party.

Republican Party (18th–19th century political party) One of the nation's first two political parties; supported a strict interpretation of the rights given to the federal government by the Constitution; generally supported state superiority over the federal government; led by Thomas Jefferson; unrelated to modern Republican Party.

reservations Areas of land set aside by the federal government for the resettlement of Native American tribes.

return to normalcy Campaign promise made by successful Republican presidential candidate Warren G. Harding during the election of 1920; implied a return to traditional values and ideas after the period of wartime upheaval and ensuing economic worries.

Revenue Act of 1918 Legislation passed in 1918 that raised direct federal incomes tax on personal incomes to support the war effort.

Revenue Act of 1942 Legislation expanding the direct income tax to affect most Americans and creating the payroll deduction system for income taxes.

Romanticism Artistic and literary movement of the antebellum era that focused on emotions over reason, self-improvement, and a belief in human goodness; major U.S. writers included Walt Whitman, Henry Wadsworth Longfellow, Herman Melville, and Edgar Allen Poe.

Roosevelt Corollary Expansion of the Monroe Doctrine in 1904 that asserted the right of the United States to intervene in the affairs of Latin American nations to prevent European powers from using military force to collect debts.

royal colony English colony under the direct control of the English crown or its official; came to include the majority of the thirteen colonies as the crown assumed control of them from joint-stock companies or proprietors.

Russian Revolution Overthrow of the czarist Russian government and institution of a communist government led by the Bolsheviks in 1919; led to Russia's withdrawal from World War I in Europe and heightened concerns over communism in the United States.

Sacco and Vanzetti Two Italian immigrant anarchists tried and convicted for murder in a highly publicized 1921 trial; although executed in 1927, debate over their possible innocence and mistrial continued for decades.

Saratoga Site of an important colonial victory in 1777 that convinced the French to offer open support to the rebelling colonists; considered the turning point of the American Revolution.

Saturday Night Massacre Controversial Nixon order for the attorney general to fire a special prosecutor into the Watergate scandal; the attorney general's resignation and subsequent execution of the presidential order generated much controversy.

Savings and Loan Crisis Financial crisis in 1989 brought about by the making of numerous bad real estate loans by savings and loan institutions; led to hundreds of bank closures and cost the economy an estimated $300 billion.

scalawag Southern derogatory term describing Southerners who worked to help Reconstruction efforts.

scientific management Principle of business and industrial management, set forth by Frederick W. Taylor, that instituted specific times required for the completion of various workplace tasks; helped increased industrial efficiency during the 1920s.

Scopes Trial Trial held in 1925 over the ability of science teachers to teach the then-controversial theory of evolution rather than the religious theory of creation; galvanized national attention and displayed the changing morals and beliefs of the era.

secession Act of formally removing a political unit from participation in a larger unit; used by Southern states, beginning with South Carolina, that wished to detach from the Union, sparking the Civil War.

Second Continental Congress Meeting of colonial leaders that began in Philadelphia in May 1775, to discuss possible actions against the British; despite disagreement among leaders over the advisability of warring with Britain and the Olive Branch Petition to King George III in an effort to avoid war, it resulted in increased preparations by colonial militias for war.

Second Great Awakening Revival of religious feeling that began in 1801; encouraged beliefs in personal salvation, direct connection to God, and individual religiosity; embraced by women and African Americans; encouraged the growth of later reform movements.

Second New Deal Legislation enacted as part of FDR's New Deal program from 1935 onward; included the Social Security Act, the Wagner Act, and others.

sectional tensions Term used to describe the disagreements and conflicts between the North and the South before the Civil War; primarily stemmed from the economic, political, and social differences stemming from Southern reliance on slavery.

Sedition Act of 1918 Legislation criminalizing and criticizing the government, the U.S. flag, or military uniform, regardless of the outcome of this criticism; curtailed civil liberties; famously led to the imprisonment of Socialist leader Eugene V. Debs for making an anti-war speech.

Selective Service Act Legislation passed in May 1917, allowing for a wide-scale federal draft into the U.S. armed forces.

separation of powers Political system dividing governmental authority among various branches; in the United States, three branches work to together in a series of "checks and balances" under separation of powers.

settlement house Reform institutions that worked to provide support and services to immigrant communities; typically founded in large, urban immigrant neighborhoods; most famous was Jane Addams' Hull House in Chicago.

Share Our Wealth society Society created by Huey Long that called for redistribution of wealth through confiscation and heavy taxation; fizzled after Long's assassination in 1935.

Shays' Rebellion Farmers' revolt led by Daniel Shays in western Massachusetts; caused by economic problems and high taxes resulting from war debts; rebels temporarily closed court to prevent seizure of land and sentencing of debtors to prison; resulted in widespread concern and illustrated the failings of the Articles of Confederation.

Sherman Anti-Trust Act Legislation passed in 1890 that subjected corporate monopolies to federal prosecution if they worked to restrict trade and competition.

Sherman's March Campaign led by General George T. Sherman that caused significant devastation through much of the South, including the sacking and burning of Atlanta and Savannah.

slave state State that permitted slavery.

slave uprisings Revolts by enslaved people against white owners or white society in general; rarely succeeded by any measure, but caused a great deal of fear among whites in the South; best-known slave uprisings include those of Gabriel Prosser in 1800, Denmark Vesey in 1822, and Nat Turner in 1831.

Social Darwinism Theory proclaiming that success in life was based on survival of the fittest; used to justify the unequal distribution of wealth resulting from capitalism and rapid industrial development during the Gilded Age.

Social Gospel Reform movement based in Christianity that encouraged sweeping reform efforts in the late nineteenth and early twentieth centuries; included settlement houses, improved health services, and improved schools, along with other reform areas.

Social Security Act Legislation passed in 1935 that created government old-age pensions, unemployment insurance, and support for the disabled; funded by federal payroll taxes.

Solid South Term describing the consistent support of the South as a Democratic voting bloc from the end of Reconstruction until the Civil Rights era.

Sons of Liberty Group of American colonists who formed in the wake of the passage of the Stamp Act to work against what they saw as unfair British taxation on the colonists, who were unrepresented in Parliament; formed by Massachusetts colonist Samuel Adams.

Spanish American War War between the United States and Spain that took place in 1898, primarily in Cuba and the Philippines; ended by the Treaty of Paris of 1898, which granted the

United States Guam and Puerto Rico, and gave up Spanish claims over Cuba and the Philippines; helped begin U.S. imperialism.

spoils system System of rewarding party supporters with government civil service jobs; largely ended by the Pendleton Act.

stagflation Combination of stagnant growth and high inflation that negatively affected the U.S. economy during much of the 1970s.

Stamp Act British law passed in 1765 that levied the first direct tax on the American colonists; imposed taxes on printed goods such as newspapers; greatly angered colonists, who saw the taxes as unfair due to their lack of representation in Parliament; led to the meeting of the colonial Stamp Act Congress, at which representatives from several colonies met to discuss their grievances; later repealed.

Statute of Religious Freedom Document guaranteeing freedom of religion and establishing separation of church and state in Virginia; written by Thomas Jefferson; served as basis for the freedom of religion clause of the First Amendment.

steamboat Transportation innovation of the early nineteenth century; used steam to power engines on large ships; eased trade and long-distance travel, particularly along new canals.

Stonewall Riots Violent demonstrations in New York City in 1969 that began after a police raid on a bar popular with homosexuals; considered the starting part of the U.S. gay rights movement.

Strategic Defense Initiative (SDI) system Computer-controlled missile defense system proposed by President Reagan to protect against Soviet missiles; derisively termed "Star Wars." Strategic Arms Limitation Treaty (SALT) Treaty between the United States and the Soviet Union, signed in 1972, that reduced the number of antiballistic missiles controlled by each power.

Strategic Arms Limitation Treaty (SALT) II Treaty between the United States and the Soviet Union in 1979 that limited armaments and weapons systems; failed to be ratified by Congress.

Student Nonviolent Coordinating Committee (SNCC) Civil rights group formed in the early 1960s that worked to end segregation and attain African American voting rights through sit-ins and other peaceful protests.

Students for a Democratic Society (SDS) Left-wing student activist group founded in 1960; aimed to encourage participatory democracy and social change among young people.

Suez Canal crisis International crisis stemming from Egyptian nationalization of the Suez Canal and Egypt's opening of diplomatic relations with communist powers; involved a brief period of military action by the Egyptians, Israelis, British, and French.

Sugar Act British law passed in 1764 that imposed higher taxes on imported goods in the colonies; aimed at raising revenue; enforced in admiralty court, which was not subject to due process or trial by jury; also known as the Revenue Act.

Sun Belt Region of the United States spanning the South and West; experienced significant population growth after World War II.

supply-side economics Economic system promoted under Ronald Reagan that favored low taxes and less government spending; sometimes termed "Reaganomics." Taft-Hartley Act Legislation passed in 1947 that limited many of the pro-union provisions of the Wagner Act; protected the right of workers to unionize, but outlawed the closed shop, required waiting periods for strikes, and enacted other pro-management measures.

Tea Act British law passed in 1773 that allowed direct importation of tea to the colonies by the British East India Company, resulting in lower tea taxes and prices; aimed at forcing Americans to recognize the right of Britain to tax their goods; resulted in colonial resistance to the importation of the tea and, ultimately, the Boston Tea Party.

Teapot Dome Scandal Scandal that took place during the Harding administration in which the Secretary of the Interior accepted bribes from the oil industry in exchange for leasing them oil fields at Teapot Dome, Wyoming.

Teheran Conference Meeting of FDR, Churchill, and Stalin in 1943 to discuss Soviet commitment to aiding the Allied efforts and to make war strategies.

temperance Moderation or abstinence in the use of alcohol; major reform movement during the nineteenth and early twentieth centuries.

Tennessee Valley Authority New Deal–era public corporation that built numerous dams along the Tennessee River and engaged in other natural resources efforts.

Tet Offensive Major Vietcong attack on U.S. and South Vietnamese holdings in South Vietnam in early 1968; named for the Vietnamese New Year (Tet); contributed to the turn of U.S. public opinion against the war.

Texan Revolution Begun in 1836 by white Texans who wished to form their own nation outside of Mexican rule; resulted in the creation of the short-lived Republic of Texas.

Thirteenth Amendment Amendment officially abolishing slavery.

Three-Fifths Compromise Constitutional provision providing for the counting of each enslaved person as three-fifths of a free person for purposes of direct taxation and congressional representation.

Townshend Acts Series of laws passed in 1766 that imposed taxes on goods imported to the American colonies; provided for trial in the admiralty courts in the case of offenses, the imposition of writs of assistance, and payment of customs officials from fines collected over violations; later repealed.

Transcendentalists Mid-nineteenth-century movement based in Massachusetts that aimed to go beyond traditional intellectual boundaries to achieve a higher state of thought and connection with God; major proponents included Ralph Waldo Emerson and Henry David Thoreau.

Treaty of Greenville Treaty between the United States and Ohio-area Native Americans, signed in 1794; forced the region's Native Americans to move elsewhere.

Treaty of Paris of 1783 Treaty between Great Britain and America ending the American Revolution; granted independence to the new United States; established the new nation's western boundary at the Mississippi River and southern boundary at the northern border with Florida; the British granted Florida to Spain; allowed private British lenders to collect colonial debts; encouraged the return of confiscated property to British loyalists in the United States.

Tripartite Pact Agreement forming an alliance of Germany, Italy, and Japan as the Axis Powers; signed in September 1940.

Truman Doctrine Foreign policy statement under President Harry S. Truman that the United States should support all free peoples who resisted communist domination.

Tuskegee Institute Educational institution founded by African American leader Booker T. Washington in Tuskegee, Alabama; worked to educate African Americans.

Uncle Tom's Cabin Anti-slavery novel written by Harriet Beecher Stowe in response to the Fugitive Slave Law; increased anti-slavery feeling in the North.

underconsumption State of economic imbalance in which workers produce more goods than consumers purchase.

underground railroad Network crossing the United States through which escaping slaves could find shelter or assistance as they tried to reach freedom and safety; best-known "conductor" was Harriet Tubman.

United Farm Workers Union of Mexican American farm laborers organized by Cesar Chavez in 1962; led major national grape boycott to call attention to problems associated with migrant labor system.

unlimited submarine warfare Policy of attacking all ships, regardless of their involvement in World War I, in a large portion of the Atlantic Ocean; a major point of contention between the then-neutral United States and belligerent Germany; contributed greatly to U.S. entry into the war.

urbanization Transfer of population from rural areas to cities; led to the growth of major industrial hubs with associated problems such as crime, disease, sanitation, overcrowding, and the growth of political machines.

USA Patriot Act Legislation passed in response to the 9/11 terrorist attacks that greatly increased the powers of the federal law enforcement agencies to conduct intelligence operations and fight suspected terrorist activities; generated controversy over potential civil liberties infringements.

Utopians Movement aimed at creating a perfect world away from the increasingly impersonal industrial world; members typically lived in simple, self-sufficient communes; major communes included Brook Farm, New Harmony, Nashoba, Oneida Community, and Amana; Shakers are perhaps the best-known utopian group.

Versailles Treaty (1919) Treaty ending World War I; mostly shaped by the United States, Great Britain, France, and Italy; despite Wilson's objections, placed heavy reparations and blame on Germany for World War I; failings contributed to the rise of nationalism and, later, World War II in Europe.

Vietnam War Conflict between the United States and democratic South Vietnam and communist North Vietnam; U.S. involvement escalated from military advising and support in the 1950s to full-scale combat in the mid-1960s; unpopular with large segments of the U.S. public, particularly the counterculture movement; U.S. involvement ended under Nixon.

Vietnamization Strategy used under the Nixon administration to shift the bulk of fighting the Vietnam War from U.S. troops to South Vietnamese forces.

Virginia Plan Plan for government proposed by Edmund Randolph in 1787; called for a Congress with two houses; representation based on population.

Volstead Act Legislation passed in 1919 that allowed for federal enforcement of Prohibition through the treasury department.

Voting Rights Act of 1965 Federal legislation that allowed the attorney general to select federal officials to register voters and oversee election practices; primarily aimed at ensuring voting rights for African Americans in the South.

Wade-Davis Bill Legislation passed by radical congressional Republicans in 1865, requiring a majority of Southerners who had been registered voters in 1860 to swear a strong oath that they had never been disloyal to the Union; rejected through a pocket veto.

Wagner Act Legislation passed in 1935 to guarantee the right to unionize, prohibit unfair labor practices, and encourage better labor-management relations through the National Labor Relations Board.

War Industries Board Federal agency created in 1917 to oversee business matters such as raw material use, production, prices, and labor relations to the benefit of fighting World War I; led by Wall Street broker Bernard M. Baruch.

War Labor Board Federal agency created in 1918 to prevent labor strikes and work stoppages in wartime industries; encouraged higher wages, shorter working hours, and the growth of union membership.

War of 1812 Conflict between the United States and Great Britain over the British practice of impressment and other perceived violations of U.S. rights; saw the new capital of Washington,

D.C., burned by the British; inspired the writing of the "Star-Spangled Banner"; ended by the Treaty of Ghent in 1814, two weeks before the final battle of the war took place under General Andrew Jackson at New Orleans.

War Powers Act Legislation passed in 1973 that required congressional approval for any commitment of U.S. combat troops for longer than 90 days.

War Production Board Federal agency created in 1942 to manage the use of raw materials during World War II.

Warren Court Supreme Court of the 1950s and 1960s under Chief Justice Earl Warren; supported an interpretation of the Constitution that saw increased rights for ethnic minorities, women, accused criminals, and others.

Warsaw Pact Treaty signed by the Soviet Union and numerous other communist nations providing for mutual self-defense in response to the creation of NATO.

Washington Naval Conference Major international conference held in 1921 that resulted in treaties calling for naval arms reduction, affirming the sovereignty of China, and barring most aggression in the Pacific.

Watergate Scandal Presidential scandal that began with a break-in at Democratic national headquarters in 1972; in time, President Nixon and other administration figures were accused of a massive cover-up, leading Nixon to resign in 1974 before facing certain impeachment proceedings; contributed to a general decline in public trust of the federal government.

Whig Party Political party that emerged in the early 1830s to oppose actions taken by Andrew Jackson; declined after the election of 1852.

Whiskey Rebellion Popular uprising that took place in Pennsylvania in 1794; began as a response to excise taxes on whiskey imposed under Hamilton's new economic program; ended when Washington sent a large federal militia to deter the angry farmers from interfering with tax collectors.

White House tapes Series of recordings made in the Oval Office that Congress repeatedly tried to subpoena as part of the Watergate investigation; Nixon's refusals on the basis of executive privilege led to a Supreme Court decision against him.

Whitewater Affair Scandal during the Clinton administration over the propriety of the Clintons' involvement in certain real estate transactions in Arkansas; led to a congressional investigation and the appointment of an independent prosecutor.

Wilmot Proviso Legislation proposed during the Mexican American War barring slavery in any territory acquired by the United States from Mexico; failed to pass Congress, but further riled sectional tensions.

woman suffrage Right to vote for women; after decades of activism, granted by the ratification of the Nineteenth Amendment in 1920.

Women's Liberation Movement Social movement of the 1960s and 1970s that supported new roles and rights for women, such as equal pay and access to abortions; supported the ultimately unsuccessful Equal Rights Amendment (ERA) that would have guaranteed equality between men and women in the U.S. Constitution.

Works Progress Administration (WPA) New Deal program that employed people on relief in construction and arts jobs; led to the creation of a great deal of infrastructure, public buildings, and murals, among other works.

Writs of Assistance Series of search warrants used by British colonial officials to inspect American merchants' goods with the purpose of stopping colonial evasion of British trade restrictions; angered colonists, who believed the Writs intruded upon their natural rights.

XYZ Affair Scandal of 1798 resulting from French efforts to obtain bribes from a U.S. delegation to Paris seeking to end French interference with U.S. shipping; resulted in popular feeling against France; the name refers to the three unnamed French officials who attempted to obtain bribes, codenamed "X," "Y," and "Z." Yalta Conference Meeting of FDR, Churchill, and Stalin in 1945 to make plans for the postwar world; called for free elections in liberated Europe and the creation of a United Nations.

yellow journalism Form of popular journalism based on sometimes exaggerated stories that appealed to emotion; force for reform during the late nineteenth and early twentieth centuries.

yeoman farmers Class of white, independent small farmers in the South before the Civil War; made up the largest part of the region's population; owned few, if any, slaves; typically grew corn rather than cotton.

Yorktown Site of the decisive battle of the American Revolution that resulted in the surrender of British General Charles Cornwallis to American General George Washington on October 17, 1781.

Zimmermann Telegram Secret communication between Germany and Mexico in which Germany offered Mexico the return of its previous lands in Texas, Arizona, and New Mexico if Mexico fought alongside Germany against the United States in the event of war; intercepted by the British and given to U.S. authorities in early 1917; release to the press greatly stirred U.S. public opinion in favor of war.

Index

NOTES

NOTES

NOTES

NOTES

NOTES

NOTES